MANAGEMENT OF HUMAN SERVICE PROGRAMS

MANAGEMENT OF HUMAN SERVICE PROGRAMS

JUDITH A. LEWIS
PROFESSIONAL ASSISTANCE FOR CORPORATIONS AND EMPLOYEES

MICHAEL D. LEWIS
GOVERNORS STATE UNIVERSITY

BROOKS/COLE PUBLISHING COMPANY
MONTEREY, CALIFORNIA

To our parents and our son, Keith

Brooks/Cole Publishing Company
A Division of Wadsworth, Inc.

Printed in the United States of America
10 9 8 7 6 5 4

Library of Congress Cataloging in Publication Data

Lewis, Judith A., 1939–
   Management of human service programs.

   Bibliography: p.
   Includes index.
   1. Social work administration. 2. Social work administration—Case studies.
I. Lewis, Michael D., 1937–   . II. Title.
HV41.L46   1982   361'.0068   82–14684
ISBN 0-534-01335-X

Subject Editor: *Claire Verduin*
Manuscript Editor: *Sylvia E. Stein*
Production Editor: *Richard Mason*
Interior and Cover Design: *Katherine Minerva*
Typesetting: *Graphic Typesetting Service, Los Angeles*

PREFACE

The survival of human service programs depends on how well they are managed. This book was written because of the authors' recognition that human service professionals have no choice but to accept increased responsibility for management and supervision in their own settings.

The book provides an overview of the managerial functions that make human services work. It has been designed primarily for use by people who see themselves as professionals in service delivery and as amateurs, even if enlightened amateurs, in management. Most human service programs are managed by professional helpers rather than by experts in the field of management. Even those human service providers who avoid moving into full-time supervisory positions find that they must perform a variety of administrative functions and that they must understand how human service systems are planned, organized, and evaluated.

Because of an increased recognition that services must be effectively run, most human service training programs now offer courses that introduce students to the field of management. This text is appropriate for such a course, whether students are expected to work in community agencies, in educational institutions, in health care organizations, in mental health centers, or in any of a number of other settings that fall under the definition of human services.

Readers are introduced to theory and practice in relation to the functions that form the basis of human service management. Each chapter is followed by discussion questions and suggested activities. A human service casebook provides a number of realistic situations, allowing readers to examine the kinds of challenges and conflicts that human service workers face every day. The questions following the case descriptions do not have "right" answers, but serve to guide explorations of the subtle issues involved.

These cases, as well as the examples included within the body of the text, have all been based on ideas and suggestions provided by over 50 practicing human service managers. The settings and people described, however, are fictitious. The problems and events depicted are illustrative of real issues, but they are hypothetical.

We have tried to balance theory and practice throughout the book and to include illustrations that apply to a number of human service settings. We hope readers will gain an awareness of management and its applications and will be able to add to the effectiveness of their own organizations.

We would like to thank the following reviewers, who read our manuscript in its various stages and contributed their helpful comments: Professor Nicholas Colangelo, University of Iowa; Dr. Jeffrey S. Haber, Metropolitan State College (Denver); Dr. Herbert H. Jarrett, University of Georgia; Mrs. Jeannette Kimbrough, St. Louis Community College; Dr. Larry Loesch, University of Florida; Dr. Kermit Nash, University of Washington; Dr. Robert H. Pate, University of Virginia; Dr. Norman D. Sundberg, University of Oregon.

Many other people also contributed to the development of this book. University faculty and students were always willing to share resources and respond to new ideas. We tried out all of our concepts and exercises in our classes, and used the excellent visual materials provided by the graphics department of Governors State University. Practicing human service managers—too numerous to be named—also gave up valuable time to share their experiences and provide practical suggestions. J. J. Fussell and Karen Wiley assisted in the development of case materials, and J.J. provided invaluable assistance at all stages of the preparation of the text. As the book neared completion, Keith Lewis acted as a reliable and painstaking assistant. Finally, the editorial and production staff at Brooks/Cole have consistently shown vision and technical excellence. Working with them has been a pleasurable experience, from beginning to end.

Judith A. Lewis
Michael D. Lewis

CONTENTS

CHAPTER **3**
BUDGETING TO MEET PROGRAM GOALS   51

CHAPTER **4**
DESIGNING AN ORGANIZATIONAL STRUCTURE   74

CHAPTER **8**
CONSULTING WITH THE HUMAN SERVICE NETWORK 173

HUMAN SERVICE CASEBOOK   197

CHAPTER **1**

FACING THE CHALLENGE OF MANAGEMENT

The management of human service programs is a major concern, not just for agency directors and supervisors, but also for the people who actually deliver helping services. Human service professionals used to cringe when they heard the term *management*. That word raised, for many, the specter of the "pencil-pushing bureaucrat," surrounded by paper and cut off from the lifeblood of day-to-day work with clients. Unfortunately, this stereotype led many human service deliverers to avoid becoming competent in management for fear that they might somehow be turning their backs on their clients or losing their professional identification as helpers.

In fact, management can be defined rather simply as the process of (1) making a plan to achieve some end, (2) organizing the people and resources needed to carry out the plan, (3) encouraging the helping workers who will be asked to perform the component tasks, and then (4) evaluating the results. This process can be shared by managers and by people who currently and essentially identify themselves as human service professionals.

Today most people recognize that awareness of managerial functions is important in any human service organization. Many professionals find themselves in supervisory roles because such positions in human service agencies and institutions are normally filled by people with training in the helping professions. Even professionals who spend all their time in direct service delivery need to understand how their organizations work. As Demone and Harshbarger (1974, p. 4) point out, "It is seldom that a human service professional, even a solo practitioner, can avoid administrative concerns."

The need for managerial competency

Everyday incidents tend to remind professional helpers that they must learn how to manage people, programs, and resources, if only to safeguard the humanistic, people-centered orientation that should permeate human services. Many human service workers are being forced to choose either to participate actively in the administration of their own programs or to leave leadership in the hands of others who may have little understanding of the helping process. Many are being forced to manage their programs or to lose them altogether.

The following incidents—all typical of the kinds of conflicts professional helpers face every day—speak for themselves.

As soon as he had earned his master's degree, Keith Michaels decided to put all his time and energy into the creation of a center that would serve the youth of his community. Now, in the fifth year of its existence, that center has grown from a storefront office where Keith saw a few walk-in clients into a major community center, complete with recreational facilities, a peer counseling project, an ongoing consultation program, a busy staff of individual and group counselors, and a major role in the local youth advocacy movement. Most of the clients, counselors, and community members involved with the center are convinced that the explanation for this growth lies in the fact that the staff has always been close to the community's young people and responsive to their needs. They feel that Keith, with the help of the energetic staff he recruited, can realize a dream they all share, and they want his promise that he will stay with the center as director.

Keith is hesitant, for the agency no longer "runs itself" the way it used to. There is a need to departmentalize, to organize staff hiring and training, to lay out appropriate plans for further change. Keith is afraid to place the management of the center solely in the hands of a professional administrator because he fears that the community responsiveness that has been a hallmark of the program might be lost. He wants to continue to have an impact on the center's future, but he knows that he will have to learn how to plan, organize, and budget on a larger scale.

Shirley Lane has spent several years working in a community agency for developmentally disabled adults. Shirley has developed an approach for working with her clients that she has found highly effective. She knows that her approach might be helpful to others. In fact, it would provide a major innovation in the field if research showed it to be as effective as she thinks it is.

Because her approach is so promising, Shirley has consistently been encouraged to submit a proposal for federal funding. Finally, her proposed project has been funded; she will have the chance to implement a training and research project that can have a great impact on the field. She knows, however, that if the project is to be successful, she must develop effectiveness in project planning, in supervising the trainees who will help carry out the project, in maintaining the budget, and in evaluating the results of interventions. She can meet this challenge only if she can successfully carry out the required managerial functions.

As the harried director of a small community mental health project, Bill Harvey never has enough time. He spends half his time in direct service, working with individuals and groups, and this is an aspect of his job that he would not want to give up. He finds his work with clients to be a positive part of his workday; it is what keeps him going and makes his efforts all worthwhile.

Bill has a small staff of professional service deliverers, all of whom are highly competent. Perhaps it is because of their high level of competence that the number of clients they have to deal with has grown so large. They now have a waiting list for appointments, which conflicts with Bill's belief that counseling should be readily accessible for community members. Yet their funding does not allow them enough financial resources to hire additional counselors. They have to make do with present staff, but they are all stretched too thin as professionals.

Bill has just been approached by a local citizens' organization whose members are interested in serving as nonpaid, volunteer counselors at the center. If they could participate in this way, Bill's time problems would be solved. He would finally have enough personpower available to provide the immediate service to counselees that he thinks they should have. With the pressure off, he could still devote some of his time to direct services, instead of succumbing to the pressure to spend all his time dealing with pressing administrative problems and fund raising.

Bill has no doubt that these volunteers could do an effective job of serving clients if he provided training and supervision. It is his own skill in supervising and coordinating their efforts that he doubts. In fact, he recently turned down the opportunity to have doctoral-level psychology students complete internships at the center because he was not sure that he could handle their needs. Now, however, the situation is desperate. He needs the help of these volunteers, but he must be able to train, supervise, and coordinate them. If he performs his managerial functions more effectively, he can spend less time on them.

Lillian Star began her career as an elementary-school teacher. She spent many years working with young children and found the work fantastically rewarding. Yet when she received training as a counselor, she wanted the chance to experience that side of helping, too. She accepted a position as a high school counselor because her city did not employ school counselors at any other level.

That work, too, has been rewarding. Yet she has always wished that she could combine the joy of working with children and the fulfillment of working as a counselor. She knows that the elementary school is the place where effective counselors should be working, for only at that level might there be a chance to prevent the personal and educational problems her clients all seem to be facing.

Suddenly, Lillian has the opportunity of a lifetime. A new elementary school is being built in her area, and the potential principal—a longtime professional colleague—has asked her to join the staff as the district's first elementary-school counselor. She will build her own program in the direction she thinks best and perhaps have the chance to consult with other schools in the development of additional programs.

Lillian has no doubt that this position would be a dream come true. She has always wanted to counsel at the elementary-school level, and now she can create a truly innovative program based on the concept of prevention.

Still, she hesitates. She knows she can counsel the children effectively. She does not know whether she can build a program where none existed before. She will need to learn how to plan effectively, how to provide leadership for teachers and parents, how to consult beneficially with other counselors, and how to evaluate her efforts. The only way that she can have the opportunity to practice her child counseling skills is if she develops administrative skills at the same time.

David Williams is one of a group of human service workers conducting a preventive program under the auspices of a child and family service center. In recent years, the financial situation of the center has changed. The agency is being forced to cut back services in some areas in order to maintain adequate funding levels for other programs.

David and his colleagues have been called in to the executive director's office and told that, as much as she appreciates their fine work, their program might be eliminated within the next year or two. She recognizes that the preventive program is very popular in the community; constant calls from schools, churches, and recreational centers have been coming in to request assistance from it. Although the director knows that the program is doing something right, she does not really know just what it is. She does not know how important it is in comparison with the functions being performed by workers providing direct, clinical services to troubled families.

David and his colleagues now have a real challenge before them. They know that they are helping the community; the informal feedback they have been receiving from young people, parents, and community agencies tells them that. They also know that right now they have no way of proving it, no way of showing that the prevention program is accomplishing something important. They have a short time in which to prove themselves, and they know that their only chance is to plan their program on the basis of goals that the administration agrees are important, coordinate their efforts with those of other programs, and develop an accurate evaluation method. If they are going to survive, they need to learn how to carry out these tasks. If they are going to survive, they need to be able to manage.

Keith Michaels, Lillian Star, Shirley Lane, Bill Harvey, and David Williams are all typical human service professionals. They are not interested in changing their professional identities or in moving up some administrative ladder. They are interested in improving and enhancing their human service delivery systems.

It could be argued that they should not make the professional moves they are contemplating. Perhaps Keith should turn the management of his counseling center over to someone whose original training was in business administration. Possibly, Lillian should stay at the high school level, where she can spend all her time on direct service, and wait until the program is fully established by someone else before moving into an elementary-school situation. Conceivably, David and his fellow human service workers should seek employment at an agency where preventive programs are already appreciated and they have no pressure to prove themselves or to sell their program.

If they do make these decisions, however, they should make them freely, based on their evaluation of all the possible options. They should not be in the position of having to choose inaction just because they lack the skills needed to bring about change either in their careers or in their programs. Human service professionals who have the ability to perform management functions may choose to avoid them. The choices they do make, however, can be based upon their values, priorities, and professional judgment.

Functions of human service management

Human service programs deal with the personal and social development of individuals, families, and communities. Sometimes they enhance this development through the provision of direct services, such as education, training, counseling, therapy, or casework. Often they work indirectly, through consultation, advocacy, referral, information dissemination, community development, or social action. The ultimate purpose of these programs, regardless of methods used, is to enhance the well-being of clients or consumers.

Currently, most human service programs are based either in public organizations, such as schools and tax-supported agencies, or in nonprofit agencies that have been created to meet specific community needs. Whether programs provide direct or indirect services and whether they are housed in public or in private, not-for-profit agencies, they tend to share similar managerial functions. The management of human service programs includes the following major components:

- Planning: Setting goals and objectives and working out strategies for attaining them
- Budgeting: Planning the use of financial resources for reaching goals and controlling expenditures
- Organizing: Identifying, arranging, and coordinating the work that needs to be done in order to carry out plans
- Developing human resources: Mobilizing the people needed to make the program work and taking steps to enhance their productivity
- Supervising: Enhancing the skills and motivation of less experienced service deliverers
- Evaluating: Comparing program accomplishments with the standards set at the planning stages; using the results as the basis for change
- Consulting: Assisting other programs or workers to accomplish tasks more effectively; enhancing the effectiveness of the human service network

Human service professionals who know how to perform these functions can play important roles in managing their programs. They can make plans to achieve human service goals, organize the people and resources needed to carry out the plans, encourage and assist individuals delivering services, and evaluate the results.

Planning

"Good management is concerned with achieving results, not with doing tasks. It is therefore necessary to know what results are required before doing anything. The more precisely the results can be defined, the easier it is to plan, organize and control work and motivate people" (Nickson, 1978, p. 177). As Nickson points out, desired results should, when possible, be described in terms of outputs rather than inputs. In other words, performance standards should be based on what is finally achieved, not on the methods or activities leading to the achievement.

A major problem in the human services has been that professionals tend to base their plans not on the results they seek to achieve, but on the means they intend to use. However, "activities . . . must be stated as costs, not accomplishments" (Krumboltz, 1974, p. 640). For human service workers, the planning process must begin with identifying needs and setting goals that can be defined by the ultimate results that are desired. A human service professional must ask not how many clients will be seen for how many hours, but what kind of impact he or she hopes to have on these clients' lives.

The planning process in human service settings begins with the assessment of community needs. Planners use a variety of methods to determine what problems exist among a given population and, just as important, what community members see as their most pressing priorities. If currently offered services are also analyzed, planners can recognize gaps in the human service system.

This assessment of needs provides the basis for selecting the potential goals of the agency or program. It is important that community members, potential consumers, and service deliverers, as well as policymakers, be involved in setting service goals. Actual programs, or collections of related activities, can be developed on the basis of these goals. Instead of assuming that a given activity should form the heart of a human service program, planners examine alternate methods for achieving the objectives that have been set. Only then can specific plans for service implementation be laid.

The questions that need to be answered as part of the planning process include the following:

- Who should be involved in planning?
- How can we determine what potential clients' needs really are?
- What outcomes are most important for the clients who will be affected by the program?
- What resources are available to help in the efforts to reach programmatic goals?
- What constraints should be taken into account?
- Given available resources and constraints, what program objectives would be realistic, clear, and measurable?
- What alternate methods could be used to meet the objectives?
- What are the best methods for meeting program objectives?
- What steps need to be carried out in order to meet each objective?
- How can program success be evaluated?

Human service professionals who develop skill in implementing such a step-by-step planning process find that the effectiveness of their programs is enhanced because all their activities relate to carefully selected programmatic goals. The same kinds of planning procedures are carried out, whether the process is applied to deciding on an agency's central mission and focus or choosing a method for meeting one program's objectives, developing a long-range strategy or setting objectives for one individual's work, solving an annoying problem or creating a startling innovation.

Budgeting

Human service professionals can understand their own programs only if they know how they are budgeted. When they are directing specially funded projects, full-time service deliverers control the allocation of limited financial resources. Even when their programs make up only parts of total agency structures, however, human service workers should try to gain access to and understand the financial reports that might affect them.

The process of setting and controlling the budget is closely related to planning and evaluation. The more closely related the budget is to goals of people who hold a stake in the agency's success, the more effectively it is likely to work.

A budget must be seen as the concrete documentation of the planning process, bringing ideals into reality. Budget reforms in recent years have shown that an annual budget does not have to be based simply on a slight increment over the previous year's figures. Instead, it can be based on a recognition of program goals and of the costs of activities expected to attain those goals. For instance, zero-based budgeting requires that each set of activities be justified in its entirety before resources are allocated. Program budgeting places accountability on programs by allocating resources for the attainment of specific objectives rather than simply to "line items" such as personnel costs or supplies.

Budget making is thus a decision-making process through which allocations are made to one service rather than another. If it is to be closely related to the program development process, human service deliverers should be involved. At the very least, they need to be aware of how the planning process has been translated into financial terms.

Even if traditional, line-item budgets are used, planners can ensure that the budget reflects program priorities by following careful procedures for allocating resources to specific activities. The objectives that have been set as part of the initial plan can be analyzed in terms of the activities that need to be performed before the objectives have been met. Each activity can then be broken down in terms of time span, personnel costs, and nonpersonnel costs until a total cost for the activity has been determined. Once this has taken place, the costs for these activities can either be budgeted according to program or placed in the context of a line-item budget. In either case, the budget that finally sees the light of day is one that has been derived not from assumptions about what types of items should always be included in a budget, but from analyses of program goals and priorities.

Once an effective annual budget is in place, ongoing financial reports help determine whether expenditures and income are as expected or whether there are significant deviations from what was planned. The human service worker who understands the budget does not need to give it a great deal of time after the initial stages. Special attention needs to be paid to money matters when there are variances that need to be accounted for or acted upon.

Closely related to budgeting is the whole question of funding mechanisms. Public agencies depend for their funding on legislative appropriations as well as on other possible sources of revenue. Private, nonprofit agencies tend to depend on some combination of grants, contracts, contributions, and fees paid for services, either by clients or by third parties. The brand of funding can have major impact on an agency's programs because funding sources vary in terms of long-range predictability and the kinds of services they tend to encourage. Program planners and budget makers need to be aware of the agency's major focus and should not lose sight of programmatic goals when new funding possibilities appear. The integrity of agency goals is especially difficult to maintain in times of resource scarcity. At such times, it is most important to recall that budgeting and fund raising should remain subsidiary to planning.

Organizing

If the planning and budgeting functions help human service workers determine what should be accomplished, the organizing function helps them carry out the plan. The methods used for organizing an agency or program grow out of the planning phase.

Kohn (1977) suggests that managers performing the function of organizing carry out the following tasks in the order listed:

1. Consult the original plan for answers to such basic questions as: What has to be done? How? What resources are required? . . .
2. Define enterprise activities that will be essential and the tasks required to implement them.
3. Obtain the appropriate people and equipment to do the job.
4. Assign and condition these resources to their respective tasks.
5. Integrate the personnel and tasks into some sort of structural order to make coordination and control possible . . . [Kohn, 1977, p. 174]

The result of this organizational effort is the creation of a structure that allows all people and units involved to understand what part they are to play in the organization, how ongoing coordination of effort is to be maintained, and what the lines of authority and responsibility are expected to be.

Within these parameters, the types of structure possible vary tremendously in accordance with the goals, needs, resources, size, and environment of the organization. They also vary in accordance with the theoretical approaches of structure designers.

Traditional management theorists believed that there were guiding principles that could be considered universally applicable to organizations. For instance, Fayol's (1949) classical principles stressed specialized division of work, clear lines of authority, unity of command, and a clearly hierarchical structure, with a narrow span of control. Even today many large, bureaucratic organizations—private, as well as public—depend on the traditional, hierarchical, controlled, and specialized approach to management.

These assumptions, however, have been challenged over the years by such theorists as McGregor (1960), Argyris (1965), and Likert (1967), who suggest that alternative methods of organization are appropriate if managers work on the basis of differing assumptions about what motivates people and what makes organizations work. These human relations approaches tend to place less emphasis on authority and specialization and greater emphasis on creativity and on worker involvement in decision-making processes.

A number of theorists (Woodward, 1965; Burns & Stalker, 1961; Lawrence & Lorsch, 1967) have presented evidence that the type of structure most appropriate for any organization depends on the specific situation. Traditional, mechanistic approaches may be suitable for organizations dealing with stable conditions and unchanging environments. More organic, nontraditional structures are needed when conditions are in a state of rapid change and when creativity is needed.

Human service professionals need to be aware of the alternatives available in organizing their agencies or programs. Although bureaucratic organizational structures offer a kind of rationalism and unity of purpose that might have some appeal, rigid hierarchies and overspecialization do not allow the kind of creativity and flexibility most needed in today's agencies. Human relations approaches tend to be more consistent with the philosophies of professional helpers, although they are not always easy to implement. Contingency theories, as well as open systems theories, aid in the recognition that human service programs are heavily affected by constantly changing environments.

Human service workers can be most effective in building organizational structures if they try to be as clear as possible concerning individual roles within their programs, design structures that allow for responsiveness to the need for change, and emphasize coordination both within the agency and between the agency and its environment. There are many ways to divide the work of individuals and departments. The decisions made in any one organization depend on the designer's theory and on the special needs the structure must meet.

Developing human resources

Human service programs are labor intensive. A major part of each budget goes toward salaries and benefits for service deliverers and support personnel. The success of services depends on the manager's ability to mobilize valuable human resources so that the immediate and long-term needs of the organization and its clients are met. Especially in times of retrenchment, when financial resources dwindle, human service managers must plan carefully both to bring needed people into the organization and to enhance their development once they have begun to provide services.

One way to expand an agency's human resources is to encourage volunteer participation. This approach works as long as recruitment and assignment of volunteer service deliverers is planned as carefully as the hiring of professional employees. Volunteers can add significantly to a program's thrust because they provide fresh ideas and strong links to their communities. Community members' participation in voluntarism and self-help increases the agency's service delivery capacity, but only if these contributions are respected as highly as those of paid personnel.

1. Volunteers should be encouraged to examine their own needs and to develop work styles and assignments that can meet those needs most effectively.
2. Volunteers should receive immediate training during an orientation period and then obtain in-service education.
3. Volunteers should have the opportunity to use their work as part of their own career development.
4. Volunteers should be allowed to use their own creativity in developing roles and programs that meet the community needs they have observed [Lewis & Lewis, 1977, pp. 92–93].

Careful selection and appraisal processes should be used both for volunteers and for paid employees. Hiring practices normally take into account the abilities, experiences, and characteristics of potential human service workers, but managers sometimes forget to consider the unique needs of the organization. Job responsibilities and priorities should be defined precisely, even before vacancies are advertised. This analysis should then form the basis for screening applicants and for hiring those candidates whose qualities best fit the actual jobs to be performed. Once people have been hired, their performance appraisals should also be based on objective analyses of the tasks and behaviors that lead to successful job performance.

Fair and objective performance appraisals serve dual purposes. They can be used for evaluation of individuals and also for identifying areas of needed development. Human service workers need access to ongoing training programs because community and client needs can change rapidly. Performance appraisals can point the way toward new behaviors that should be learned and practiced, allowing services to keep pace with client needs.

Human resources are too valuable to be wasted. Especially in service delivery organizations, workers should have the opportunity to grow and develop in their jobs. They need fair appraisal systems, access to training, and the kind of support and assistance that effective supervisors can give.

Supervising

The process of supervision involves helping a less experienced person increase his or her effectiveness in service delivery. Through the vehicle of the supervisory relationship, the supervisor provides support and encouragement, helps build skills and competencies, and oversees the supervisee's work. The nature of the relationship depends on the supervisor's leadership style, the supervisee's motivation, and the organization's problems.

A number of theorists have presented conceptualizations that help point up similarities and differences in leadership styles. Blake and Mouton (1978) use the Managerial Grid™ to distinguish between managers with a primary concern for production, or task, and those whose orientation involves a primary concern for people, or process. Their team management concept, involving a leader with high concerns for both people and production, is based on an understanding that a highly committed and interdependent work force may be exceptionally effective in task accomplishment. McGregor (1960) bases his distinction on two separate sets of assumptions. Managers working under Theory X assume that people dislike work and must be coerced and controlled to work toward organization objectives. Theory Y managers assume that people want to achieve and to work creatively and thus need very little direct supervision or control. Hersey and Blanchard (1977) use a contingency approach, pointing out that the most important factor in the relationship between supervisor and supervisee is the level of task-related maturity that has been reached by the person being led or supervised.

Several theorists also have helped shed light on the question of what tends to motivate supervisees toward effective performance. Herzberg (1975) distinguishes between factors that produce job satisfaction and motivation (growth factors) and those that simply prevent job dissatisfaction (hygiene factors). McClelland's (1965) distinction is among differing personal needs, including achievement, power, and affiliation—all present in differing degrees among workers. Many management theorists also use Maslow's (1954) hierarchy of needs to indicate that workers may strive for self-actualization in the work setting only after more basic needs have been met.

Within the context of their own styles and assumptions, human service professionals face unique problems in supervising in service-oriented settings. Human service organizations tend to employ many professionals, which has strong implications for the supervisory process.

> And what distinguishes the professional employee from the non-professional worker, whether skilled or unskilled? It is primarily that he is a professional, that is, that his work, its standards, its goals, its vision are set by the standards, the goals, the vision of a profession, that in other words, they are determined outside the enterprise. . . . Moreover, the professional employee cannot be "supervised." He can be guided, taught, helped—just as a manager can be guided, taught, helped. But he cannot be directed or controlled [Drucker, 1968, p. 398].

Supervisors in human service settings need to take into account the special focus of the professional personnel with whom they must deal. They must also take into account the unique motivating forces that drive people—whether professionals, paraprofessionals, or volunteers—to enter helping fields.

Evaluating

An integral part of the managerial process, from planning through budgeting and implementing, is evaluation. Evaluating involves comparing program accomplishments with criteria and standards set at the planning stage. Evaluation is not necessarily a specialized activity carried on only at special times by experts descending upon an organization from the outside. It should be seen as an ongoing self-assessment process in which all human service workers participate.

This process, when placed in the management cycle, permits the staff to know the effect of the program's operation on the community, and whether that operation is working as planned. With this knowledge, the staff member can more easily improve the program operation, respond quickly to changing community needs, and justify the importance of the program in regard to budget priorities. These factors are all part of the management cycle [Caines, Lewis, & Bates, 1978, p. 15].

Evaluation of human service programs is meant to improve the quality of existing services by distinguishing among activities in terms of their effectiveness and efficiency.

Essentially, then, there are three basic objectives of program evaluation:

1. To provide descriptive information about the type and quantity of program activities or inputs (*program effort*)
2. To provide information about the achievement of the goals of the current stage of program development (*program effectiveness*)
3. To provide information about program effectiveness relative to program effort (*program efficiency*) [Tripodi, Fellin, & Epstein, 1978, p. 39].

The evaluation process includes both a constant monitoring of agency activities and an assessment of the impact of services on clients. Human service professionals need to know whether the services being carried out are in accordance with what was planned within a certain time and budget. They also need to know whether the program is meeting its objectives in terms of client change. Finally, they need to know how the factors of program effort and program effectiveness interact with one another. Whether the evaluation is oriented toward activities or outcomes, similar steps must take place.

First, program goals and objectives must be specified, whether the objectives in question are related to desired outcomes or to operations. The program objectives can form the basis for evaluation only if they are specific, concrete, and measurable. A statement of program goals and objectives thus includes specification of the criteria and standards to be used in determining success.

When criteria and standards are clear, evaluators can identify the kinds of data needed to measure the degree to which objectives have been attained. Once the needed data have been identified, the next step becomes identifying the source of the data and designing a system for obtaining and reporting information.

If an ongoing information system is in place, evaluations of effort and effectiveness can be implemented, either by external consultants or by agency workers. Once evaluation results have been reported, needed program changes can be identified and implemented.

It is difficult to separate evaluation from planning because an effective plan must include an evaluation component, but an effective evaluation must be based on the goals and objectives identified as part of a plan. Most important, human service professionals must be aware of the need to gather appropriate data as part of normal, ongoing program operation. Only then can evaluation gain its rightful place in the management and coordination of all activities. When this takes place, human service workers who already "know" that their services are effective will be able to prove it to others.

Consulting

The consulting process involves helping individuals, groups, or organizations improve their effectiveness in dealing with specific clients or in solving long-range problems. Because of the unique nature of the consultant-consultee relationship, consulting is not usually considered a managerial function.

> In consultation, the basic power relationship between the consultant and the consultee is that of peers. Although the consultant does have expert power in the relationship, the consultee is not obligated to accept the consultant's ideas or suggestions. The consultant has no administrative or professional responsibility for the consultee's work (an important difference from supervisory or educational relationships), and he or she should have no need to modify the consultee's approach to the problem posed [Goodstein, 1978, p. 24].

Because the consultant is always responding to a request for help and because the consultee's participation and acceptance of suggestions are always voluntary, consulting is considered to fall well outside the normal definition of management. In fact, however, the managerial functions human service professionals practice are often based on voluntary, rather than enforced, participation of others. Human service workers' consulting skills are necessary to the carrying out of programmatic goals; so we are considering consultation as an important, if quasi-administrative, function.

Human service professionals in agency settings act as consultants both to individuals and to organizations. Their help to individuals is usually concentrated on assisting professional or paraprofessional service providers to work more effectively with specific clients or to improve their skills. Consultation with organizations tends to focus on improving the problem-solving capabilities of the organizations, as well as on helping deal with immediate problems. Interventions might include working on group process, providing training programs, gathering and disseminating data, or suggesting changes in organizational structure.

Human service consultation takes place in varying settings. Professionals might find themselves called on as internal consultants, helping colleagues in their own agencies to work more effectively or trying to enhance the climate of the agency as a whole. Increasingly, human service workers are also engaged either in consulting or in acting as consultees with other members of the community's helping network. Consultation among members of the human service network tends to involve both the sharing of expertise and information and the development of linkages among agencies. Human service professionals also act as consultants to community groups, helping them enhance their self-help capabilities. Whether the immediate focus is on helping a colleague deal with a simple problem or helping a total organization redefine its strategies, the consulting process depends on the careful formulation of an agreement between consultant and consultee. Both parties to the process need clear awareness of the goals and the methodologies forming the basis of the relationship.

The human skills of management

In an era of accountability and limited resources, human service professionals cannot afford the luxury of attending to their own customary activities in isolation from general agency goals and operations. Service deliverers must know how their activities relate to programs and how these programs, in turn, relate to agency and community priorities. Human service professionals, like everyone with a stake in an agency's continued existence, must be aware of the managerial process.

Managerial tasks do not have to be painful. The practical, human skills that underlie managerial functions are closely allied with the skills of helping. The managerial functions previously described need to be implemented in order for programs to be effectively maintained. Underlying every managerial activity is the need for human relations and decision-making skills.

Human relations skills

Management is never a "solo" performance. It involves the orchestration of complex human elements into a whole that is characterized by harmony rather than discord.

In any organization, managers must be able to work effectively with individuals and groups. They must encourage communication, build personal motivation, and form cooperative problem-solving groups. These processes are as important in planning and budgeting as in direct supervision.

The planning function can hardly be carried out in isolation. In human service settings, plans are designed to meet identified needs by specifying the activities that have to be performed in the interest of reaching objectives. If a plan is to be a living document, its formation must involve active participation of the people who will be affected by it, including potential service consumers as well as policymakers, board members, funding sources, managers, and agency employees. The human service professional who is involved in developing any kind of program plan or innovation must be able to encourage and work closely with a variety of individuals and groups, each of whom might have a special priority in mind.

Budgeting requires far greater skill with people than with dollars and cents. Although the budget is closely involved with the planning process, it invariably attracts more conflict than any other planning components. Allocation of scarce resources means that funds are distributed to some programs, services, or individuals at the expense of others. Even when the most rational possible procedures are used to make the necessary decisions, both the processes and the results need to be sold to participants. When more traditional budgeting approaches are used, political processes and the balancing of conflicting interests come to the fore and need to be accepted as realities. No one can build a budget without being in close touch with the needs of funding sources, consumers, and workers.

The balancing of human and organizational needs is also important in the creation of an agency's structure. Organizing involves dividing and coordinating the efforts of individuals and departments. These tasks can be done successfully only if the manager is sensitive to the needs of the people contributing to the work effort. The degree of centralization or decentralization, of specialization or generalization, of control or independence built into the organization's structure is a function of the needs being met. These needs include both those dictated by the tasks to be performed and those dictated by the human characteristics of the people performing them. Like a plan or a budget, an organizational structure depends as much on interpersonal dynamics as on technical concerns.

Human relations skills interact even more directly and clearly with leadership functions. A key to management is that tasks are performed not just by the manager, but by and through the efforts of other people. Motivating, affecting, and supporting others' behaviors require strong interpersonal competency, whether the object of the leadership activity is a supervisee or a local citizen, an individual staff member or a group participating in a problem-solving meeting.

Similarly, consultation requires the ability to work effectively both with individuals and with groups of varying sizes. The basis of the consultative process is the relationship formed between consultant and consultee. The human service professional involved as part of the consulting network must be able to form such relationships with colleagues within the agency as well as with community members and employees of other organizations. He or she must have the ability to intervene comfortably either with individuals or with organizations. Awareness of group process variables and the way they affect work settings becomes especially important.

Finally, human relations skills affect the human service manager's ability to carry out evaluation processes. Not surprisingly, many workers find evaluation threatening. Yet the active participation of all agency employees, at least in data gathering, is necessary to carrying out the evaluation function. If evaluations are to be accurate and if their results are really going to be used as a basis for managerial decisions, cooperative efforts are essential.

The skill of working effectively with individuals and groups runs through the performance of every managerial function, and human service professionals may well find their backgrounds more useful than expected. Professional training can also enhance the development of skills in individual or joint decision making.

Decision-making skills

Management is, in a very basic sense, a process of making decisions. From deciding whether to spin off a new agency to choosing the location of a water cooler, from selecting a new staff member to considering alternate data forms, the manager is in the position of constantly choosing among alternatives. Deciding, along with communicating, is what a manager actually does with his or her time.

Decision making involves identifying and weighing alternate means for reaching desired ends. In human service settings, the selection of the best means for achieving an objective is often far from clear. Because of the high degree of uncertainty that will always be present in dealing with human needs, completely rational decision making is impossible. Basic values, desired goals, and the wishes of sometimes opposing factions need to be taken into account. In this context, decision-making skill requires sensitivity as much as rationality.

When carrying out the planning function, human service professionals need to decide what kinds of approaches to use in assessing needs, how to involve community members and other stakeholders in the goal-setting process, and what reasonable objectives for a program might be. These decisions actually precede the real decision-making challenge: choosing the most effective combination of services to meet the specified objectives. No one administrator or service deliverer makes these decisions alone. Involvement in cooperative decision making, however, is, if anything, more complex than choosing alternatives on the basis of one person's judgment.

Budgeting is also a decision-making activity. Whether working alone or as a member of a planning group, the human service professional must help decide how resources are to be allocated. Especially in times of economic stress, each positive choice can bring with it the need to make a negative decision somewhere else. Choosing to fund one activity means choosing not to fund another.

The decisions that are made as part of the organizing function also have far-reaching implications. In organizing, the manager must weigh the benefits of varying methods of dividing tasks among individuals and departments. The choices made invariably have major effects on the behaviors and productivity of all members of the service-delivering team.

In providing leadership for this team, as well as in implementing internal or external consultation, the manager continues to choose among alternate interventions, methods, and targets of change. Each decision made affects both the immediate situation and the life of the agency as a whole. Ultimately, evaluation completes the administrative cycle by measuring the effects of past decisions and laying the groundwork for new choices.

Many new choices are being made as the human service network adapts to changing needs. Those who desire to affect the directions taken can do so only if they are willing to recognize the impact of agency management, only if they are willing to use their skills in implementing functions that might make a difference.

Discussion questions

1. Chapter 1 presented several examples of human service professionals dealing with conflicts about their own development. What choices would you make if you were faced with similar situations? Would you feel that you had to choose between being a helper and being a manager?
2. What do you perceive as the main differences between managing a human service organization and managing a business? Would the same skills, attitudes, and body of knowledge be appropriate for each?
3. Think about a human service organization with which you are familiar. Is it well managed? How could its effectiveness be improved? Which managerial functions are being performed most effectively?
4. What skills would you need to develop in order to manage a human service program?

Group exercise

Work in groups of about six to eight people. Brainstorm as many answers as you can generate to the question "What are the characteristics of an effective professional helper?" Be sure to write down any ideas that anyone in the group suggests.

After completing this list, use a brainstorming approach again, this time to answer the question "What are the characteristics of an effective human service manager?"

Compare the two lists, discussing the following questions:

1. How great are the differences between effective helpers and good managers?
2. To what degree are our ideas about human service managers affected by our own stereotypes of business managers?

Cases

Examine Case 1-1 ("Deinstitutionalization") and Case 1-2 ("Meeting the Needs of Battered Women"). Use the cases as the basis for individual thinking or group discussion.

References

Argyris, C. *Organization and innovation.* Homewood, Ill.: Irwin, 1965.

Blake, R. R., & Mouton, J. S. *The new managerial grid.* Houston: Gulf Publishing, 1978.

Burns, T., & Stalker, G. W. *The management of innovation.* London: Tavistock, 1961.

Caines, K., Lewis, J. A., & Bates, L. E. *A manual for self-evaluation of human service agencies.* San Francisco: University of San Francisco Press, 1978.

Demone, H. W., & Harshbarger, D. Issues in the management and planning of human service organizations. In H. W. Demone & D. Harshbarger (Eds.), *A handbook of human service organizations.* New York: Behavioral Publications, 1974.

Drucker, P. F. *The practice of management.* London: Pan Books, 1968.

Fayol, H. *General and industrial management.* London: Pitman, 1949.

Goodstein, L. D. *Consulting with human service systems.* Reading, Mass.: Addison-Wesley, 1978.

Hersey, P., & Blanchard, K. H. *Management of organizational behavior* (3rd ed.). Englewood Cliffs, N.J.: Prentice-Hall, 1977.

Herzberg, F. One more time: How do you motivate employees? In Harvard Business Review (Ed.), *On management.* New York: Harper & Row, 1975.

Kohn, M. *Dynamic managing: Principles, process, practice.* Menlo Park, Calif.: Benjamin/Cummings, 1977.

Krumboltz, J. D. An accountability model for counselors. *Personnel and Guidance Journal,* 1974, *52,* 639–646.

Lawrence, P. R., & Lorsch, J. *Organization and environment.* Cambridge, Mass.: Harvard University Press, 1967.

Lewis, J., & Lewis, M. *Community counseling: A human services approach.* New York: Wiley, 1977.

Likert, R. *The human organization.* New York: McGraw-Hill, 1967.

Maslow, A. *Motivation and personality.* New York: Harper & Row, 1954.

McClelland, D. Achievement motivation can be developed. *Harvard Business Review,* 1965, *43,* 6–8, 10, 12, 14, 16, 20, 22, 24.

McGregor, D. *The human side of enterprise.* New York: McGraw-Hill, 1960.

Nickson, R. W. *How to be a successful manager.* London: Thorsons Publishing, 1978.

Tripodi, T., Fellin, P., & Epstein, I. *Differential social program evaluation.* Itasca, Ill.: Peacock, 1978.

Woodward, J. *Industrial organization: Theory and practice.* London: Oxford University Press, 1965.

CHAPTER 2

PLANNING FOR AGENCY EFFECTIVENESS

Management in human service settings is a highly challenging task, primarily because the factors that differentiate nonprofit organizations from profit-making firms are the very factors that tend to make management difficult. Administrative problems exist in human service organizations. Some of these problems are so common that they might be considered inherent in the nature of human services.

But human service agencies are not necessarily doomed to a future of mismanagement and inefficiency. Many of the problems that plague them can be solved or at least cut down to manageable size through more effective planning. A glance at the kinds of difficulties most frequently cited demonstrates the close connection between administrative difficulties and lack of planning.

1. *Human service organizations have unclear, "fuzzy" goals.* Several writers (Cohen & March, 1975; Harshbarger, 1975; Drucker, 1977; Newman & Wallender, 1978) have pointed out that the goals guiding human services tend to be less clearly stated than those of their profit-making counterparts. Perhaps because such objectives as profit maximization are eliminated from consideration in not-for-profit organizations, there is a tendency for human service goals to be vague and difficult to measure. In some instances, goal statements are too general to have a great deal of meaning either to consumers or to service deliverers. In other cases, more specific objectives are stated, but they

are not accepted unanimously by all stakeholders in the agency's work. This situation causes obvious managerial difficulty because those charged with the responsibility for delivering services might actually be working at cross-purposes.

2. *There are conflicts in values and expectations among the groups involved in human service delivery.* Among the role groups interested in human services are citizens, consumers, service deliverers, managers, funding sources, and policymakers, all of whom may have differing ideas about service priorities (Cohen & March, 1975; Cyert, 1975; Harshbarger, 1975; Barton, 1978; Kouzes & Mico, 1979). A major difficulty in human service organizations has involved failure to bring together the varying expectations of each of these groups. The problems are made even more complex by the fact that human service agencies tend to employ many professionals. These workers sometimes have conflicting loyalties between their professional training and their concern for agency policies (Whittington, 1973; Carver, 1979).

3. *Human service agencies tend to demonstrate more concern for means than for ends.* Drucker (1977), McClure (1979), and Carver (1979) have all recognized a tendency for human service deliverers to concentrate more on the nature of the services being delivered than on the ultimate purposes of these services. Familiar methods are often used long after changes in community needs or agency mission should have dictated changes in professional services. The result can be a lack of connection between the agency's avowed purposes and its employees' activities.

4. *It is difficult to measure the outputs of human service agencies.* If it is difficult to state the goals and objectives of human service organizations, it is certainly problematic to attempt to measure outputs (Cyert, 1975; Newman & Wallender, 1978; Rossi, 1978; Kouzes & Mico, 1979). Because the results of human service programs are often intangible, administrators are hard pressed to ensure accountability either on the part of the agency as a whole or on the part of individual employees.

5. *The connections between agency effectiveness and resource allocation are tenuous or nonexistent.* Drucker (1977), Cyert (1975), Harshbarger (1975), Newman and Wallender (1978), and many others have pointed out that a major problem in human services lies in the fact that nonprofit agencies do not need to respond to the marketplace. If clear goals are also missing, there is no way to make decisions concerning resource allocation, except by political considerations, personal preferences, or luck.

All these problems are cited again and again as factors that make many human service organizations ineffective in meeting consumer needs. Yet these characteristics are not inherent in human service organizations; they are inherent in organizations that have not engaged in meaningful planning processes.

Agencies that plan develop clear goals based on assessment of community needs and on input from a variety of stakeholders. They attempt to reach a broadly based consensus concerning the efficacy of these goals. They translate their missions into achievable and measurable objectives, and then they use these objectives as the bases for resource allocation and program evaluation. In short, the planning process meets head on the problems that plague human service administrators, service deliverers, and community members. This planning process can be considered generic, in the sense that the same kinds of steps are followed whether the procedure is being applied to strategic planning, program planning, problem solving, management by objectives, or innovation.

The generic planning process

The generic planning process can be identified by its use of the following basic steps: (1) needs assessment, (2) definition of goals and objectives, (3) identification of alternative methods for meeting goals, (4) decision making, and (5) development of plans for implementation and evaluation. Each of these steps involves a major commitment both from agency personnel and from community members. Each step also depends on the effective completion of the previous task, beginning with the all-important process of needs assessment.

Needs assessment

Human service agencies can be effective only if they allocate resources and build expectations based on clear and comprehensive goals. These goals must be responsive to the realities of the given community. Because the services being delivered must be the services that community members require and want, needs assessment is the initial basis upon which programs must be formed. "A comprehensive needs assessment is an activity through which one identifies community problems and resources to meet the problems, develops priorities concerning problems and services, and [begins the process] of program planning and development of new or altered services" (Stewart, 1978, p. 294).

The needs assessment might be a broadly based attempt to measure and evaluate the general problems and needs of a total community, as in the instance of a community mental health center or a health agency beginning operation. The needs assessment might involve a specific measurement of the needs of a narrowly defined target population, as in the case of an existing agency or institution deciding on the efficacy of an innovative service. In either situation, the needs assessment should be comprehensive in the sense that an attempt is made to identify problems, to measure relevant community characteristics, to analyze consumer perceptions of problems and goals, and to determine whether needs are being met by current programs and services.

Problem identification.   Needs assessment involves a recognition that services are being planned in order to bring about some change in the current situation. The planning process must begin with a definition of the problem being addressed. There must be some measurable area of difference between the current state of affairs and what is desired.

Using a variety of tools and mechanisms, the individual or group conducting a needs assessment tries to determine the extent to which a specific disability, dissatisfaction, or unmet goal exists within the community. Attempts are made to establish the size of the potential target population, the nature and severity of the problems being addressed, and the likelihood that specific kinds of services would be used. In the hope that potential services might be preventive rather than strictly remedial in nature, focus is placed not just on current disabilities, but on health-related goals. Interest is centered both on what is and on what can be.

Ideally, the result of this initial diagnostic stage "changes the question from 'What does the staff have to offer that the client can be given?' to 'What help does the client need, when and where, and what must be done to provide the service?' " (Littlestone, 1973, p. 20).

Community and institutional characteristics.   The problems addressed by human service agencies take place within environmental contexts that must also be assessed. Knowledge of the environment allows planners to recognize demographic characteristics of the target population, to discover resources available for problem resolution, and to isolate social, political, or economic factors that might be causally related to difficulties consumers experience. A comprehensive needs assessment must identify both problems and the environmental factors that affect them.

Analysis of consumer perceptions.   As Barton (1978, p. 38) points out,

> Many conditions in society are not perceived as social problems. Only a few conditions become social (or community) problems for which policy is developed. For conditions to become recognized as problems, there must be a process of perceived, collective definition in which a given condition is selected and identified as a social problem.

Barton (1978, p. 40) defines a community need as "the lack of a positive condition or the presence of a negative condition which affects the health, social, or economic well-being of the community or society." Human service professionals often believe that they can identify the negative or positive conditions that exist in a community. Yet the identification of problem situations is affected by a variety of perceptions, values, experiences, and sociocultural factors. Only members of a given community can decide whether a condition is tolerable or unacceptable, central to the quality of life or tangential. Needs assessment must also take into account potential consumers' perceptions of their own needs.

Current programs and services. Each needs assessment, whether it has been designed to provide a sweeping picture of a total area or to examine the prevalence of a single, concrete problem, must take into account the current efforts being undertaken. Examination of service utilization can help shed light on the prevalence of a specific need. A survey of locally available services can also help determine whether additional programs are necessary. Analyzing current offerings can be as important as identifying problems because needless duplication of effort can be avoided.

> The process of need identification and assessment involves two distinct steps: (a) the application of a measuring tool or an assortment of tools to a defined social area; and, following this attempt at measurement, (b) the application of judgment to assess the significance of the information gathered in order to determine priorities for program planning and service development [Siegel, Attkisson, & Carson, 1978, p. 216].

There is an "assortment" of tools available to be used in the gathering of data concerning problem identification, environmental factors, community perceptions, and current services. The choice of instruments or approaches depends on how the information will be used and the time and resources available.

Assessment instruments

Most needs assessments utilize a combination of approaches because comprehensiveness requires different tools for the measurement of separate factors. Each of the many types of tools available has the ability to expand or contract, to run the gamut from the narrow and simple to the broad and complex. The human service professional who hopes to be involved in program planning should be aware of the nature of the options available. These options fall into several basic types that are appropriate in most situations.

Social indicators. *Social indicators* are quantitative measures of aspects of the community that are thought to correlate with needs for service. A needs assessment based on the use of social indicators normally uses secondary data rather than gathering all needed information specifically for the purpose of the study. The needs assessor would decide what kinds of information might be useful for shedding light on the problems of a target group or geographic area. Then information would be gathered, possibly using a combination of locally gathered data and national statistics. Data that are relevant for needs assessment are found through such sources as census reports and other governmental publications, statistics gathered by local or national organizations, needs assessments carried out by local health or planning departments, and a variety of nationally distributed publications.

Some of the aspects of community life that can be measured, at least indirectly, in quantitative terms include demographic characteristics, socioeconomic variables, health, educational level, housing, employment patterns, family patterns, safety, and use of leisure and recreational facilities. Bloom (1977), in a landmark needs assessment using census tract data to estimate mental health service needs in Pueblo, Colorado, gathered information concerning demographic characteristics, community participation, family characteristics, housing characteristics, socioeconomic characteristics, and personal disruption, measured through such variables as delinquency, suicide rate, school dropouts, and number of divorced or separated individuals. Using cluster analysis, he was able to identify specific areas in terms of such variables as socioeconomic affluence and social disequilibrium.

Bloom's study is considered a landmark because it resulted in a comprehensive description of a community and because the variables measured can be correlated with other statistics to make predictions concerning service needs and to identify high-risk areas or population groups. Data in public records should also be used as a beginning resource even in very limited program development efforts. For instance, a service agency developing an outreach program for youth would need, at the least, data concerning school dropout rates, youth employment trends, drug and alcohol use, delinquency rate, and family characteristics. A senior center considering the development of a drop-in recreational center would need information concerning transportation availability, health, education, population density, and socioeconomic characteristics of the community. Gathering data from secondary sources might not, in itself, make a comprehensive needs assessment program, but it does provide an appropriate beginning.

Surveys of community members. When surveys are utilized, community members are asked directly to provide information concerning their characteristics, needs, and desires. Surveys can be used with a sample of persons living in a community or administered to all members of a target population (for example, when school or university counselors distribute a questionnaire to the entire student body). The survey can take the form of a mailed questionnaire, a series of telephone interviews, or personal contacts.

Surveys that are carefully designed and conducted provide the most direct, scientifically valid, and reliable information about the needs and utilization patterns of individuals and families. Of all the approaches to need assessment, the citizen survey approach alone is capable of eliciting from individuals specific information about their own needs and utilization of services [Bell, Nguyen, Warheit, & Buhl, 1978, p. 287].

Surveys can be used to gather data concerning any or all the needs assessment purposes: problem identification, measurement of community characteristics, analysis of community member perceptions, and use of current programs and services. Survey design determines what kinds of information will be elicited. This kind of approach would probably be too expensive to use for every new program or service being considered. It is appropriate, however, for the purpose of cyclical reassessment of changing community needs. An agency, or even a small program, would benefit by using surveys in some form at regular intervals so that needs assessment data would be up to date and available whenever services were being designed or reevaluated.

Surveys of local agencies. Survey approaches can also be used to identify the services currently being offered and used in the local community. When surveys are conducted for this purpose, questionnaires asking managers to identify the kinds of services provided, the number and types of consumers served, and other agency characteristics can be sent to known agencies and institutions. This process can have a two-pronged purpose: to gather utilization data that can illuminate client needs and to determine what kinds of resources are currently available within the community. This step is especially important if an agency or institution is considering branching out into a new service area because the question of whether existing programs would be duplicated is an important one to answer.

Open forums and meetings. The views of community members concerning their own needs and priorities can be determined through community meetings. In such settings, a variety of ideas that would not be heard through other mechanisms might be developed. The forum or meeting approach can run the gamut from small, informal get-togethers, to block club meetings, to open hearings. What is important is that many elements of the community be encouraged to voice their views. A desirable side effect of this type of needs assessment is that community commitment to service delivery can be enhanced.

For example, the Woodlawn Organization of Chicago, a citizens' community group, conducted a series of hearings and meetings to develop a Model Cities program in the late 1960s (Lewis & Lewis, 1978). The mechanisms used included a series of large public hearings, followed by ongoing work on the part of committees composed of a combination of community members and consultants. The result of this process was a written plan that laid out the community's priorities in terms of education, employment, income maintenance, social services, and environment. The report also included an unusual aspect: a statement of the citizens' preferred *strategies,* including citizen responsibility for planning and implementation and wide use of non-professionals and semiprofessionals to deliver services. In the ensuing years, the priorities have remained uppermost in the community. Although the organization is now much larger and more complex, the priorities are still part of the community's commitment, and active participation in community meetings remains a norm.

Community meetings appear to be most workable as an approach if several types are used, depending on the stage in the needs assessment process. For instance, the program planning model of Delbecq and Van de Ven (1971) is often cited as a model of effective community participation in needs assessment. This model uses the nominal group technique. Individuals, working independently, write down their responses and suggestions and then share them with other group members. The Delbecq and Van de Ven model includes varying participation at different stages in the process, starting with problem exploration, which involves large groups of consumers and staff members, and followed by separate meetings for specialists, for key administrators and resource controllers, for organizational staff, and for all the constituencies together. Each meeting has a different function to perform. Each function fits the stage in the development of the needs assessment. Each stage leads toward a final implementation that is responsive to the needs and desires of all the relevant stakeholders.

Use of key informants.   Sometimes a needs assessment can begin with contacting key informants, or people who can be expected to be well informed concerning unmet needs and local opinion. The people involved are often local leaders; sometimes they are individuals whose positions make them particularly sensitive to local needs. Human service deliverers are often in close touch with community needs because they begin to see repetitions in the kinds of problems their clients are presenting.

Key informants can help with the needs assessment process through meetings, individual interviews, or questionnaires. Their sensitive analyses of the current situations can never replace more broadly based needs assessments, but they can help narrow the focus of the assessment so that appropriate meetings, surveys, or social indicator approaches can be designed.

Ultimately, the needs assessment tools used play a part in laying the groundwork for subsequent planning processes. "Assessment provides one important informational input to a much broader planning process that leads to (a) the selection of and priority setting among problems and target populations to be addressed; (b) the selection and operationalization of specific community program activities; and (c) the evaluation of these program activities" (Siegel, Attkisson, & Carson, 1978, p. 221). Needs assessment makes the selection of goals possible.

Selecting goals and objectives

The heart of the planning process is the selection of the goals and objectives upon which the work of the agency or program will be based. Goals provide the direct link between consumer needs, as identified through the needs assessment, and agency services, which are selected through decision-making procedures.

It might be an ideal situation if the choosing of goals and the making of decisions concerning the best means for achieving them could be accomplished in a completely rational manner. In reality, such rationality would presuppose a certainty about means and ends that the human services do not possess.

> Rational action is rooted on the one hand in known or agreed upon outcomes or ends, and on the other hand in certainty about cause-effect relationships. To the extent that people agree on the outcomes desired of an organization and the activities performed are believed to produce the desired outcomes, one can speak of rational behavior. Thus, rational decision making . . . is based on: (1) defining and agreeing upon the organization's domain and (2) determining cause-effect relationships among means and outcomes [Van de Ven & Ferry, 1980, p. 92].

Citing the work of Thompson and Tuden (1959) and Pfeffer (1978), Van de Ven and Ferry (1980) point out that when agreement on desired ends exists, some degree of rationality in planning is possible; relatively effective decision making can take place, even if uncertainty regarding appropriate means to the desired ends is also present. When members of the organization disagree concerning ultimate goals, however, decision making becomes an exercise in power, conflict, and negotiation among rival factions.

This conceptualization has special meaning for human service organizations, particularly because clear means-ends relationships are not really present in such agencies. We cannot say unequivocally that a specific service will consistently bring about a specific client outcome. We can say that, given a specific set of objectives concerning desirable client outcomes, we can select from among a number of alternate interventions and build a program with a reasonable chance for success.

Many programs fall short of this promise of success simply because the important step of gaining commitment to clear goals and objectives is omitted. This omission brings with it several serious and related problems.

Human service deliverers tend to become caught in what Odiorne (1974, p. 6) calls the activity trap, when "they become so enmeshed in activity they lose sight of why they are doing it, and the activity becomes a false goal, an end in itself." Professionals, in particular, "having spent years mastering one class of activities, called a profession . . . persist in practicing those activities, as learned, even when the objectives practically cry out for some other kind of behavior" (Odiorne, 1974, p. 7).

As human service professionals tend to focus attention on means rather than on the desired end results of their activities, they are joined in this attitude by other stakeholders in the agency's work. "Traditionally, human service practitioners have been concerned with methods and techniques. . . .

Just as human service professionals have been involved in technologies of counseling, human service managers have been involved in management processes ... often losing sight of the specific problems and needs of case-workers and their clients" (McClure, 1979, pp. 15–16). The focus on activities, rather than on goals, keeps agencies wallowing in uncertainty. This uncertainty, in turn, maintains the separateness of the concerns of such varying groups as consumers, policymakers, service deliverers, and managers and also encourages conflict among human service professionals concerning the most appropriate approaches to service. Decisions tend to be made on the basis of the power temporarily held by one coalition or interest group, and as power alignments change, program continuity is affected.

Planning processes in human service agencies can be made more effective only if goal setting is a high priority. If goals are to lead the way toward successful program development, they should be characterized by their responsiveness to the expectations of a number of individuals and role groups and by their ability to be translated into measurable objectives.

Goal agreement. The people who have a stake in the outcomes of human services should have an opportunity to have input into the decision-making processes concerning goals and objectives. Just as community members, policymakers, service consumers, and service deliverers should participate actively in the needs assessment procedures, they should also have the chance to maintain their commitment through the selection of agency or program goals. In the example of the Woodlawn Organization needs assessment previously cited, local citizens participated in hearings and task forces that began with discussions of community needs and then translated the resulting needs statements into statements of goals and priorities (Lewis & Lewis, 1978). In most situations, the surveys and open forums that allow community members to share their views concerning needs can be expanded or continued so that they are also encouraged to discuss their perceptions of priorities concerning meeting those needs. Emphasis should continue to be placed not on the kinds of service mechanisms desired, but on the outcomes that citizens and consumers desire.

It is also important that service deliverers share in the process of setting the goals that their work will help meet. Only when they have been active participants in setting agency or program goals can service providers see their own work objectives in the context of the work of the agency as a whole. Many agencies have been successful in involving human service workers in goal setting; so a balance between the work of individuals and the work of the agency can be found.

Lorei and Caffey (1978) discuss a survey of staff opinion regarding goals that was sent to 6435 professional staff members of the Veterans Administration mental health services. The survey, which was designed to provide the basis for service evaluation, asked respondents to select from among a number of listed goals the ones they considered most important. "The focus of concern about goal clarity is on the end product of treatment and not the intermediate conditions (such as development of insight) for achieving it. . . . The goal-oriented approach . . . provides a common framework for communications among people with diverse professional and theoretical positions" (Lorei & Caffey, 1978, p. 1289). This orientation helps eliminate a great deal of conflict over service methodologies by focusing attention on goals that are shared among professionals with widely varying approaches to treatment.

Conflict between individual professional concerns and loyalty to agency goals can also be lessened through active participation of human service workers in setting priorities. Hurst, Moore, Davidshofer, and Delworth (1976, p. 314) elucidate the concern many human service professionals feel.

> Counselors who work in counseling or mental health agencies sooner or later experience some dissonance between what their individual interests and skills would have them do professionally and what they are asked to do as staff members of their agency. . . . A second quandary . . . is that of seemingly endless requests for varied services by the parent institution or the clientele being served. . . . The result is that individual and agency resources are consumed by immediate demands and little or no resources are left for investment in more long-range goals and directions.

The solution the authors cite was used in a university counseling center, where a careful planning process involved identifying institutional and agency objectives, identifying the center's programs and resources, determining the proportion of agency resources to be used for each of several "intervention modes," and then negotiating the amount of time each staff member would spend on each intervention modality. This approach was seen as a way to maintain a coherent direction for agency work without sacrificing the professionalism and individuality of the human service professionals called upon to deliver services.

Common commitment to agency goals is important because the individuals involved can have negative or positive effects on goal attainment through their behaviors. Just as important is the clarity of the goals and objectives selected.

Goal clarity. Goals are broad statements of the outcomes sought by an agency or program. Objectives are more specific and measurable statements regarding outcomes. The objectives identify the accomplishments that relate to a particular goal, so that, ideally, if all the objectives have been reached, the goal will automatically have been attained.

Sometimes the words *goal* and *objective* are used interchangeably. What is important is that some statement of outcome be used to determine the selection of agency activities. Outcomes should be stated so that they are:

- *behavioral,* clear, concrete, specific, operational
- *measurable,* or in some way at least verifiable—it is clear when they have been accomplished
- *realistic,* not set too high, capable of being accomplished with available resources
- *worthwhile,* not set too low, not petty or meaningless
- *adequate,* that is, goals that are substantial translations of the mission of the system and that de facto satisfy real needs and wants (Egan & Cowan, 1979, p. 126)

If goals are not clearly stated, the benefit of wide agreement is lost. Stakeholders' commitment to the attainment of specific goals must be based on a clear understanding of what those goals really are. Vagueness brings with it a pervasive sense of confusion as individuals find that their perceptions of agency mission differ from those of other people.

Goals also fail to serve their real purposes if they are not operational and realistic. The function of goals in the planning process is to provide the basis for all decisions regarding programs and services. When objectives are clear, alternative methods for reaching them become readily identifiable.

Identifying and selecting alternatives

With clear objectives in mind, those responsible for planning services and programs can identify possible alternatives, specify any constraints that affect decision making, and identify the kinds of services most likely to be feasible, efficient, and effective for meeting consumer needs.

Many program planners find it helpful to use brainstorming to identify alternatives rather than to set immediate limitations on the kinds of options to be considered. In human service settings, it is especially important to consider a wide range of choices in terms of services or programs, even if some of the suggestions do not immediately appear practical. In order to meet a human service goal, a planner or group of planners can consider a variety of direct and indirect services. Untried approaches should receive the same initial consideration as customary methods. "The established way of doing something ... must be assessed as one alternative rather than as a sacred cow" (Elkin, 1977, p. 74).

Human service workers do tend to see their customary approaches to helping clients as sacred cows; so they may stop short of considering all the possible helping strategies that could meet their objectives. They are using what Simon (1976) terms a "satisficing" approach to decision making, rather than an "optimizing" approach.

When decision makers choose to satisfice, they set minimal criteria for effective courses of action and then consider alternatives until they find one that meets the criteria. Usually, the requirements are few; sometimes, in fact, only one criterion is used as a basis for decision making. The result of this strategy is that once a reasonable alternative has been found, the search stops, and many choices are never considered at all. This approach can be contrasted with an optimizing decision-making strategy, which calls for examining as many alternatives as possible in an attempt to find the most beneficial.

Optimizing cannot be used for all decisions. In deciding questions of major importance, however, one should attempt to identify and consider as many choices as possible. In human service planning, it is inappropriate to halt the decision-making process before innovative services and delivery systems have been considered. In short, the human service planner should try to meet the criteria for effective decision making identified by Janis and Mann (1977, p. 11):[1]

> The decision maker, to the best of his ability and within his information-processing capabilities
>
> 1. thoroughly canvasses a wide range of alternative courses of action;
> 2. surveys the full range of objectives to be fulfilled and the values implicated by the choice;
> 3. carefully weighs whatever he knows about the costs and risks of negative consequences, as well as the positive consequences, that could flow from each alternative;
> 4. intensively searches for new information relevant to further evaluation of the alternatives;
> 5. correctly assimilates and takes account of any new information or expert judgment to which he is exposed, even when the information or judgment does not support the course of action he initially prefers;
> 6. reexamines the positive and negative consequences of all known alternatives, including those originally regarded as unacceptable, before making a final choice;
> 7. makes detailed provisions for implementing or executing the chosen course of action, with special attention to contingency plans that might be required if various known risks were to materialize.

The effective decision maker generates as many alternatives as possible, considers the potential consequences of each, actively searches for all relevant data, and exhibits openness to new information.

This openness is especially important for human service planning. If this process is to be effective, it must be based on a high degree of acceptance of varying service modalities. Alternatives should be rejected not because they are unfamiliar, but because they fail to meet reasonable criteria set by policymakers, service providers, administrators, and consumers.

---

[1] From *Decision Making: A Psychological Analysis of Conflict, Choice, and Commitment,* by I. Janis and L. Mann. Copyright © 1977 by The Free Press, a Division of Macmillan Publishing Co., Inc. Reprinted by permission.

Broad participation should be involved in selecting the criteria that will be used to assess alternate services. These criteria can involve constraints or set requirements that each feasible alternative must meet. In human services, decision makers do not necessarily have a completely free rein in choosing services that can be considered or populations that can be served. They are limited by legislation, by the policies of larger institutions within which a program might be housed, by ethical standards, and by a host of other factors, even before limitations of resources are considered.

All these limiting factors must be considered, and some attempt has to be made to measure the costs of various alternatives, not only in terms of money, but in terms of the trade-offs that must be involved if limited resources are earmarked for one service rather than for another.

The kinds of decisions made in human service settings cannot be based solely on rational considerations. Causal relationships are not always clear enough to allow us to say that one approach, and only one, can lead to a desired outcome. Many human factors impinge on the decision-making process.

> In the nonprofit sector, investment projects or public policies generally have ramifications in three directions: economic, social, and political. They cause reallocation of scarce resources from one use to another, distribute desirable and undesirable effects, and create conflicts among partisan interests. [Because of this] the alternative chosen must be economically efficient, socially acceptable, and politically feasible [Prakash, 1979, pp. 295–296].

Thus, actually deciding among alternative methods for reaching goals involves balancing a number of factors so that the options selected are both in tune with objectives and realistic in nature.

Depending on the situation and on the resources available, the decision-making procedure might be as complex as a computer-based cost-benefit analysis or as simple as the use of an individual rating system. At its most basic level, decision making includes some kind of procedure for considering alternative solutions in terms of the criteria selected. Whether a simple matrix, with each alternative measured in terms of its feasibility, or a decision tree, with all alternatives considered in terms of their costs and probable outcomes, is used, the outcome of the process should be selection of services that are appropriate to agency objectives, acceptable to stakeholders, and economically feasible. Each alternative should have stood the test of stringent questioning, with both innovations and sacred cows being considered, at minimum, in terms of the following questions:

· Does this service fit agency or program goals and priorities?
· Are available or potential resources adequate for service provision?
· Can the service be accepted by community members and consumers?
· Can the service be delivered by available or potentially available service providers?

- Does the service meet the policy constraints within which the agency or program must work?
- Do the potential benefits of the service appear to outweigh the estimated costs?
- Can we measure service effectiveness?
- Can we develop an implementation plan?
- Are there serious risks involved in implementing the service?

When this decision-making process has been completed, the procedure of planning for actual implementation becomes reasonably uncomplicated.

Developing an implementation plan

The earlier steps in the planning process result in the identification of goals and objectives and in the specification of the kinds of methods or services that will be used in order to reach the desired outcomes. Once these general methods have been identified, the planner must begin to lay out a program of action that can provide for the implementation of new or changed services.

Implementation procedures depend on clarity, and some kind of formal or informal document should be in the hands of those responsible for carrying out any aspect of the plan. Each general goal statement should now have its own list of objectives because the achievement of all objectives will lead to goal attainment. Each objective, in turn, should have a specified method, service, or program that has been selected to meet the objective. Each service or method depends for its achievement on an organized set of implementation activities. There must be a plan for implementing the plan.

Young suggests that a set of key decisions must be made now, including the following:

1. What are the major activities necessary to implement the methods selected?
2. Who will be responsible for performing each activity?
3. What are the starting and completion dates for major activities?
4. What are the basic resources needed to perform each activity? [Young, 1978, p. 16]

The answers to these questions provide the basis for an implementation plan that specifies who is to perform what activities, when, and using what resources. The plan should be flexible enough to meet unexpected situations, but it should also provide clear and concrete statements concerning individual responsibilities and time frames for completing actions.

In most human service situations, simple time lines with milestones for task completion are adequate for illustrating projected implementation activities. For example, a program for providing newly designed counseling services to young people recruited from the community could not actually begin until counselors were hired and trained, clients were recruited, and clients and counselors were oriented to the program. The time line would need to specify the number of days or weeks needed for recruiting, interviewing, and selecting counselors; for designing the counselor training program; for implementing the counselor training program; for planning client recruitment; for carrying out client recruitment; for screening potential clients; for implementing an orientation session; and so on. The implementation plan would need to specify exactly what procedures would be carried out and by whom. A typical time line model based on this example and dealing with a hypothetical agency called the Neighborhood Youth Center is shown in Figure 2-1.

When planning is complex, more sophisticated approaches might be needed. For instance, the Program Evaluation and Review Technique, commonly known as PERT, might be used to specify the events that need to take place in order for a specific event—in this case, the start of the counseling program—to occur on time. Activities are assigned expected times for completion and graphically arranged so that it is apparent which events depend on the completion of others. In our current example, event A (counselors recruited), event B (training program designed), event C (counselors selected), and event D (counselors trained) must all precede the beginning of the counseling program. The clients must also be recruited, oriented, and screened before the program can begin. The critical path, however, involves events A, C, and D. Here there is no slack time. Recruitment and selection of counselors, as well as design of the training program, must take place on time if the program is to begin on schedule (See Figure 2-2). The charts shown in Figures 2-1 and 2-2 indicate the activities that need to be performed, the individuals responsible for carrying them out, and the time frame for implementation. Similar formats should be used to determine resource allocations, with budgets based on the planned activities (see Chapter 3).

Developing an evaluation plan

At the same time that the initial planning is being implemented, planners should consider the methods that will be used to evaluate the success of the services to be delivered. The objectives identified as part of the planning process also provide the basis for evaluation of program outcomes. Thus, evaluation criteria have, at this point, been identified. If the planners also use this opportunity to plan for the gathering of relevant data on an ongoing basis, effective evaluation can become a reality.

Littlestone (1973) points out that each phase of the planning cycle should have a concurrent "evaluation action" so that, as goals are specified and preferred solutions selected, criteria and data requirements are also being specified. "If, from the outset, evaluation is considered concurrently with other planning steps, a rigor is introduced that will aid in testing the feasibility of each step in the planning process" (Littlestone, 1973, p. 13).

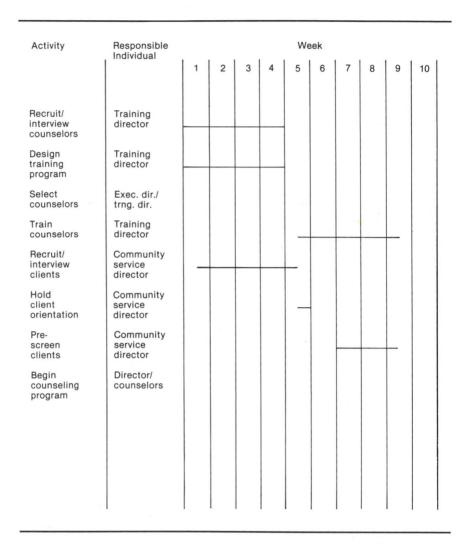

FIGURE 2-1   Time Line Model, Neighborhood Youth Center Career Counseling Project

This generic planning process, from needs assessment to goal definition, to decision making, to planning for implementation and evaluation, can prevent many of the problems normally associated with human service organizations. Effective planning lessens the use of unclear, fuzzy goals, brings commonality of purpose and expectation to various concerned groups, focuses concern on ends rather than solely on means, helps specify desired outputs, and attempts to relate resource allocation to goals. This approach provides

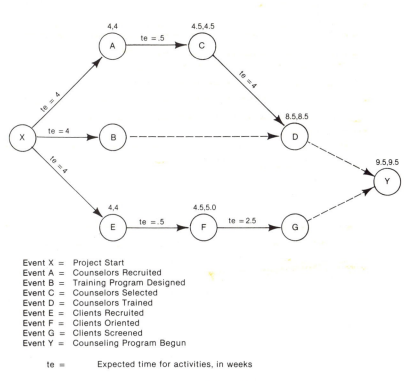

Event X = Project Start
Event A = Counselors Recruited
Event B = Training Program Designed
Event C = Counselors Selected
Event D = Counselors Trained
Event E = Clients Recruited
Event F = Clients Oriented
Event G = Clients Screened
Event Y = Counseling Program Begun

te =   Expected time for activities, in weeks

Digits Above Each Event = Earliest expected time, latest expected time for event, in weeks

FIGURE 2-2   PERT: Start-Up Time for Neighborhood Youth Center Counseling Project

a basis for planning behaviors, whether the specific task is strategic planning, program development, problem solving, implementation of management by objectives, or innovation. The same basic process is readily adaptable to the needs of each situation.

Adaptations of the planning process

There are a number of basic steps that should be followed in order for effective planning to take place. Although these steps provide the needed guidelines for each situation, adaptations must also take place—for instance, strategic planning requires a broader approach than other planning.

Strategic planning

"Strategic planning . . . involves the organization's most basic and important choices—the choices of its mission, objectives, strategy, policies, programs, goals and strategic resource allocations" (King, 1979, p. 341).

When the generic planning process is applied to strategy development, stress is placed on setting the broad basis for agency policy. The goals set at this level provide the basis for the objectives of each subsequently planned agency program; the methods selected determine the activities of each service component.

Strategic planning begins with needs assessment, a procedure that should be repeated at scheduled intervals. Needs assessment identifies the needs and priorities of the entire target population, both as they are perceived by the host community and as they are demonstrated through objective measures.

Based on this broad needs assessment, as well as on an understanding of the nature of the agency itself, a statement of the organization's mission should be developed. The mission statement answers that most basic of questions, "What business are we in?" (Drucker, 1977). It sets the tone of agency policy and provides the constraints under which more specific program planning must work. The choice of the organization's mission is the choice of its identity.

The selection of the agency's broad goals and policies should be scrutinized repeatedly, whenever new programs or activities are being considered. The effective agency uses its basic mission statement as a living document rather than as an impractical set of ideals honored only through verbalizations. The values and philosophy implicit in the agency's mission have the practical purpose of giving a system "concrete focus" (Egan & Cowan, 1979, p. 125) and of setting decision making in motion.

At the broad, agencywide level, the activities planned are the strategies or the general directions that will be used to reach goals. These strategies should be based both on their adherence to agency mission and on their relevance for the organization's interactions with its environment. Strategic planning must involve at least an attempt at forecasting, with planners trying to estimate what the future holds for the agency and for the population being served. It is at the strategic planning level that changes in resources, in community demography, and in available methodologies should be considered so that long-range thinking becomes possible. At this level policies can reflect whether the environment within which the agency works is likely to be stable or changing. The broad strokes painted by strategic or long-range planners now make possible the designing of detailed pictures at the program development level. The strategic planning steps depend on completion of the stages illustrated in Figure 2-3.

In carrying out the strategic planning process, an agency such as the hypothetical Neighborhood Youth Center would have to decide what basic

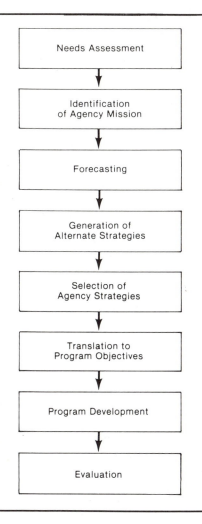

FIGURE 2-3   Steps in Strategic Planning in Human Service Agencies

need and population it would seek to serve. Suppose such an agency received seed money from the state government, with the idea that the agency would seek to "meet the needs of local youth." The problems faced by young people within the assigned geographic area would need to be identified through a variety of assessment methods, and input would be sought from young people, their parents, and other community members. Attempts would be made to determine how the needs of youth were currently being served through the schools, recreational programs, churches, the legal system, and human service agencies. This assessment of the current situation would provide the basis for deciding on the agency's basic mission. Would emphasis be placed on out-of-school youth, on young people with special problems, on the whole range of normal children and teenagers? Would the purpose of the agency's programs be to enhance mental health, to prevent specific problems, such as delinquency or substance abuse, to deal with problems already in existence, to meet the career development and employment needs of teenaged youth? The basic idea of "meeting the needs of local youth" would need to be clarified so that the agency's relationship to its environment would be clear both to service deliverers and to consumers.

Our hypothetical agency might discover that the local human service network offers a variety of services to troubled youth but that no agency or institution is attempting to *prevent* the problems being faced. The mental health system and the courts are becoming overloaded with cases involving younger and younger clients, and attempts at forecasting seem to indicate that, if current demographic patterns remain, the problems will be exacerbated within the next few years.

The reality of this situation might provide the basis for the agency's mission: to prevent mental health problems and delinquency through a focus on normal, school-aged youth. With this overall goal in mind, planners must now generate and select among alternate strategies. Given this agency's mission, there is a myriad of possibilities for potentially effective programs, including both direct services that can help young people develop more effective living skills and indirect services that can improve the quality of life for youth in the local community. After obtaining input from a broad cross-section of community members and after considering what strategies had been utilized in other locales, the Neighborhood Youth Center planners might decide to focus on (1) reducing youth unemployment, (2) increasing children's interpersonal and problem-solving skills, and (3) improving the responsiveness of judicial, educational, and human service systems to the needs of youth. The first goal might be reached through a combination of direct service (career counseling and placement) and indirect service (encouraging local employers to hire young people). Children's skill development might take place either through programs offered directly by the center or through cooperative projects with the schools or other institutions. Increased responsiveness of local systems might be brought about through youth advocacy and consultation programs.

Use of strategic planning by the Neighborhood Youth Center would have obvious results. Without the planning process, the formers of the agency might either flounder into a number of unrelated or unneeded service areas or assume that only one type of service, such as counseling young people with problems, would be appropriate. With a sense of its own mission, however, the agency would have guidelines for program development in place. General agency strategies would form the basis for further development, with each objective providing the rationale for a specific program and each program being based on the existence of measurable objectives. These objectives, in turn, would allow for effective evaluation.

Program development

The generic planning process also provides the basis for the steps followed in the development of each agency program. "Programs are the resource-consuming *collections of activities* through which strategies are pursued to achieve objectives" (King, 1979, p. 2). All of an agency's work is accomplished through programs or sets of service-related activities that meet agency goals. Every program has its own set of goals, each of which is considered the objectives that will lead to the accomplishment of the agency's more general mission. Normally, each program has resources that have been allocated at the agency level to lead to the accomplishment of its own objectives.

As the planning process is applied to program development, needs assessment remains an important first step. The goals and objectives selected must now be based both on recognition of client needs and on the overall goals of the parent agency. The selection of alternative services also depends on such constraints as the agency's policies, existence of other programs, and sharing of scarce resources. The adaptation of the generic planning process to program development needs is illustrated in Figure 2-4.

At the program level, planning mechanisms remain important. The generic process is affected, however, by the fact that plans should be more detailed in nature. The broad goals and strategies identified at the strategic planning level provide constraints that affect goal setting and decision making.

For instance, one of the objectives of the Neighborhood Youth Center is to decrease youth unemployment. At the program development level, planners would assess local characteristics in terms of the specific variable of employment patterns and would then base services on the problems and potentials identified. Realistic goals and objectives would have to take into account both needs assessment results and agency mission as a whole. Planners in this context would recognize that the thrust of services would be directed toward the needs of a broad range of normal youth and would see useful employment as a mechanism for preventing such problems as delinquency.

The methods identified would also take into account the existence of other agency programs. It might be decided to use the youth advocacy program as the base for advocating the hiring of young people. The actual direct service program might provide career counseling and placement services for young people contacted through communitywide advertising campaigns. Given the nature of the agency's mission, counseling would be focused on the development of normal young people. Clients requesting psychotherapy would be linked with other agencies. Thus, within the context of broad agency goals,

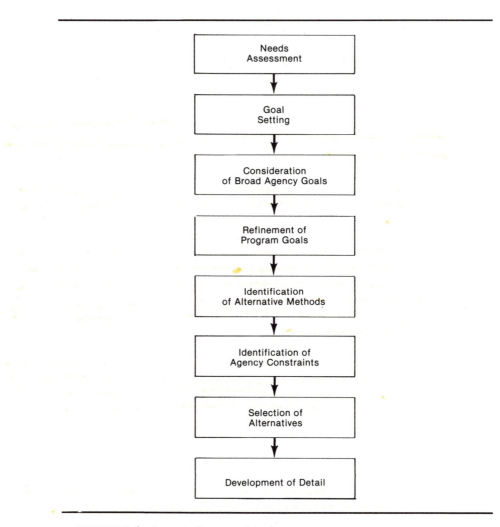

FIGURE 2-4   Steps in Program Development

program developers would set in motion a detailed program for the implementation of a career development and placement program that would lend itself to effective evaluation in terms of outcomes for clients.

Problem solving

Utilization of a planning approach also influences the effectiveness of the agency in dealing with situations defined as problematic. A "problem" can be defined as "a discrepancy between what is (current performance) and what could or should be (expected performance or organizational goals).

Once the gap between what is and what should be goes beyond some threshold, a problem is perceived" (Kiltmann, 1979, p. 218).

Although effective planning can help prevent many problems, discrepancies and frustrations will always exist in any agency. In fact, clearer goals can bring with them increased sensitivity to shortcomings in delivery systems. The generic planning steps are as applicable to problem resolution as they are to long-range strategy or program development. The adaptation that must be made for problem-solving purposes is a stress on problem definition. In many human service agencies, problems are recognized by managers, policymakers, service providers, or consumers. Although the existence of a problem is noted, the definition of the problem is less clear. There is a tendency to identify potential problem solutions prematurely or even to state solutions as problems. (For instance, an agency administrator might state a problem as "The counselors need training in group work" rather than "There is a long waiting list of clients who desire counseling. Could working with clients in groups, rather than individually, provide a partial solution? Do counselors need more training in order to implement this potential solution?")

As Kiltmann (1979, p. 220) points out, "More often than not . . . individuals assume that their view of the world (their specialty) defines the essence of the problem. . . . Alternatively, some top manager or person 'close to the problem' defines what it is and all attention . . . is devoted to solving that definition of the problem." In fact, the definition of the problem is not always so easily found. Greater attention to determining the real nature of the problem can make a great deal of difference in the generation of alternative solutions. When focus is placed initially on a discrepancy, rather than on a potential solution, a more vigilant approach to decision making can result. The steps to be followed in problem solving, as indicated in Figure 2-5 are very much like the generic planning processes.

Problem solving is a brand of planning. Definition of the problem is a needs assessment, and potential solutions parallel the program activities identified in strategic or program planning.

Suppose it were found that the career counseling program at the Neighborhood Youth Center had failed to attract the number of young people expected. If the program were not planning oriented, the problem might be stated incorrectly as "There is no need for career counseling services for young people in this area," "The quality of the counseling and placement services has not lived up to expectations," or "We need to improve our mechanisms for getting information about the program out to young people." If the problem were stated in terms of the discrepancy between the desired and existing state ("The program has served 125 clients instead of the projected 300"), planners would be free to explore a number of possible explanations and solutions. If one likely solution were to be tried, planners would be able to evaluate it by measuring its impact on the specific problem. The agency might still "improve mechanisms for getting information about the

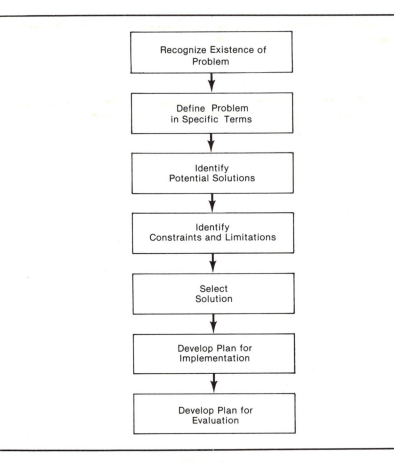

FIGURE 2-5   Problem Solving

program out to young people," but the alternatives would have been carefully considered and the likelihood for a successful solution would be increased.

Management by objectives

Management By Objectives (MBO) is both a way of managing the efforts of people in an organization and a method for ensuring active involvement and coherence in the planning process. The approach is an adaptation of generic planning procedures, particularly with regard to the identification of strategic, program, and individual goals. "Objectives start at the highest level and cascade downward throughout the organization. The idea is that lower-level objectives, when achieved, will contribute to higher-level objectives, and that the upward summation of achievement will equal achievement at the highest level of the overall goals of the organization" (Barton, 1981, p. 231).

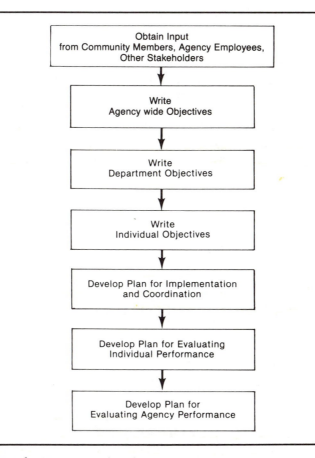

FIGURE 2-6   Management by Objectives

The planning process, as it is applied in the MBO approach, includes much input into the setting of organizationwide objectives, which are then used as the basis for setting the objectives of each department or program. The objectives to which all stakeholders have agreed are used as the basis for planning the work of each member of the organization. Each individual, in concert with his or her supervisor, decides on the part he or she will play in meeting organizational objectives, and this agreement provides the basis upon which the individual's work will be evaluated. Although MBO was pioneered in profit-making organizations, it also holds great promise in the nonprofit sector (McConkey, 1975).

Figure 2-6 shows that the steps followed in MBO have much in common with the generic planning process. The needs assessment step is subsumed under the stage of obtaining input for the writing of agencywide objectives, which can be identified as policies. The selection of alternative implementation strategies is also present, although the activities are identified as objectives and subobjectives rather than as programs or services. If we reexamine the planning processes of the Neighborhood Youth Center, we can see that much of the groundwork for MBO has been laid through strategic planning and program development. The remaining step would be to develop objectives for each individual staff member, with these objectives being tied closely to the objectives of his or her program. A major strength of this planning approach lies in its attention to results, rather than to the methods for obtaining these results, and in its involvement of all employees in the planning process.

Innovation

Planning procedures can be used effectively whenever an individual, program, or agency considers the possibility of implementing an innovative approach to service delivery. An approach can be considered an "innovation" if it involves a "deliberate, novel, specific change aimed at accomplishing the goals of the system more effectively" (Mueller, 1971, pp. 3–4).

Human service agencies are often characterized by faulty efforts at innovation. Some programs try out each new service delivery "fad," whether it appears to meet recognized client needs or not. Others seem unable to cut through the entrenched commitment to specific methods or to deal effectively with social and political barriers to change, with the result that innovative methods are never tried.

As Delbecq (1978) makes clear, introducing innovations into human service organizations is a complex task that involves securing initial mandates, exploring both problems and available knowledge, developing proposals on the basis of broad input, designing programs, and implementing programs, often through carefully selected approaches such as pilot studies or demonstrations. Only after this process is diffusion of the innovation considered.

Designing an innovation to be utilized in the context of human service delivery systems thus requires careful planning, with emphasis both on the development of clear problem definitions and goals and on awareness of attempts to use the innovative method in other settings. Another important consideration in planning for innovation is the recognition of forces within the organization and its environment that might encourage or discourage the change being implemented (see Figure 2-7).

If the youth employment program were to attempt an innovation in the form of replacing individual career counseling with group-oriented career development curricula delivered in the school setting, a number of variables would have to be taken into account. In addition to examining the use of such approaches in other locations, planners would need to consider the implications of such a change for stakeholders in the local program. The new

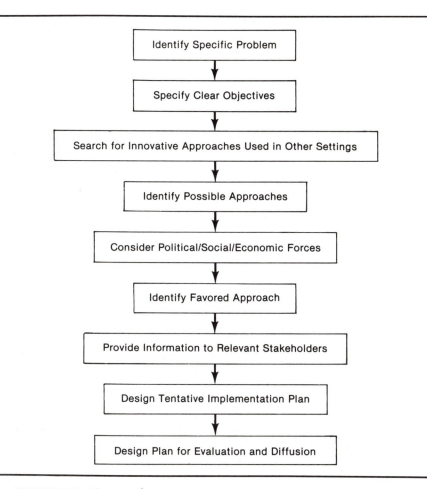

FIGURE 2-7   Planning for Innovation

program could not be implemented effectively unless agency employees, school personnel, parents, youth, funders, community members, and employers understood and believed in it. Even then, careful implementation would require that the program be tried on a pilot basis in one class or one school before being offered throughout the community.

Planning processes must be based on concerted, conscious, and cooperative efforts, whether they are being applied to the broadest possible statements of agency mission or to specific innovations in service delivery. A focus on planning, rather than on ad hoc attempts to "muddle through," can make the difference between an efficient and effective service delivery system and a victim of change.

It is not easy for an agency to begin to implement greatly needed planning procedures, but effectiveness demands it. As Slevin (1979, p. 16) puts it, "It's easy to be constantly worrying about alligators and to keep putting aside swamp drainage."

Discussion questions

1. Think of a human service agency with which you are familiar. If you were director of that agency, what needs assessment data would you find useful? What types of instruments would help generate information you could use in planning?
2. To what extent do you think professionals get caught in the "activity trap"? Is it possible to maintain professionalism without placing definite limits on the types of activities an individual is willing to perform?
3. Human service organizations are often accused of having vague and unclear goals. Given the nature of the problems HSOs address, is it realistic to think that goals can be clear and measurable? Do we have to sacrifice clarity in order to deal with issues of real concern to people?
4. If you were managing a human service program, what steps would you take to ensure that you were responsive to the community?

Group exercise

Work in small groups of no more than three or four participants. Each group should identify one hypothetical human service organization that you would like to see in existence. With this fictitious agency in mind, develop an initial plan by writing down answers to the following questions:

1. What is your ideal of what this organization should be like?
2. What do you see as the primary goals toward which the agency should work?
3. Give some examples of specific, measurable objectives that would help meet the goals you have identified.
4. What are some activities or services that would be helpful in meeting objectives?

Give your hypothetical agency a name and share the results of your work with the other groups.

Save your work on this so that you can use the same hypothetical agency as a basis for later activities.

Cases

For further exploration of planning issues, see Case 2-1 ("Community Action and Mental Health") and Case 2-2 ("The Model College Counseling Center").

References

Barton, A. K. A problem, policy, program model for planning community mental health services. *Journal of Community Psychology,* 1978, *6,* 37–41.

Barton, R. F. An MCDM approach for resolving goal conflict in MBO. *Academy of Management Review,* 1981, *6,* 231–241.

Bell, R. A., Nguyen, T. D., Warheit, G. J., & Buhl, J. M. Service utilization, social indicator, and citizen survey approaches to human service needs assessment. In C. C. Attkisson, W. A. Hargreaves, M. J. Horowitz, & J. E. Sorensen (Eds.), *Evaluation of human service programs.* New York: Academic Press, 1978.

Bloom, B. L. *Community mental health: A general introduction.* Monterey, Calif.: Brooks/Cole, 1977.

Carver, J. *Mental health administration: A management perversion.* Address to the Association of Mental Health Administrators, annual meeting, September 8, 1979.

Cohen, M., & March, J. G. *Leadership and ambiguity: The American college president.* New York: McGraw-Hill, 1975.

Cyert, R. M. Management of non-profit organizations: With emphasis on universities. In R. M. Cyert (Ed.), *The management of non-profit organizations.* Lexington, Mass.: Lexington Books, 1975.

Delbecq, A. L. The social political process of introducing innovation in human services. In R. C. Sarri & Y. Hasenfeld (Eds.), *The management of human services.* New York: Columbia University Press, 1978.

Delbecq, A. L., & Van de Ven, A. H. A group process model for problem identification and program planning. *Journal of Applied Behavioral Science,* 1971, *7,* 466–492.

Drucker, P. F. Managing the public service institution. In D. Borst & P. J. Montana (Eds.), *Managing nonprofit organizations.* New York: AMACOM, 1977.

Egan, G., & Cowan, M. A. *People in systems: A model for development in the human service professions and education.* Monterey, Calif.: Brooks/Cole, 1979.

Elkin, R. A systems approach to planning and managing programs for the handicapped. In D. Borst & P. J. Montana (Eds.), *Managing nonprofit organizations.* New York: AMACOM, 1977.

Harshbarger, D. The human service organization. In H. W. Demone & D. Harshbarger (Eds.), *A handbook of human service organizations.* New York: Behavioral Publications, 1975.

Hurst, J. C., Moore, M., Davidshofer, C., & Delworth, U. Agency directionality and staff individuality. *Personnel and Guidance Journal,* 1976, *54,* 314–317.

Janis, I. L., & Mann, L. *Decision making: A psychological analysis of conflict, choice, and commitment.* New York: Free Press, 1977.

Kiltmann, R. H. Problem management: A behavioral science approach. In G. Zaltman (Ed.), *Management principles for nonprofit agencies and organizations.* New York: AMACOM, 1979.

King, W. R. Strategic planning in nonprofit organizations. In G. Zaltman (Ed.), *Management principles for nonprofit agencies and organizations.* New York: AMACOM, 1979.

Kouzes, J. M., & Mico, P. R. Domain theory: An introduction to organizational behavior in human service organizations. *Journal of Applied Behavioral Science,* 1979, *15,* 449–469.

Lewis, M., & Lewis, J. *The Woodlawn experience: Community organization and mental health.* Chicago: Governors State University Press, 1978.

Littlestone, R. Planning in mental health. In S. Feldman (Ed.), *The administration of mental health services.* Springfield, Ill.: Charles C Thomas, 1973.

Lorei, T. W., & Caffey, E. M. Goal definition by staff consensus: A contribution to the planning, delivery, and evaluation of mental health services. *Journal of Consulting and Clinical Psychology,* 1978, *46,* 1284–1290.

McClure, J. F. Introduction: The problem of product. In J. F. McClure (Ed.), *Managing human services.* Davis, Calif.: International Dialogue Press, 1979.

McConkey, D. D. *MBO for nonprofit organizations.* New York: AMACOM, 1975.

Mueller, R. K. *The innovation ethic.* New York: AMACOM, 1971.

Newman, W. H., & Wallender, H. W. Managing not-for-profit enterprises. *Academy of Management Review, 3*(1), 1978, 24–31.

Odiorne, G. S. *Management and the activity trap.* New York: Harper & Row, 1974.

Pfeffer, J. *Organizational design.* Arlington Heights, Ill.: AHM Publishing, 1978.

Prakash, P. Cost-benefit approach to capital expenditure. In G. Zaltman (Ed.), *Management principles for nonprofit agencies and organizations.* New York: AMACOM, 1979.

Rossi, P. H. Some issues in the evaluation of human services delivery. In R. C. Sarri & Y. Hasenfeld (Eds.), *The management of human services.* New York: Columbia University Press, 1978.

Siegel, L. M., Attkisson, C. C., & Carson, L. G. Need identification and program planning in the community context. In C. C. Attkisson, W. A. Hargreaves, M. J. Horowitz, & J. E. Sorensen (Eds.), *Evaluation of human service programs.* New York: Academic Press, 1978.

Simon, H. A. *Administrative behavior: A study of decision making processes in administrative organizations.* New York: Free Press, 1976.

Slevin, D. P. Management functions: What to do and when. In G. Zaltman (Ed.), *Management principles for nonprofit agencies and organizations.* New York: AMACOM, 1979.

Stewart, R. The nature of needs assessment in community mental health. *Community Mental Health Journal,* 1978, *15,* 287–294.

Thompson, J. D., & Tuden, A. Strategies, structures, and processes of organizational decision. In J. D. Thompson et al. (Eds.), *Comparative studies in administration.* Pittsburgh: University of Pittsburgh Press, 1959.

Van de Ven, A. H., & Ferry, D. L. *Measuring and assessing organizations.* New York: Wiley, 1980.

Whittington, H. People make programs: Personnel management. In S. Feldman (Ed.), *The administration of mental health services.* Springfield, Ill.: Thomas, 1973.

Young, K. M. *The basic steps of planning.* Charlottesville, N.C.: Community Collaborators, 1978.

BUDGETING TO MEET PROGRAM GOALS

The process of budgeting is inextricably attached to that of planning. As Wildavsky (1974, p. 2) puts it, "A budget . . . may be characterized as a series of goals with price tags attached." At its best, an agency's operating budget is a mirror of its mission and objectives. At its worst, it "rigidly controls expenditures, limits the discretion of the executive and imposes a stereotyped, mechanical framework upon administrative behavior" (Feldman, 1973, p. 30).

The budget itself is simply a projection of operational plans, usually for a one-year time span, with the plans being stated in terms of the allocation of dollars for varying functions or activities. Whether the budget helps or hinders the agency's efforts to set and meet its goals depends on the degree to which it is placed in perspective as a tool at the service of program planners.

> A budget is a "plan of action." It represents the organization's blueprint for the coming months, or years, expressed in monetary terms. This means the organization must know what its goals are before it can prepare a budget. . . . All too often the process is reversed and it is in the process of preparing the budget that the goals are determined [Gross & Jablonsky, 1979, p. 359].

The budget, then, should be the servant, rather than the master, of planning. As a decision-making tool, it helps transform goals into service realities.

Approaches to the planning/budgeting process

The actual approaches to making decisions concerning resource allocations vary greatly. These methodologies can, however, be categorized in terms of two basic frameworks: (1) the traditional, incremental approach to budgeting and (2) reforms utilizing rational decision-making procedures.

Incrementalism

The traditional budgeting process, still operational in most human service settings, involves the yearly submission of a proposed budget to the manager, board, funder, or governing body controlling resource allocation. The same type of routine tends to be followed whether the budget maker is a project director appealing for funds from a funding agency, a program manager vying with other departments for a share in an agency's total budget, a nonprofit agency executive presenting a proposal to the board of directors, or a public administrator seeking legislative appropriations of tax dollars.

The budget request is usually formulated in response to notification from the next higher authority that the document is to be developed by a particular deadline. The budget for the current year generally provides the basis for beginning analysis of needs for the following year. Usually, the final results of the current year, in terms of expenditures, need to be estimated. These estimations, along with reports of expenditures to date, help the budget developer recognize "how he will do this year compared with what he said he'd do, and what he wants to do next year compared with what he will do this year" (Sweeny & Wisner, 1975, p. 71). The current year's budget is the building block upon which analysis of the next year's need is based.

The budget format used in this approach is normally the "line-item budget." Expenditures are categorized in terms of functional groupings, typically including such categories as personnel (salary and fringe benefits), consultant costs, equipment, supplies, travel, capital outlay, and other expenses. Each of these categories is a line item in the budget, and the decision maker focuses on accepting or reducing the dollar amounts proposed for each. There is a natural tendency for those submitting budget proposals to request more than they expect to receive and for resource allocators to engage in routine cutting of the originally proposed amounts. Throughout the process, attention is focused on the dollars expended rather than on agency programs. "This focuses information for budgetary decision making upon the things government buys, such as personnel, supplies, etc., rather than upon functions performed and accomplishments of activities. In other words, responsibility is achieved by controlling inputs; outputs are generally ignored" (Otten, 1979, p. 525). Thus, although the budget maker might utilize an analysis of program goals in developing his or her proposal, the give-and-take process between those making requests and those deciding on allocations does not really stress program results or even activities. Instead, accountability is based on success in maintaining expenditures within proper limits.

The decisions in question at this stage of the budgeting cycle tend to be oriented not toward the budget as a whole but toward the difference between the current and the proposed budget. Traditional budgeting approaches are termed "incremental" because they normally accept current funding levels as bases to which agencies are entitled and then scrutinize only the differences between current and requested funds.

> Applying the incremental approach to the budgeting process suggests that attention is directed to the changes that occur between the existing state and the proposed state. The marginal difference between what is and what is proposed is examined. This process accepts the existing base and examines in detail only the increments which extend the current budgeting program into the future. This procedure results in a continually upward-sloping expenditure line containing few declines or breaks [Pattillo, 1977, p. 5].

It is in regard to these increments, or small changes in resource allocation, that political processes come into play. Competing programs, projects, and agencies, each with its own accepted base, must share limited resources. The questions asked change from "What is the appropriate funding level for program X?" to "Whose appropriation should be cut or whose taxes raised to finance an increase in program X?" (Skok, 1980, p. 448). Then preferences must be expressed, support bases sought, bargains struck, and agreements reached.

Through these procedures, incrementalism focuses on small, yearly funding increases that are allocated without a great deal of attention to program goals or effectiveness. When resources are extremely scarce, however, attention may need to shift from the idea of providing for steady increases to the notion of creating a *downward-sloping* expenditure line. What McCaffery (1981, p. 179) terms "decremental budgeting" must go into effect when "needs must go unmet and budgeting ... becomes the grim business of deciding which needs not to meet." Decremental budgeting, a process that one can expect to become increasingly common, utilizes the same steps as its more growth-oriented predecessor. Now, however, political forces will help determine not which programs gain the most, but which sets of activities sacrifice the least.

The traditional approach to budgeting, whether used to allocate increases or decreases in expenditures, depends on bargaining mechanisms, focuses on small changes rather than on total policies, and stresses expenditure rather than results. Over the years, many budget makers and funders have found these methods practical. Decision making is simplified when attention is paid to modifications in existing practices rather than to reexamination of total programs and policies. Uncertainty concerning means and ends—always a problem in human service delivery systems—is lessened when changes are designed in small increments, for major, irrevocable errors are avoided. In short, decision makers are freed from the responsibility for making major commitments in terms of the value of alternate programs and freed from the need to engage in highly complex calculations. "It is much easier to agree on an addition or reduction of a few thousand or a million than to agree on whether a program is good in the abstract. It is much easier to agree on a small addition or decrease than to compare the worth of one program to that of all others" (Wildavsky, 1974, p. 136).

Yet the inherent weakness in incrementalism lies specifically in its failure to force consideration of major policy questions as part of the budgeting process. Traditional approaches fail to make distinctions between effective and ineffective programs or between necessary and unneeded services. This shortcoming has especially serious consequences when resources are scarce because the method does not help decide what programs or services should be cut, in what order, and to what extent.

Because of the recognized need to consider agency goals in the budgeting process, several reforms have been suggested and tried in recent years.

Budgetary reforms

If the primary purpose of incremental budgeting is to control agency expenditures, the focus of recent reform movements has been to tie budgeting more closely to planning, to "convert the annual routine of preparing a budget into a conscious appraisal and formulation of future goals and policies" (Schick, 1972, p. 17).

A major reform thrust has been in the direction of *program budgeting,* which involves categorizing expenditures and resources by program area rather than by line item. A program budget replaces such items as personnel costs, travel, and postage with groupings such as youth counseling program, educational outreach program, and legal advocacy program. Although a typical line-item budget might show personnel costs for a whole agency without distinguishing among staff members tied to various programs, the program budget ties resources to specific sets of activities.

More important, the budgeting process itself is tied closely to planning and evaluation. When resources are related to programs, the programs themselves are considered accountable for achieving objectives that lead to accomplishment of the agency's overall goals. Thus, the program budgeting approach requires that attempts be made to determine which programs are effective in terms of outcomes achieved and efficient in terms of resources consumed in pursuit of objectives. The development of the budget document itself depends on prioritizing programs in terms of goals, activities, and costs.

Program planning, in the form of the Planning Programming Budgeting System (PPBS), was used widely after its introduction in the federal government in the 1960s, but it has been largely replaced by a related budgetary reform, *zero-based budgeting.*

Zero-based budgeting also focuses on the unification of planning, budgeting, and evaluating.

> By packaging expenditures into programs, PPB was intended to establish the linkage between these inputs of program resources and outputs of program results. . . . Zero-based budgeting takes the program concept a step further by packaging expenditures into decision packages within programs that should make the input-output relationship between resources and results even more detailed [Binner, 1978, p. 166].

Zero-based budgeting provides a dramatic alternative to traditional procedures in that it emphasizes the need for each program to justify its very existence as part of the planning process. Instead of comparing a request for funds to the previous year's expenditures, decision makers compare and contrast every proposed program in terms of overall agency goals. Existing programs are, theoretically at least, in equal competition with untried innovations. Through analysis of comparative effectiveness, activities are prioritized so that decision makers can decrease expenditures on ineffective functions and reallocate these resources to programs identified as having higher priority. The process is zero based because each program must start from zero in justifying any commitment of resources.

Zero-based budgeting is accomplished through the use of decision packages, which describe a set of related activities that lead to the accomplishment of a given goal. The information is organized so that alternate levels of effort are described, with the form itself including the following:

- a description of the function
- the goal(s) or objective(s) of the function
- specific measures of performance
- the benefits to be derived from its funding
- the consequences to result from its nonfunding
- the projected costs of the package
- alternative ways of performing the same activity [Pattillo, 1977, p 11]

For instance, if a human service goal involved placing 100 high school students in part-time jobs, decision packages would allow decision makers to analyze the costs and effects of eliminating the program altogether, increasing or decreasing the number of students placed, and using alternative methods (having the service provided by volunteers from the business community, by paraprofessionals, or by professional human service workers; using mail, telephone, or personal contacts; interviewing students in the schools or in centralized office settings). All the choices, including program elimination and program expansion, would be analyzed, with priorities set on the basis of this analysis. The agency's entire budget would then be devised on the basis of rankings, under the assumption that resource allocation would then be tied closely to programmatic goals.

Budget reforms, as they have been practiced in complex organizations, depend on the use of *cost-benefit* or *cost-effectiveness analysis.* Both types of analysis attempt to relate costs to program outcomes. They can either begin with a desired level of performance and compare alternative activities in terms of the cost of reaching this level or begin with specification of available resources and consider alternatives in terms of the performance level that can be reached with a given amount of funding. In either instance, costs are related to measurable outputs or activities, which are, in turn, related to program outcomes or results.

In cost-benefit analysis, decision makers must translate goals into monetary terms so that programs are evaluated according to their economic benefits to the community or to some specified group. Thus, cost-benefit analysis can be used only in situations that allow for the translation of benefits into dollar terms, as in "the benefits from a program for training welfare recipients for jobs, which might be reflected in the extent to which the recipients received jobs, and the money thus saved from welfare department expenditures, as well as the money contributed to society through taxes and so forth" (Tripodi, Fellin, & Epstein, 1978, p. 97).

In contrast, cost-effectiveness analysis considers the relationship between costs and outcomes without translating results into monetary values. Alternative activities are analyzed in terms of cost; so analysts can compare their efficiency in reaching specific goals. In the example given by Tripodi, Fellin, and Epstein (1978, pp. 101–102), "Group therapy for a designated population is cheaper than individual therapy in achieving a 70 per cent rate of reduction in psychological symptoms."

The decision-making data generated through these rational methods are potentially helpful for balancing priorities and for distinguishing between efficient and inefficient programs. In its ideal form, a rational planning/budgeting approach can reallocate scarce resources so that agency services improve. Innovations can be emphasized, and the end results of programs can receive more attention than they have in more traditional procedures. When resources diminish, such methodologies as zero-based budgeting can provide sorely needed guidelines for change.

Binner (1978, p. 164) points out that when zero-based budgeting takes the place of incremental traditions, "Instead of . . . having only to concentrate on justifying as much of the requested increase as possible, the administrator has submitted a blueprint for cutting his or her own budget below the current level." Although no administrator welcomes a budget cut, most would prefer to control the nature of needed cuts on the basis of program effectiveness, rather than await across-the-board cuts ordered by others.

Rational analyses have not proven themselves as panaceas for human service delivery systems. In small agencies, the expertise and resources for carrying out highly complex analyses are not really present. In larger organizations, analyses can be carried out, but an unwelcome side effect has often been that people concerned with programs bow out of the planning process, leaving power concentrated in the hands of technicians concerned more with costs than with effectiveness, more with dollars than with human needs.

Finally, rational analysis is difficult to use in human service settings because we do not have clear enough knowledge concerning the means for reaching particular ends and because we cannot always label one goal or need as more important than another.

> If one can state objectives precisely, find quantitative measures for them, specify alternative ways of achieving them by different inputs of resources, and rank them by desirability, one has solved the social problems for the period. One has only to bring the program budget up to date each year. Is it surprising that program budgeting does not perform this sort of miracle? [Wildavsky, 1974, pp. 206–207]

Adaptations for human service agencies

If one does not expect Wildavsky's "miracle," budget reforms can have something to offer to human service agencies. Even in an agency without technical expertise or complex information systems needed for sophisticated analysis, the basic ideas of program budgeting can have utility. Even in a small, isolated program tied to line-item budgeting through government funding, the idea of budgeting as a priority-setting process can be a reality.

Budget makers do not have to choose between traditional, line-item budgeting on the one hand and comprehensive rational systems on the other. Instead, they can adapt the ideas of zero-based budgeting to a simpler technology. The key is in the questions asked as part of the planning/budgeting/evaluation cycle. Feldman (1973, p. 44) points out that

> In preparing his budget, the mental health executive would ... be concerned with the following issues:
>
> 1. What are the objectives of this organization?
> 2. What programs are available to move toward these objectives?
> 3. What will each of these programs cost in human and material resources and what will each contribute toward accomplishing the desired objectives?
> 4. Which of these programs should be implemented and to what extent?
> 5. Do we have a feasible plan for implementing them?
> 6. Can we evaluate at appropriate times the relationship between the proposed and actual accomplishments?

These questions are asked as part of the planning process, and the answers should provide the beginning point upon which the agency's budget is built.

Accountability must then be based not solely on the efficiency of agency management in spending no more and no less than was budgeted, but on the effectiveness of agency programs in meeting specified goals through resources allocated for those purposes. The success of this kind of process depends not just on the actions of agency administrators and service deliverers, but also on the relationship between the agency and its funding sources.

Funding

Human services are funded most frequently through appropriations, grants and contracts, fees (including third-party payments), contributions, or a combination of two or more sources. The nature of an agency's funding has major implications for the planning and budgeting processes, as well as for how the agency's accountability is perceived.

Appropriations

Appropriations are made by the legislative branch of government, usually on a yearly basis, for the support of mandated public services. Appropriations are a factor only for public administrative entities, with human service programs most likely to be affected through tax-supported parent agencies.

Normally, a public entity can expect support on a long-term basis, with yearly appropriations primarily affecting the level of increment or decrement. This continuity, however, can sometimes limit the flexibility of the human service organization attempting innovation. As Brager and Holloway (1978, p. 43) point out, "The functions of public organizations are prescribed by legislation and often leave little room for deviation even when outside funds are available to support growth and change."

Dependence on legislative appropriations also means that an agency is subjected in a very direct way to changes in funding level brought about by broad economic and political changes. Governmental bodies are immediately affected by economic stress and by shifting political tides, and the level and allocation of resources becomes a focal point for political processes. Planning at the agency level, then, requires that directors, administrators, and service deliverers maintain an awareness of economic, social, and political forces so that appropriations adjustments can be foreseen well in advance. Agencies that do well in times of economic stress tend to have strong, cohesive, and politically active consumer groups. Public agencies cannot lobby, but citizen support groups can.

Funding by appropriation has strong impact on the budgeting process and on the nature of agency accountability. Ongoing use of public funds does tend to allow for continuity and consistency in agency mission and goals. There is still a strong tendency, however, for accountability to be measured in terms of traditionally understood services rather than in terms of community impact. Because agencies are held accountable for the means they use rather than for the ends they seek, they tend to have difficulty reforming budgetary processes or attempting innovations in service delivery unless these innovations have gained political acceptance.

Grants and contracts

Grants and contracts can come either from public funding sources, such as federal agencies, or from private foundations. The differences between grants and contracts are in the degree of control and specificity on the part of the funding agent. A *grant* is a sum of money provided for the achievement of a set of objectives through the recipient's activities. A *contract* is similar but usually lays out the specifics of activities to be performed even before the recipient of the funds is selected. The differences between the two are illustrated clearly by Lohmann's (1980, p. 63) example:

> The essential difference is that . . . contracts spell out more clearly and in greater detail the requirements of the program of work to be conducted under the grant. While a grant might call for a "demonstration of the effectiveness of casework in public housing," a comparable performance contract might specify the delivery of 1,000 hours of casework to 250 clients during a ninety-day period.

Thus, when a funding source utilizes a performance contract or subcontract as a funding mechanism, its own personnel might first spell out the specific activities to be performed and then select as the recipient of the allocated funds the agency deemed most likely to be successful in carrying out the specified functions.

Even in the case of a grant, however, a project being funded must meet priorities set by the funding agency. For instance, in the case of monies funded through federal programs, projects are expected to be helpful in carrying out objectives specified at the level of national policy. Thus, when a human service agency submits a proposal or application for funding to a federal funding agency, the proposal will be considered first in terms of its appropriateness to the funding organization's priorities and guidelines. If the proposal does not fit funding priorities, it will be eliminated without consideration, regardless of its merits. If the proposal does have potential for helping meet the funding program's goals, it will be considered, in most instances, on the basis of the following questions:

- How well does the applicant demonstrate that there is a real need for the proposed project?
- How clear and attainable are the project's objectives?
- Does the proposal spell out a plan of action that suits project goals and objectives?
- Is the applying agency likely to be able to carry out the proposed project and meet the specified goals within the suggested time frame?

- Is the budget clearly thought out and appropriate for the scope of the project?
- Are plans for evaluation and dissemination well documented, feasible, and appropriate?

The questions potential funding agents ask bear obvious similarities to those human service planners ask in the context of budget preparation. Careful planning and goal clarity are valued in the process of awarding grants and contracts. This factor provides one of the major strengths of the project grant as a funding mechanism for human services. There is a potential for tying resource allocation and goal accomplishment together through this type of funding. Although this potential has not always been met, mechanisms for accountability could be developed so that the success of funded projects might be measured more by accomplishments than by methods alone. There is nothing in the mechanics of the funding process itself to prevent this, and funding agents are beginning to show greatly increased interest in project evaluation.

There are, however, a number of almost unavoidable problems associated with grants and contracts when they form the agency's fiscal base. Most immediately apparent is the uncertainty of funding. Grants are designed for the support of short-term projects, and although ongoing support is often possible, it is not built into the official funding process. An agency that depends on grants or contracts for its survival is virtually unable to make long-range plans because of the lack of a financial base.

Agencies funded by grants also tend to have multiple sources of fiscal support. This factor makes even the keeping of normally simple reports a complex endeavor. The American Accounting Association (1971, p. 87) suggests that not-for-profit organizations provide yearly statements that "cross fund lines and combine or consolidate fund information in ways that provide appropriate supplementary information relative to the composite not-for-profit operating entity as a whole." It is often difficult for agencies to consolidate information concerning a number of totally separate funding sources and projects, especially when time lines are different and when reporting procedures vary among funding agencies. Separate financial statements are needed for each earmarked fund; yet in the interests of accountability and control, combined statements should also be available.

Finally, the lure of grants can interfere with agencies' efforts to maintain the integrity of their missions and goals. What Lohmann (1980, pp. 77–78) calls "planning on the run" can involve the following scenario:

> In the face of pressures from the grantor to scale down (or increase)
> the amount of a grant request, adapt a proposal to changing guidelines,
> modify the work plan, revise the personnel plan, or make other
> changes in a grant proposal, the administrator must constantly consider
> the impact of such revisions on the agency and its programs. . . . In the

present system of grant negotiations, last-minute decisions challenge the planning skill of human service administrators and may virtually nullify the deliberation and planning that went into the original proposal.

In this context, it is challenging to keep a clear picture of the agency's primary mission in mind. The need for funding often encourages human service planners to take on projects that would not ordinarily fit the scope of their agency. When this happens repeatedly, agency administrators, service deliverers, and consumers suddenly find that the very nature of the agency's programmatic thrust has inadvertently been changed. Even unrestricted funds can become tied to grant-funded projects as matching money.

Most nonprofit agencies depend on grants and contracts for at least a sizable proportion of their total funding. This factor impacts on the agency's budgeting process by enhancing the planning for specific projects but also by making agencywide coordination and long-range vision difficult to implement.

Fees

Many human service agencies charge direct fees for services rendered. When these fees are charged to individual clients, they are often based on sliding scales, with individuals paying differing amounts depending on their financial status. Frequently, fees are paid not by consumers themselves, but by outside organizations, or third parties. Third-party payments can come from insurance companies, Medicare, public agencies purchasing services for clients, or other sources.

Sometimes third parties can have the same kind of effect on agency practices as other funding sources might have. For example, an insurance company might pay for counseling services only if they are provided by licensed psychologists, despite the fact that skilled paraprofessional counselors normally provide such services in a particular agency. Such "strings" attached to payments can provide restrictions on an agency's activities. With this exception, however, fees for service tend to have the same kind of impact on budgeting whether they are paid by consumers or outside organizations.

A rarely noted problem faced by agencies that depend on fees for a significant percentage of their fiscal base is the tendency to stress direct services at the expense of alternate activities, such as community education, consultation, and advocacy. Although grants or appropriations might provide some support for such indirect services, fees are most closely associated with such traditional treatment modalities as individual counseling or therapy. Fee-based human service agencies have difficulty moving into innovative service areas when their funding depends almost completely on the number of individuals personally served. This is true not only when fees are charged to consumers, but also when agencies receive contracts from public organizations to provide treatment for a specific number of clients.

Another implication of the use of fees as a funding base is the inherent difficulty in predicting income. Planners must be able to estimate very accurately the number of clients likely to be served in a given time period, with estimations becoming even more complex if sliding scales mean that not all clients generate the same amount of revenue. Some agencies can use a flexible form of budgeting, but this works only if service costs are highly variable. (For example, if a training program uses part-time trainers on a consultant basis, hires them only when enough trainees are enrolled, and rents temporary facilities at the same time, then each training implementation can have its own budget.) Normally, however, human service agencies have fixed costs, especially personnel costs, that must be met; so revenues must be predicted with a high degree of accuracy when the yearly budget is developed.

Contributions

Contributions to an agency's operating budget can run the gamut from $5 donations by individuals to multimillion-dollar endowments. The process of fund raising can mean anything from direct mailings, to knocking on the doors of corporate offices, to mounting campaigns for special-purpose funds. Agencies that depend on large contributions for their fiscal bases often use the services of professional fund-raising or development specialists as well as encouraging the fund-raising efforts of board members. Regardless of the size of the fund-raising operation, however, human service professionals and administrators are likely to be affected, at least indirectly.

The implications of contributed funds for the budgeting process depend more on the type of contribution than on its size. Unrestricted donations can be used to carry out any of the normal agency functions; so they become part of the operating budget. Sometimes, however, contributions are restricted to use for specific purposes, with these funds earmarked either for specific current activities or for specified future use. Endowment funds may be restricted or unrestricted in terms of activities supported, but involve the use of only the income earned from assets. An agency depending on various types of large contributions that include endowments must either develop or purchase investment expertise. In addition, an agency depending on contributions for a major proportion of its revenue must also develop mechanisms for recording pledges or bequests (monies promised to the agency but not yet available).

For smaller agencies, participation in consolidated fund-raising efforts is the norm. Contributions are received indirectly, through participation in such programs as United Fund, United Way, or local community chests. In reality, receiving funds from such campaigns is more similar to obtaining grants than it is to mounting direct campaigns for donations. Agencies apply for funding, indicate the objectives to be met by the funds, follow specified reporting procedures, and, in fact, must fit the funder's funding priorities.

Diversified funding

Each of the typical methods of obtaining revenues brings problems, both for planning and for recordkeeping. Many agencies are experimenting with alternate methods that can help in the maintenance of agency autonomy. For instance, many nonprofit organizations are finding it useful to maintain connections with profit-making corporations that contribute part of their profits to the upkeep of the not-for-profit agency. Such arrangements are legally complex and would not necessarily meet the needs of all human service programs.

The important factor in obtaining revenues is to maintain agency independence to the degree possible. This means that agencies should attempt to diversify their funding procedures so that the "drying up" of one funding source does not cause a fiscal crisis in the agency. Although multiple funding makes planning and reporting complex, it also prevents dependence on one source or one mechanism.

Planners must attempt to maintain the integrity of the agency's mission, understanding that funding is only a means toward this end. Care needs to be taken to avoid letting possible new revenues dictate the taking on of activities that might be tangential or unneeded. In the final analysis, it must be remembered that funding, like all aspects of the budgeting process, must also be the servant of planning.

Creating the annual budget

The creation of the actual budget document is based on estimates both of expected revenues and of needs for the coming year. Budget needs depend on the objectives that have been developed as part of the planning process. By closely scrutinizing their implementation plans, budget makers can come close to estimating precisely what the budgetary needs of various activities might be.

In our discussion of planning, we considered a career counseling project being implemented for the first time by a hypothetical agency, the Neighborhood Youth Center. Figure 3-1 shows a time line indicating the activities to be performed during the ten weeks preceding the actual start of service delivery.

The agency's training director is responsible, during the first 4.5 weeks of the project start-up, for recruiting potential counselors, for designing their training program, and for selecting the counselors, in concert with the community service director. A subsequent 4 weeks are to be spent in actually delivering the training program to the counselors. By week 10, the trained counselors will be ready to begin delivering services. The budget designer might estimate that the training director will be spending half his or her time on the start-up of the career counseling project for the equivalent of two full

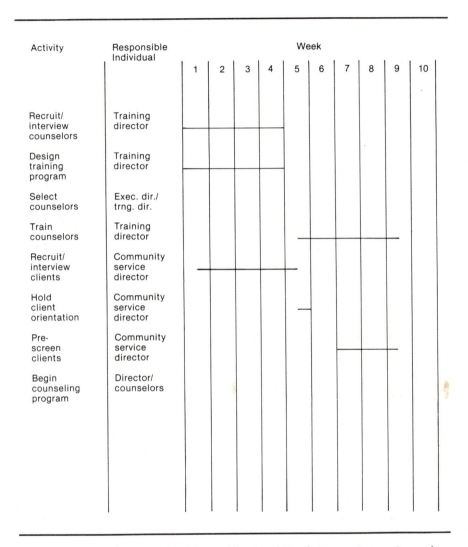

FIGURE 3-1   Time Line Model, Neighborhood Youth Center Career Counseling Project

months. If the training director's yearly salary is $20,000, the fraction of that salary spent on training the career counselors would be 1/12, or approximately $1666.66. The training director's fringe benefits would also need to be computed. If they amount to, say, 18% of salary, the fringe benefits for salary earmarked to this project would be approximately $299.99. The cost of the training director's involvement in setting up this program would be $1966.65.

The community service director is also heavily involved in the start-up of the counseling project because he or she is in charge of client recruiting and intake. It might be assumed that for two months the community service director would allocate 1/4 of his or her time to the project, meaning that 1/24 of his or her salary would be earmarked. If his or her salary is also $20,000, the earmarked salary would be $833.33, the fringe benefits, $149.99, and the total, $983.32.

The budget maker would also need to take into account other costs of this set of activities, including clerical costs; a percentage of the agency direc-tor's time; costs of recruiting clients and counselors, including printing, pos-tage, newspaper advertisements, and telephone; stipends or salaries paid to counselors during the training program; supplies; and overhead.

With all this taken into account, the financial planner would be able to make a reasonably accurate estimate of the cost of getting the counseling program in motion. These estimated costs could then be integrated into the amounts budgeted for the counseling program as a whole and/or for the agency's line-item budget as a totality (that is, specifying the total personnel costs for the agency by adding together the salary expenditures for this and all other agency programs). Whether these planning data are used to develop program budgets or for subsequent translation into line-item terms, the same kinds of procedures can be followed. The only major factor involved is that the agency's budget must fit the reality of its planned activities. If plans include carefully designed implementation strategies, the creation of a budget simply means translating activities into monetary terms.

There is tremendous variation in the forms that budget documents, once completed, can take. We will use as an example a line-item budget for a federally funded project (see Table 3-1). We have selected this type of budget as an example because almost all human service professionals come into contact with government grants at some time in their careers. Budgets for specially funded projects do have some unique features.

This budget is for a project to train volunteer counselors working in a crisis intervention project in their community. The grant is to pay the training expenses for the project; so other aspects of the program, such as services to clients, cannot be charged to this account.

The project director will spend 100% of his or her work week on this specific project; the volunteer coordinator and curriculum development spe-cialist will spend 50% of their time on this project and 50% on other programs. The secretary is to spend 100% of his or her time on the project; so he or she should not be expected by the agency to do clerical work for non-project-related employees. The fringe benefits paid to project staff are based on the normal employee benefits offered by the agency, in this case, 18% for pro-fessional personnel and 15% for nonprofessional personnel, as determined by union contracts.

TABLE 3-1   Budget for Volunteer Training Program

PERSONNEL COSTS

Position	% Time	Salary	Fringe benefits	Total
Director	100%	$25,000	$4500 (18%)	
Volunteer coordinator	50%	10,000	1800 (18%)	
Curriculum development specialist	50%	9,000	1620 (18%)	
Secretary	100%	11,000	1650 (15%)	
Total personnel costs		**$55,000**	**$9570**	**$64,570**

CONSULTANT COSTS

Visiting lecturers (5 at $100/day)	500
Travel: $160 × 5 trips	800
Per diem: $40/day × 2 days per trip × 5 trips	400
Evaluation consultant (local)	
10 days at $100/day	1000
Total consultant costs	**2700**

EQUIPMENT

Norelco transcriber	465
Norelco recorder	160
Overhead projector	150
Secretarial desk	298
Secretarial chair	102
IBM typewriter	811
Total equipment	**2086**

SUPPLIES

General office supplies	300
Total supplies	**300**

The total personnel costs make up the bulk of the costs for the entire project. Listed under consultant costs are both consultant fees and consultant travel and per diem costs. The federal agency funding this project places consultant travel in this category. Other programs might place consultant travel in a separate category, along with staff travel. The budget submitted to a specific funder must meet that program's requirements, even if separate materials must reorganize the same information to fit the agency's record-keeping systems.

Equipment, supplies, travel, and other expenses are itemized specifically. Often, the form used to submit a budget to a federal or other funding source requires that only the total line items are listed. Personnel costs, consultant costs, equipment costs, supplies, travel, and other expenses are listed as totals,

TABLE 3-1 *(continued)*

	Total
STAFF TRAVEL	*Total*
Travel to field site at $150/trip × 3 trips	$450
Per diem: $40/day × 2 days per trip × 3 trips	240
Travel to two national conferences at $300/trip × 2 trips	600
Per diem: $40/day × 10 days	400
Local travel: Est. 500 miles/month × 20¢ mile × 12 mos.	1200
Total staff travel	2890
OTHER EXPENSES	
Telephone:	
Long distance calls @ $100/month × 12 months	1200
Postage:	
Letters: $30/month × 12 months	360
Brochures	300
Printing/reproduction	
Program brochures	500
Training manuals	300
Reprints	200
Duplication of training materials	200
Total other expenses	3060
TRAINEE EXPENSES	
Tuition and fees for community college credit:	
$200 × 30 trainees	6000
Total trainee expenses	6000
Total direct costs	81,606
INDIRECT COSTS	
8% of total direct costs minus $6000 tuition/fees	6,048.48
Total indirect costs	6,048.48
Total project budget	$87,654.48

with specifics appearing on a separate budget justification sheet. Whether these details appear on the budget document or on the attachments, they must be available both for the use of the funder and for the use of the agency's own information system.

In this particular budget, trainee expenses include $6000 to be paid as tuition to a local college so that the volunteers being trained through the project can receive academic credit. It will be noted that this amount is eliminated in the consideration of the project's "indirect costs." Indirect costs are designed to help pay the project's share in the total overhead of the agency housing the program. The amount of indirect costs can vary tremendously, depending on the agreements worked out between the agency and the funding source. In this instance, because the project is a training program, the government funder has agreed to pay only 8% of the total direct costs. The $6000 earmarked for tuition is eliminated because it has no relationship to the agency's own overhead.

The form a budget takes and the information included depends on the funder's and the agency's requirements. The agency must meet the guidelines of the funding source. In this instance, the requirements are relatively simple. In many instances, agencies are required to provide matching funds, either in money or in "in kind" contributions. When that takes place, another column, showing local contributions, appears on the budget. Basically, however, budget format follows need, and the most important factor to consider is whether the items and figures are readily understandable to the people who need to make decisions regarding allocations, expenditures, reports, or accountability.

Financial reports

Financial reports serve the dual purpose of expediting the management process and ensuring accountability. Interim statements serve the internal purpose of helping monitor expenditures, and yearly reports can also provide information about the agency's fiscal condition to funding sources, policymakers, and concerned citizens.

Interim statements

Individuals who have any responsibility at all for controlling a program's expenditures should have access to regular financial reports, at least on a quarterly basis and preferably each month. Such reports help decision makers maintain a high level of awareness concerning the current state of expenditures so that they can make adjustments on a timely basis.

In nonprofit organizations, expenditures should closely match revenues. Obviously, the budget should not be overspent. Less obviously, expenditures should approximate budgeted amounts throughout the year so that agencies are not placed under pressure to spend a great deal of money very quickly at the end of the fiscal year. Whether variances from budgeted amounts are negative or positive, knowledge of departures from initial plans can enable planners either to adjust the budget or to change spending patterns. A typical interim report is shown in Table 3-2.

The report shown in Table 3-2 covers a one-year project funded for a fiscal year beginning July 1 and ending June 30. This report appeared on April 6, meaning that the project had just finished its third quarter. The budgeted amount for personnel is slightly underexpended in comparison with what might be expected. Only $48,631.37 has been spent to date, but the expectation might have been that approximately $52,500.00 would have been spent if salaries and wages were spread out evenly through the year. This variation

TABLE 3-2 Interim Report for University-Based Training Project

	Allocation	Outstanding obligation	Expended year-to-date	Free balance
Personnel	70,000.00	.00	48,631.37	26,511.63
Contractual services	6,600.00	1,339.72	4,014.68	1,245.60
Commodities,	1,815.00	80.55	291.12	1,443.33
other	.00	26.55	.00	(26.55)
Travel	1,984.00	943.00	1,026.47	14.53
Retirement	5,933.00	.00	3,734.45	2,198.55
Tele-communications	900.00	75.00	600.00	225.00
Indirect costs	7,240.00	.00	4,028.70	3,211.30
Student financial assistant	2,625.00	.00	150.00	2,475.00
Total	102,240.00	2,464.82	62,476.79	37,298.39

is due to the late start of the secretary, whose position was unfilled at the start of the project. It might be possible to allow some overtime at this point if additional clerical assistance is needed.

The line item described as commodities seems drastically underspent at this point, and the decision maker receiving this report would be likely to examine the situation in order to avoid spending the budgeted amount at the last minute. Carefully laid plans would ensure more effective use of the funds. The related line item, "other," has been overspent by $26.55, as is shown by the fact that this figure appears in parentheses. Apparently, an incorrect line item or account number was used in charging a purchase. This error would now be corrected.

The budgeted travel money has been spent. The only way further travel could take place would be if special permission were obtained to change a line item or if the funds came from some other source. It would be important for the project director to be aware of this now. This situation also shows the importance of using "accrual" accounting, rather than showing only cash transactions. Although $943 has not yet been spent, the outstanding obligation means that additional funds for travel are unavailable. If the report were limited to cash as the basis for accounting, this category of expenditure might become drastically overspent through lack of information.

Finally, the project director would need to be concerned about the fact that student financial assistance had not been used up to the budgeted amount. It would be necessary to examine project activities in order to determine the relationship between this factor and the training program as an educational entity. Sometimes financial reports can serve not just to monitor the monetary aspects of a project, but also to point toward substantive areas where pro-grammatic improvement should take place.

Annual reports

Annual financial statements complete the budgeting cycle and are designed primarily as a mechanism for fiscal accountability. Such reports can include balance sheets, which show agency assets and liabilities as of a specific date, or revenue and expenditure reports. In many instances, the only actual requirement that an agency or program needs to meet is to provide the "bare bones" of information concerning expenditures. The annual report shown in Table 3-3 contains the kind of fiscal information required for federal reporting. All figures must be backed up by detailed journal entries available for audit.

This annual report indicates that, of a grant for $81,000.00, only $71,431.33 has been spent, leaving an unexpended balance of $9,568.67. Beyond this minimal information, the agency conducting the funded project would also provide programmatic data to the funder.

Even in situations where detailed financial reports are not legally mandated, agencies and funded projects should attempt to provide documents that combine programmatic with fiscal information. Such documentation can assist the agency in planning for future years. It can also provide sorely needed information to others and should therefore be in language and format that interested community members and policymakers can readily understand. Availability of information becomes especially important when agencies are faced with the need to solve problems related to economic stress and funding cutbacks.

Cutback management

Resource scarcity brings with it the need for all stakeholders in human service programs to become involved in the search for new methods. "Cutback management means managing organizational change toward lower levels of resource consumption and organizational activity. Cutting back an organization involves making hard decisions about who will be let go, what programs will be scaled down and terminated, and what clients will be asked to make what sacrifices" (Levine, 1979, p. 180). When resources decline, policymakers sometimes fall victim to the notion that indiscriminate slashing of funds can solve the problem. In reality, however, such approaches are oversimplifications of highly complex issues. How can an agency conserve resources without merely punishing the more efficient programs that have already eliminated wasteful practices?

Levine (1978) suggests that the five most commonly used cutback methods include (1) decisions based on employee seniority, (2) hiring freezes, (3) across-the-board cuts, (4) use of criteria related to program productivity, and (5) some form of zero-based budgeting. Each of these decision-making methods has clear shortcomings, especially in terms of fairness to service deliverers and clients.

TABLE 3-3 Annual Report of Training Grant Expenditures
From 07/01/— to 06/30/—

1.	Expenditures of federal funds for this budget period				
	a. Personnel	$56,778.35	h.	Alterations and renovations	.00
	b. Consultant serv.	1,939.08	i.	Other	(2) 4,085.27
	c. Equipment	1,913.45	j.	Trainee expenses	540.00
	d. Supplies	1,201.75	k.	Total direct costs	66,457.90
	e. Travel, domestic	2,000.00	l.	Indirect costs	4,973.43
	f. Travel, foreign	.00	m.	Total	71,431.33
	g. Patient care cost	.00			
2.	Expenditures from prior periods		.00		
3.	Cumulative expenditures		71,431.33		
4.	Total amount awarded		81,000.00		
5.	Unexpended balance		9,568.67		
6.	Unliquidated obligations		.00		
7.	Unobligated balance		9,568.67		
8.	Grant related income				
	a. Interest earned (enclose check)		.00		
9.	Other		.00		

If jobs are cut on the basis of the jobholder's seniority, control over the nature of program cuts is lost. Similarly, hiring freezes also leave a great deal to chance, depending on what individuals leave or retire at any given point. Use of seniority and hiring freezes provide hardship for both women and minorities, who tend to have been the last hired.

Across-the-board cuts are commonly used as first attempts at problem resolution. This approach can buy only a small amount of time, however. At some point, someone must make the difficult decisions concerning effective and ineffective programs. Although zero-based budgeting and other rational approaches are very helpful in clarifying differences in efficiency among programs, they cannot as effectively discriminate among varying levels of client need.

Finally, decisions concerning the nature of agency cutbacks must depend on the concerted efforts of individuals willing to share the responsibility for deciding what kinds of programs contribute most to the agency mission and what kinds of services must be sacrificed. If the agency is serving a community on the basis of assessment of local needs, community members must be involved in deciding which of their goals and needs have the highest priority. They must also help decide whether cuts in funding will be fought or accepted.

McTighe (1979), in his "prescription for scaling down" an organization, states that agency managers must examine the organization's mission, recognize marginal investments or programs of limited utility, use rational mechanisms for making choices, encourage the active participation of agency employees, and retain organizational openness.

The idea of openness in fiscal matters might prove to be one whose time has come. Agencies need to increase their openness, both in terms of sharing financial information and in terms of seeking input from a variety of sources.

This openness can begin to take place when human service professionals, managers, funding sources, and community members accept the fact that budgeting, far from being a mystical force only accountants understand, is merely a method for bringing plans to fruition.

Discussion questions

1. Suppose that, as director of a human service agency that had always been supported by federal funds, you learned that your funding was going to be cut drastically. Would you concentrate your efforts on fighting against the cutback or on planning for more limited programs? What factors would you take into account in making decisions about program cutbacks?
2. How useful are budgetary reforms such as zero-based budgeting and program budgeting for human service agencies? Do you foresee new types of reforms?
3. Do you think it is possible for an agency to maintain its commitment to a central mission or purpose when funding patterns change and new types of activities are supported? How would you deal with a situation in which you could get funding only if you changed the basic focus of your agency's programs?
4. If you were coordinating a program in a human service agency, what kind of information would you need concerning income and expenditures?

Group exercise

Look again at the hypothetical agency you developed as part of the group exercise on planning. In the same groups of three or four, study the activities you identified as being important for your fictitious agency. Generate a list of possible nontraditional funding sources that might help you get your programs into action. What funding sources might have an interest, for whatever reason, in supporting these activities?

Choose one of the activities on your list and try to figure out what its costs might be. Take into account the timing of the activity, the personnel costs for workers who would be involved in carrying it out, any special consultant costs, and nonpersonnel costs, such as supplies, equipment, and office space. How much money would you need to carry out this activity for a given period of time?

Each group should share the results of its discussion with the other groups.

Cases

See Cases 3-1 ("The Best Laid Plans") and 3-2 ("Budget Cut").

References

American Accounting Association. Report of the committee on accounting procedures of not-for-profit organizations. *Accounting Review,* 1971, *46* (supplement), 81–163.

Binner, P. R. Zero-base budgeting and mental health programs. *Administration in Mental Health,* 1978, *5,* 162–171.

Brager, G., & Holloway, S. *Changing human service organizations: Politics and practice.* New York: Free Press, 1978.

Feldman, S. Budgeting and behavior. In S. Feldman (Ed.), *The administration of mental health services.* Springfield, Ill.: Thomas, 1973.

Gross, M. J., & Jablonsky, S. F. *Principles of accounting and financial reporting for nonprofit organizations.* New York: Wiley, 1979.

Levine, C. H. Organizational decline and cutback management. *Public Administration Review,* 1978, *38,* 316–325.

Levine, C. H. More on cutback management: Hard questions for hard times. *Public Administration Review,* 1979, *39,* 179–183.

Lohmann, R. A. *Breaking even: Financial management in human service organizations.* Philadelphia: Temple University Press, 1980.

McCaffery, J. Revenue budgeting: Dade County tries a decremental approach. *Public Administration Review,* 1981, *41,* 179–189.

McTighe, J. J. Management strategies to deal with shrinking resources. *Public Administration Review,* 1979, *39,* 86–90.

Otten, G. L. Zero-based budgeting: Implications for social services. In G. Zaltman (Ed.), *Management principles for nonprofit agencies and organizations.* New York: AMACOM, 1979.

Pattillo, J. W. *Zero-base budgeting: A planning, resource allocation and control tool.* New York: National Association of Accountants, 1977.

Schick, A. The road to PPB: The stages of budget reform. In F. J. Lyden & E. G. Miller (Eds.), *Planning programming budgeting: A systems approach to management* (2nd ed.). Chicago: Markham, 1972.

Skok, J. E. Budgetary politics and decision making: Development of an alternative hypothesis for state government. *Administration and Society,* 1980, *11,* 445–460.

Sweeny, A., & Wisner, J. N. *Budgeting basics: A how-to guide for managers.* New York: AMACOM, 1975.

Tripodi, T., Fellin, P., & Epstein, I. *Differential social program evaluation.* Itasca, Ill.: Peacock, 1978.

Wildavsky, A. *The politics of the budgetary process* (2nd ed.). Boston: Little, Brown, 1974.

CHAPTER **4**

DESIGNING AN ORGANIZATIONAL STRUCTURE

Human service professionals do not often think of themselves as the designers of organizations. Yet that is precisely the role they play when they engage in such activities as deciding whether service deliverers in an agency should be divided according to specializations or choosing whether to depart-mentalize an agency's services according to type of client served (the youth center, the senior citizen center) or according to type of activity performed (counseling, group work, consultation, education).

Organizational design is a decision-making process. Once initial planning has been completed, an organizational structure is needed to carry out the broad strategies that have been mandated, which involves seeking the best possible answers to the following questions:

· What are the primary goals and objectives that the organization should be designed to meet?
· What continuing activities need to be performed in order to implement the strategies that have been selected as part of the planning process?
· How can the necessary activities be divided so that individuals or groups can be assigned responsibility for performing them?
· Once activities have been grouped into specific jobs, what kind of authority and responsibility should be assigned?

- How and by whom should decisions be made?
- How specialized should roles and jobs be?
- Who should control the work being performed?
- How can communication and coordination among members of the organization be facilitated?
- How can job or role descriptions be developed to take into account both functions and accountabilities?
- How can coordination and communication with the external social environment be facilitated?

The answers to these questions bring with them the ability to describe and chart interlocking roles that in turn form a structure. The result of the entire process is the creation of an *organization* or a social unit that has been purposefully designed to meet a set of goals through a regular series of planned and coordinated activities.

The nature of the structure that is finally formed varies tremendously, based on the goals, needs, size, environment, and resources of the organization. The most important determining factor, however, may well be the theoretical orientation of the people carrying out the function of organizational design.

Organizational theories

Few human service workers maintain clear awareness of the practical differences dividing organizational theorists. Although all thinkers in the field of organizational theory seek the "best" answers to our basic questions, there is little agreement about what those best answers really are. The designers of an organization are faced with a myriad of choices. They can build structures that are highly centralized and specialized or systems based on widespread decision-making responsibility and participation. They can departmentalize the organization's activities by joining all the people who perform a specific function, or they can build teams of people with differing but complementary skills. They can use traditional, hierarchical designs or experiment with task forces, committees, or even leaderless groups. The organization's form has major implications for the way its functions will be performed.

Classical theories

The earliest major thinker to formulate the concept of an ideal organization was Max Weber, who saw the "rational legal bureaucracy" as the efficient organization in its pure form (Gerth & Mills, 1958). Weber's ideal structure, developed in the late 19th and early 20th centuries, included high degrees of specialization and impersonality, authority based on comprehensive rules rather than on social relationships, clear and centralized hierarchies of authority and responsibility, prescribed systems of rules and procedures, hiring and promotion based solely on technical ability, and extensive use of written documentation.

Weber saw this pure system as a historical trend that would meet the needs posed by the increasing size of organizations and that would at the same time replace unfairness and uncertainty with rationality and clarity. Sofer (1972, p. 13) summarizes the advantages of bureaucracy as Weber saw them, including the following:

Rationality
Precision in operation
Speed
Reduction of friction between people
Steadiness
Subordination of juniors to seniors in a strict and known way
Reliability
[Employees] being trained to become experts in their particular fields and gaining a habitual and virtuosolike mastery of their subjects

Speed, precision, and reduction of friction were associated with the ideal bureaucracy because in this organization everyone would have a clear awareness of both his or her and others' functions. All aspects of the organization's work would be regulated. The repetitiveness of the work would bring with it both steadiness and high quality. Personal enmity and constant questioning would be replaced by rationality and regularity.

Although Weber's approach was philosophical, the ideals of clearly defined objectives, specialization, hierarchical chains of command, and responsibility commensurate with authority are also basic to the thinking of early management scientists, such as Taylor (1911), and practitioners, such as Fayol (1949). Over the years, classical management theorists have developed rules that they think should govern the decisions about how organizations should be structured. These rules of thumb are in common use in all types of organizations today, especially those that are large and complex. They have been summarized most clearly by Urwick, as cited by Stewart (1968, pp. 39–40), in terms of 10 basic principles:

1. *Principle of the objective.* Once an organization has determined its basic mission, every part of it must be devoted to carrying out the tasks implied. There is no room for activities not related directly and rationally to the key objectives that have been identified by those at the top of the management hierarchy.

2. *Principle of specialization.* The organization should be divided into groups based on function so that each member performs the same type of activity.

3. *Principle of coordination.* Facilitating coordination among the various groupings within an organization is the basic purpose of the organizing function. Unity of effort is brought about through the process of organizing.

4. *Principle of authority.* There needs to be a clear line of authority so that everyone knows to whom he or she is responsible.

5. *Principle of responsibility.* Each manager is responsible for the activities of his or her subordinates.

6. *Principle of definition.* Each member of the organization should have a clearly defined set of duties that is recorded in a written job description. The job description is also expected to include recognition'of the place of the job within the organization's hierarchy.

7. *Principle of correspondence.* Each position should have authority commensurate with its responsibility.

8. *Span of control.* Classical management theorists identify ideal spans of control in terms of the number of people one manager can effectively supervise. Five or six subordinates are often considered the appropriate number.

9. *Principle of balance.* Differing units of the organization can be kept in continual balance among themselves.

10. *Principle of continuity.* An organization is an ongoing activity.

Although organizational theorists may find much with which they would disagree in this list of principles, most professional managers live by them. In the private sector, as well as in government agencies, managers still tend to trust such basic concepts as every worker must report to only one superior and there should be a clear line of authority from the top to the bottom of an organized hierarchy.

> Weber's ideal bureaucracy, in which the man [*sic*] or men at the top can make a decision and be confident that the organization will move with speed and precision to carry it out, is still the goal of many practical administrators. Many of them accept his view that an organization must be built on (1) specialization, (2) a hierarchy of officials, each of whom possesses a planned amount of authority, (3) impersonal rules, and (4) managers trained for their jobs [Dale, 1969, p. 179].

Although use of the term *bureaucratic* as an epithet to describe inefficient and unwieldy administrative structures is usually reserved for the public sector, elements of bureaucracy are most commonly seen in traditionally organized private firms that are often noted for their efficiency.

With classical management theories still prevalent in so many settings, we need to ask how relevant or useful they are for human service programs and agencies.

A human service agency designed on the basis of classical principles would be organized so that all employees, including professionals, paraprofessionals, and clerical workers, perform regular, specialized tasks. A counselor assigned to perform individual counseling with adolescents might spend all his or her time in this activity; other specialists might conduct group sessions or work with parents. Although the degree of specialization would depend on the size of the agency and the resources available, each task would relate to the basic goals of the program as a whole. The activities to be performed in the interests of meeting these goals would have been identified first, and then competent individuals would have been selected and trained to carry them out. It would be understood that the resources and jobs involved in the program would not belong to individuals but would belong to the agency, with replacement of individual workers being possible without disruption in the flow of work. (Agency activities would not change because a behaviorist was replaced by an Adlerian or because a social worker was replaced by a psychologist.) Each worker would report to one supervisor or director, who would have the authority and responsibility to carry out policies chosen by the ultimate authority (in the case of a human service agency, usually delegated to an executive director by a board of directors). Each human service professional—like each other worker—would understand the precise limits of his or her function. All similar clients would receive similar services.

The major contribution that classical theories offer to human service programs is in the area of unity of effort, with the idea that all the activities of an organization should relate to its general goals. Human service organizations could benefit from increased rationality in the planning process because one of the weaknesses of human service programs has been the tendency of professionals to perform the functions that are comfortable for them rather than those that can best meet the client-oriented goals of the agency or institution. The idea that a counseling program or agency should have a clearly defined set of objectives that should be met through the coordinated efforts of all workers is one that could enhance the efficiency and effectiveness of helping professionals. Even the bureaucratic ideal of "impersonality" could have something to offer because, as Perrow (1972) points out, this involves the purging of "particularism" and discrimination in hiring and in services.

The strengths of the classical approach seem to be outweighed by its weaknesses, at least for human service programs. The major problems in applying classical management principles to helping services lie in the insistence on specialization and on centralized hierarchies of authority. Human service professionals tend to see themselves as having responsibility not just to their agencies or institutions, but to their clients and their professional colleagues as well. They are not easily able to conform to a system that expects them to obey orders that may conflict with their professional standards or with their views of their clients' best interests. The use of very specialized, routine work patterns may be of little value in dealing with human, and therefore often unique, problems. The worker who gains a "habitual and virtuosolike mastery" of his or her subject may overlook the differing needs of individuals being served, with the result that agency rules gain in ascendancy while consumer rights are lost. Human service agencies are beginning to come to grips with the fact that creative approaches are needed to deal with the problem of increasing client needs coinciding with decreasing agency resources. Unfortunately, what bureaucracies may offer in terms of rationality is lost in terms of creativity.

Some of these weaknesses are addressed by the proponents of another theoretical approach: the human relations school.

Human relations approaches

The human relations approach to organization assumes that the bureaucratic view of human beings is too narrow to be useful in real-life organizations. As Argyris (1957) points out, workers are really motivated by many factors other than economics, including desires for growth and independence. To Argyris, the organizational forms mandated by the classical theorists make for immature, dependent, and passive employees with little control over their work and thwart more mature employees capable of autonomy and independence. The purpose of the human relations approach is to develop organizational forms that build on workers' strength and motivation.

McGregor (1960) distinguishes between managers adhering to Theory X and those adhering to Theory Y. He does not say that either of these theories is correct. He does say that each is based on assumptions that, if recognized, would have major implications for organizing activities. McGregor's Theory X manager assumes that people dislike work, lack interest in organizational objectives, and want to avoid responsibility. The natural result of this situation is that managers must base their organizations on the need to control, to supervise closely, and to use reward, punishment, and active persuasion to force employees to do their jobs. In contrast, the manager who adheres to Theory Y assumes that people enjoy working, desire responsibility, have innate capacities for creativity, and have the potential to work toward organizational objectives with a minimum of direction. The implication of these assumptions is that work can be organized in such a way that personnel at all levels have the opportunity to do creative, self-directed, and responsible jobs.

The organizational implications of McGregor's model are clear. Theory X managers would use high degrees of specialization, clear lines of authority, narrow spans of control, and centralized decision making. Theory Y managers would use less specialization, less control, and more delegation of decision making and responsibility. The organization would be decentralized so that workers' natural creativity could be channeled effectively.

Likert (1967) examines a number of specific organizational variables, including leadership, motivation, communication, decision making, goal setting, and control. He divides organizations into four basic types, based on how they deal with these organizational variables. He labels his four types System 1 (exploitive authoritative), System 2 (benevolent authoritative), System 3 (consultative), and System 4 (participative group). Likert's System 1 organizations are characterized by leaders who distrust their subordinates, by decision-making processes that are concentrated at the top of the organizational hierarchy, and by communication that is almost exclusively downward, from supervisor to supervisee. Control and power are centralized in top management so that others feel little concern for the organization's overall goals. System 2 organizations also centralize power in the hands of the few at the top of the hierarchy, but add an increased degree of communication. There is more trust in subordinates, but it is condescending in nature. System 3 increases communication; employees have the opportunity to give input, although all major decisions are still made at the top of the management hierarchy. System 4, the opposite of System 1, is characterized by leaders who have complete confidence in workers, by motivation that is based on responsibility and participation as well as on economic rewards, by communication among all organization members, by extensive interaction, by decentralized decision making, by wide acceptance of organizational goals, and by widespread responsibility for control. Likert (1967, p. 46) says that most managers recognize System 4 as theoretically superior to the others. He points out that if clear plans, high goals, and technical competence are present in an organization, System 4 will be superior. The key to its superiority lies in a structure based on group decision making and on the relationship of each group in an organization to every other group through common members or linking pins.

How would an organization based on the thinking of Argyris, McGregor, and Likert differ from a bureaucratic agency? If a human service program were organized in accordance with a human relations approach, it would be characterized by greater freedom of action, both for human service professionals and for their coworkers. Instead of departmentalizing the agency by function, the organization might divide work according to purpose or population being served. An interdisciplinary task force, including various helping professionals, paraprofessionals, community members, and consumers, might work together to solve a specific problem. Such a group might design a program to improve the agency's services to court-referred juveniles or to troubled families. It might provide outreach services to displaced homemakers or to school-aged drug users. It might educate the community concerning mental health or stress management.

The task force itself might be permanent or ad hoc, but this organizational structure would allow each person to participate actively in planning and decision making while decreasing the prevalence of routine, specialized activities. Less attention would be directed toward authority and control and greater emphasis would be placed on the flow of information from person to person and group to group. In the case of a large agency, people would identify with their own projects and feel responsibility for their success. In the case of a small agency or of a program within a larger institution, all staff members would participate in setting objectives and choosing evaluation methods for the program as a whole. Although a hierarchy of authority might exist, decision-making powers would not be limited to those at the highest levels, and the boundaries between jobs and specializations would not be clear-cut. Structure would be seen as a changing force rather than as a constant factor.

A strength of the human relations approach for human service agencies is its consistency with the approach of helping professionals. Human service workers tend to favor increasing self-responsibility and options for their clients. There is consistency in their work environments if they, too, are treated as responsible adults and if they have the chance to treat their coworkers in the same way.

The human relations-based organization also has a greater allowance for change than does the bureaucratic structure. Although bureaucracies are efficient for dealing with routine tasks, they do not allow for the creative responses to change that a more fluid environment can make. In the human service field, there is a need for the development of new approaches that can help clients deal with a world in which change is constant. Professionals who have the opportunity to create and the freedom to innovate might provide better service than their highly specialized colleagues.

Of course, the human relations theories do not provide easy answers. Creating an organization based on concepts of democracy and independence is, if anything, a more complex task than developing a more traditional structure. Although people might have innate capacities for growth and creativity, they have not necessarily had the chance to develop these capacities in schools and work settings that still tend toward Theory X. The Theory Y manager must carefully create structures that can encourage workers to learn how to function without close supervision and at the same time provide effective training and leadership.

Human service organizations are often closely related to larger systems, and a structure that differs greatly from those used by others is often misunderstood. A System 4 counseling department within a System 1 school or a System 4 community agency attempting to deal with a System 1 city government faces conflicts that might seem surprising. Yet the existence of these differences should be expected, as the contingency theorists make clear.

Contingency theories

No one form of organization is appropriate for all types of settings. Several researchers have indicated that the tasks and environments differing organizations face bring with them the needs for differing structures. Determination of the most efficient and productive type of structure in a given situation depends upon the specific contingencies being faced.

Woodward (1965) categorizes companies in terms of the complexity of their technologies, distinguishing between "unit and small batch firms," which produce specialized units in accordance with customer orders; "mass production firms," which use assembly lines; and "process production firms," which engage in continuous processing of materials. Their research has led Woodward and her associates to believe that different forms of organization are appropriate for companies using different types of technology. Classical, bureaucratic forms may be appropriate for mass production firms but highly inappropriate for unit processing companies, which need to be more adaptive to rapidly changing demands.

Burns and Stalker (1961) distinguish between what they term *mechanistic* and *organic* forms of organization. The mechanistic form, comparable to the classical type of structure, depends on formal authority, specialization, and structured channels of communication. The organic form is highly flexible and informal, with communication channels based not on the hierarchical chain of command but on the need to solve immediate problems by consulting the person with the needed data. In studying a number of British firms, Burns and Stalker have found that the organic style seems most appropriate for firms such as electronic companies facing rapid technological change and the need to solve novel problems. The mechanistic form is productive for firms needing efficiency in dealing with very stable conditions.

The work of Lawrence and Lorsch (1967) provides more insight into organizational needs in varying situations. Lawrence and Lorsch have identified four organizational features that vary with the degree of environmental certainty: (1) reliance on formal rules and communication, (2) time horizon, (3) diffuse or concentrated goals, and (4) relationship- or task-oriented interpersonal styles. Lawrence and Lorsch stress that effective organizations have a good "fit" with their environment. An organization with a stable environment can use formal rules, a short time horizon, traditional communication channels, and task-oriented management. An organization with an unstable environment needs more points of contact with the external world so that changes can be recognized promptly. Such an organization needs a longer time orientation and a more complex communication pattern. Formal rules and hierarchies would interfere with the needed information flow; so it would be inappropriate to rely on them.

Lawrence and Lorsch point out that because an organization's structure should depend on the degree of certainty of the information in the environment, different units within the same organization might need different types of structure. One department might deal with a segment of the environment that has a high degree of certainty while another unit within the same system might actually be dealing with a relatively steady flow of information. For instance, within a given company, most departments might use traditional hierarchies, but the research and development section would need the flexibility of an organic structure. Lawrence and Lorsch suggest that, in such differentiated organizations, the integration of activities and units becomes especially important, and unity of purpose should be achieved through the design of special coordinating structures. The complexity of the organization depends on the degree of differentiation in interfaces with the environment more than it depends on mere size.

The contingency theorists make clear that an effective organization can run the gamut from a traditional bureaucracy to a highly organic, constantly changing structure. Which structure is appropriate depends on the organization's needs.

At its most basic level, the contingency approach offers administrators a method for clarifying their ideas about organization. If human service professionals were to use contingency theory to determine the best ways to structure the work of their programs or agencies, they would, as a first step, identify the most salient characteristics of their services and settings. Following Woodward's example, they would need to ask whether their agencies were in fact mass production firms or small batch firms. Human service workers who viewed themselves as technicians offering consistent services to a wide range of clients might be able to use mechanistic organizational structures, but such designs would be inappropriate for professionals attempting to deliver multifaceted services based on community needs assessments. Helpers would also need to determine whether their environments were characterized more by rapid change or by stability over time, recognizing that agencies dealing with shifting populations or subject to changes in funding could not afford to use slow-moving, unwieldy organizational structures.

Human service professionals might find the concepts of differentiation and integration within organizations particularly useful. In many instances, human service programs interface with their environments in different ways than other programs with which they are associated. For example, in social service settings, agencies are often divided between counseling services and income maintenance services, and differing organizational structures might be appropriate for each. Recognition of this factor might lead to creative attempts to integrate divergent departments and eliminate some of the rancor that often accompanies such units' attempts to reform each other. Similarly, counseling departments housed within traditional academic institutions might develop methods of coordinating efforts that previously had been seen to have little in common.

The contingency theories, unlike the other approaches, recognize the impact of the external environment on each organization's structure and process. They are, in effect, systems theories. These ideas have been developed further in approaches that also see organizations primarily as open systems.

Open systems theory

Systems can be thought of as sets of elements that interact with one another so that a change in any one of those elements brings about a corresponding alteration in other elements. Open systems take in and export energy through interfaces with the environment so that units within the system are also affected by changes in other systems.

Whether an organization is considered an open system has major implications for the designer's decision-making processes. Hall (1972) divides the basic approaches to organizational design into two main perspectives: approaches that view the organization as an open system versus those that see it as a closed system. The closed system is essentially classical. "The closed-system model views organizations as instruments designed for the pursuit of clearly specified goals. Organizational arrangements and decisions are geared to goal achievement and are directed toward making the organization more and more rational in the pursuit of its goal" (Hall, 1972, p. 15). In contrast, open systems theorists recognize that rationality within organizations is limited both by internal factors, such as organization members' characteristics, and by external factors, such as changes in the supply of available people and materials.

Katz and Kahn (1966) spell out the characteristics of the open system as follows:

1. *The importation of energy or input.* [Some kind of energy is brought in from the environment or other organizations in order to be processed by the system in question. In the case of counseling and human service systems, the input is largely in the form of people.]

2. *Throughput.* [Within the system, the energy is processed and changed in some way.]

3. *Output.* [The organization exports energy to the environment at large and to other systems.]

4. *Cycles of events.* [The energy exchange is repetitive so that the export of energy tends to provide the basis for a new import of energy, with the cycle then being repeated continuously.]

5. *Negative entropy.* [Organizations try to import more energy than they export. If the reverse takes place—if more energy is exported and less imported—the system dies.]

6. *Information input, negative feedback, and the coding process.* [Systems import information as well as energy. Some kind of coding system is needed to determine which information is useful and which can be ignored. Negative feedback helps the system control outputs because deviations from what is expected can be corrected.]

7. *The steady state and dynamic homeostasis.* [When a factor in the environment changes, the organization must change just enough to maintain a steady state and deal with the disruption. The basic character of the organization is maintained through changes in form.]

8. *Differentiation.* [Open systems tend to move steadily toward greater differentiation and specialization of the functions performed by units within the organization. Growth is from the simple to the more complex.]

9. *Equifinality.* [The same end state can be reached from different initial states and different means. At the same time, different final states can be reached from the same initial states.]

Managers who view their organizations from the systems perspective tend to see organization more as a process than as a structure. They know that structural changes both affect and are affected by changes in all the other components of the organization. They know, too, that the goals and activities they choose will be affected by environmental factors that are often beyond their control.

The ideas offered by systems theory might well be more important to human service agencies than to private sector firms because environmental impacts on both the program as a whole and individual clients must be considered. Human service professionals using these ideas would develop structures indicating the relationships between the agency and other systems as well as those within the agency. Methods of coordination with community groups, funding sources, governmental agencies, other helping agencies, educational institutions, professional organizations, and a variety of other systems would need to be identified. In addition, organizational strategies would take into account the progress of individual clients through the system. Methods would be developed for linking clients with various services, for following up on clients as they move into other systems, and for communicating with referring agencies as new clients are accepted. These methods would be built into the organizational structure, with communication to outside agencies being as carefully planned as communication within the program itself.

A major strength of the systems approach is the encouragement it gives to human service professionals to think of themselves as part of a network that, as a totality, can serve the individual client in a coordinated way. This does not mean that human service administrators should allow their programs to be buffeted about by external systems, all making conflicting demands. The other organizational approaches, including the classical management approach, provide some benefits as well, for they can help agencies in their attempts to clarify basic programmatic goals and to find ways to develop unity of effort in reaching those goals.

Theory Z

Ouchi (1982) developed the Theory Z concept through his study of Japanese corporations. Assuming that there must be some organizational reason for Japanese workers' productivity and commitment, he studied a number of corporations. His findings were that Japanese organizations are characterized by lifetime employment, slow evaluation and promotion, nonspecialized career paths, collective decision-making styles, collective responsibility, and an integration between work and social lives. These characteristics can be contrasted with those of an American bureaucratic structure: short-term employment, rapid evaluation and promotion, specialization, explicit control mechanisms, individual decision making, individual responsibility, and segmented concern. The American worker, according to Ouchi, is more oriented toward his or her specialization than toward loyalty to the specific organization. "In the United States we conduct our careers between organizations but within a single specialty. In Japan people conduct careers between specialties but within a single organization" (Ouchi, 1982, p. 29).

Ouchi's notion is that the Japanese approach brings with it an integration of effort and a degree of loyalty that allows workers to equate their own best interests with the interests of the total organization. Although the Japanese approach cannot be transferred completely to the American situation, a number of organizations, which Ouchi terms Theory Z companies, do share some of the characteristics of Japanese firms. These organizations depend for their integration on the common values firmly held by all members. "The socialization of all to a common goal is so complete and the capacity of the system to measure the subtleties of contributions over the long run is so exact that individuals will naturally seek to do that which is in the common good" (Ouchi, 1982, p. 71). Individual workers see themselves primarily as members of the organization and only secondarily as members of a profession or specialty. Their commitment is to work in close concert with others toward the achievement of long-range, organizationwide goals. They trust the organization and their coworkers and sense a mutual commitment. They join with others in collective decision-making processes and expect to work in a number of different areas within the organization so that they develop a sense of what each component offers.

A Theory Z human service agency would bring in new service deliverers under the assumption that the individual and the agency were both making long-term commitments. Within the agency, the human service worker would play a number of different roles over the years. For example, a community mental health center might be composed of a number of units, including an inpatient facility, a day treatment center, an outpatient program, specialized services for children and for the aged, and a consultation and education program. The individual worker would spend some time in each of these units, playing a variety of roles. No one professional would specialize in a particular type of service or clientele. Each worker would have enough familiarity with all the units that he or she would have a good picture of how the whole center operates. Center philosophy would be clear, and an important part of each employee's orientation program would be the opportunity to learn in depth about the agency's mission and theoretical approach. Within the units of the center, decisions concerning client services would be made collectively. Performance measures would revolve around group procedures rather than around individual expertise.

A Theory Z approach in a human service setting might help bring about a degree of integration that is missing in many agencies. Organizations that depend on employees who have been highly trained in professional specializations often find service deliverers immersed in their own work and unaware of the agency's total thrust. The Theory Z emphasis on development of a central philosophy and on giving workers the opportunity to experience several parts of the organization might help build commitment and enhance mutuality in the agency's work.

This high degree of integration within the organization is not without problems. If workers in a Theory Z organization hold fast to common values, they might also tend to have difficulty dealing with diversity. Although a human service agency needs a guiding philosophy, it also needs the ability to reach out for innovative ideas from other settings. Professionals who are active in their fields and who move from agency to agency bring fresh approaches that would be lost in a closed organization.

No organization is ever purely mechanistic or purely organic, completely closed or completely open. Instead, as Hall (1972, p. 27) points out, "in essence, organizations attempt to be rational, controlling their internal operations and environment to the greatest extent possible, but never achieving a totally closed, rational system."

Being aware of a variety of theoretical frameworks helps human service professionals know that, as they seek to organize their programs, they do have choices. These choices are made even more complex, however, by the very special nature of human service organizations.

Problems in organizing human service agencies

Many theoreticians recognize that general organizational theories apply to human service agencies in a somewhat limited way because there are special features of human services that make them difficult to organize, or at least to describe in organizational terms.

Newman and Wallender (1978) point out that not-for-profit enterprises differ from firms in the profit-making sector because objectives are often intangible; employees have dual commitments, being as loyal to their professions as to their employing agencies; the influence of consumers or "customers" is weak; and rewards, punishments, and funding are not fully under the control of internal management.

These factors have strong impact on the organizational process. Questions of centralization versus decentralization are difficult. Employees who have professional training can make all the decisions covered by their professional codes, but they do not necessarily take agency goals, or even changing client needs, into account. On the other hand, a centralized bureaucracy cannot be successfully implemented because the presence of a large number of professionals confounds the hierarchy and eliminates unquestioning subservience to agencywide objectives.

These special features make decision making in the nonprofit agency difficult, and the resulting organizational processes sometimes have a special character. Several organizational theorists have attempted to describe the uniqueness of the organization employing large numbers of professionals.

One way of examining such structures is in terms of what Mintzberg (1979) calls the "professional bureaucracy." Like the traditional bureaucracy, this type of organization depends on the regularity of the tasks to be performed, on standardization, and on stability. The tasks to be performed in the professional bureaucracy, however, are too technical and complex to be closely supervised by managers. Instead, the authority that is present is based on professional expertise; so the regularity of the bureaucracy is combined with a high degree of decentralization. Each professional worker controls his or her own work in terms of professional standards and training, but the skills used are repetitive.

The primary difficulty with the "professional bureaucracy" is that change becomes increasingly difficult.

> The professional bureaucracy is an inflexible structure, well suited to producing its standard outputs but ill suited to adapting to the production of new ones. All bureaucracies are geared to stable environments; they are performance structures designed to perfect programs for contingencies that can be predicted, not problem solving ones designed to create new programs for needs that have never before been encountered [Mintzberg, 1979, p. 375].

Another difficulty within human service organizations is that it is not always possible to identify where decision-making power resides. There is often a dual hierarchy, with professional employees having a power and status system separate from the official organizational management system. Kouzes and Mico (1979) identify three domains in human service organizations: the policy domain, the management domain, and the service domain. Administration is especially difficult because of the need to bring coherence to the varying goals, values, and perceptions of widely separate subgroups within the organization.

Some theorists see rationality as an overly simplistic model for use in examining human service organizations. The "organized anarchy" concept of Cohen and March (1975) identifies some organizations as characterized primarily by goals that are unclear or difficult to measure, technologies that are also changing or contested, difficulty in evaluating outcomes, and decision making that involves fluid participation, with people "wandering" in and out of the decision-making process.

Although the concept of organized anarchy was developed to describe higher education, it is also applicable to other human service organizations with high degrees of professionalization and has potential for helping shed light on the complexities of change in such settings (Berger, 1981).

Organizing the human service agency or program involves recognition both of the complex variety of organizational theories available and of the special problems inherent in nonprofit, professionalized settings.

Organizational practices

The human service professional's philosophical approach toward organizing will affect every decision that he or she makes as a structure is developed. Regardless of theoretical orientation, however, each organizer must decide how to identify individual roles within the organization, how to divide activities among groups or departments, and how to coordinate efforts both within the organization and at interfaces with the environment.

In human service organizations, given their unique characteristics, the following general guidelines might prove helpful:

1. *Develop clarity concerning individual roles within the organization.* Because it is difficult within human service organizations to identify the decision-making centers and to distinguish between agency and professional roles, it is particularly important that individuals have a clear idea of expectations. This does not mean that a bureaucratic structure must be followed. Even in a strongly decentralized decision-making structure such as Likert's System 4, participants do know what role they can expect to play, what kind of decision-making power they have, and how subsystems interact within the organization.

2. *Build a structure that allows for responsiveness to the need for change.* Both classical bureaucracies and their professional counterparts seem too unwieldy to lend themselves to the need for change. Human service agencies need to combine some degree of clarity, which is missing in the "organized anarchy," with the kind of flexibility that can bring needed adaptations to changing client needs. The key to dealing with this issue might well lie in the type of departmentalization utilized.

3. *Emphasize the coordinating function.* The effective human service organization needs to emphasize coordination, both within the agency and between the agency and its environment. It is an open system, and it can maintain its life only when this factor is recognized. The fact that agencies are interdependent with other systems can be seen as a problem, but it can just as accurately be seen as an opportunity for growth and for efficient use of resources.

Identifying individual roles

Organizations are helped to run smoothly if their individual members are aware of their own roles and know both what is expected of them and what they can expect of others. Having some type of organizational chart to provide a graphic illustration of relationships is helpful.

Organizational charts.   Traditional, mechanistic organizations depend on organizational charts to clarify the chain of command and to illustrate the expected flow of communication. Organic structures place less stress on charts but still use them to clarify roles. Organizational charts alone do not explain functions in great detail but must be joined by written job descriptions that can provide additional information. Organizational charts fail to show the degree to which decision-making responsibilities are delegated or the emphasis placed on interpersonal communication within an organization. A chart that appears to show a very traditional management structure may in fact be somewhat misleading. A clear attempt at organic structuring is illustrated by the work of Wilson (1976, p. 33), shown in Figure 4-1.

The agency Wilson depicts is one in which the director and an assistant are the only paid staff. The bulk of the agency's work is carried out by task forces, or committees, each of which is led by a volunteer. The committees, which include youth recruitment, senior citizen involvement, school aide and tutor program, a group project task force, research, office assistants, and several others, perform what would normally be considered both professional and clerical work. At the same time, they serve as a mechanism for increasing total community involvement, providing what Wilson terms a "pyramid effect" (Wilson, 1976, pp. 32–33).

A more traditional structure might appear somewhat more like that shown in Figure 4-2.

The organizational chart shows that the executive director is the chief operating officer of the agency, reporting to a board of directors either directly or through a committee structure. The assistant directors handle whatever matters the director delegates. The remainder of the duties to be performed

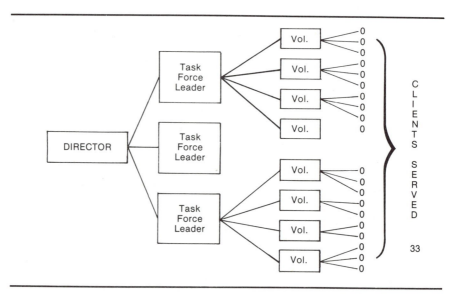

FIGURE 4-1 Organizational Chart for Volunteer Agency (*From* The Effective Management of Volunteer Programs, *by M. Wilson. Copyright © 1976 by Volunteer Management Associates, Boulder, Colo. Reprinted by permission.*)

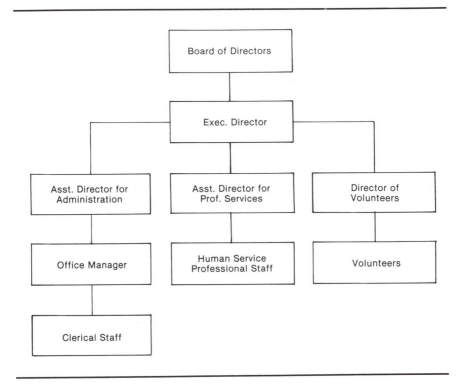

FIGURE 4-2   Organizational Chart for Traditional Human Service Agency

by the agency are handled by staff members, who are assigned duties, or by volunteers, who are supervised by their director.

If this very small but traditionally structured agency should grow in size, organizational changes would involve the addition both of more vertical levels and of more horizontal specializations. Vertically, growth would bring with it the placement of directors in charge of smaller departments, with supervisory levels added between directors and staff members. Horizontally, specialties such as training director and personnel director might be added, and the professional services department would be divided into smaller sections based on type of service offered. Another major by-product of growth in a mechanistically structured agency would be the beginnings of differentiation between line and staff positions.

Line and staff.   Many large organizations divide their personnel into the two categories of line and staff. Line managers have responsibilities in carrying out the major purposes of the organization and have the authority to direct others in carrying out these purposes. In a bureaucratic structure, they are part of the chain of command that links all levels of the managerial hierarchy. Staff personnel do not have the same kinds of authority relationships. Instead, they act in advisory capacities to line managers, either as personal staff or as experts able to give advice in specific fields. The agency illustrated in Figure 4-2 might add personal staff, perhaps in the form of an assistant to the director, or specialized staff, perhaps in the form of a research and evaluation department. The personnel department might be considered a staff, rather than a line, department.

Few human service agencies differentiate between line and staff positions. In community agencies delivering counseling or social services, human service deliverers are considered line personnel because the services they perform are directed toward the major purpose of the organization. Sometimes, however, human services fall within larger organizations. Then it becomes very important to determine whether service providers are considered line or staff personnel. For instance, in many school situations, counselors are not certain whether they are to be considered line or staff. Major conflicts between administrators and counselors arise because that distinction has never been clarified. Consider the major differences in counselor role as it would be perceived by the principal in Figure 4-3 as compared to the principal in Figure 4-4.

In Figure 4-3, counselors, along with teachers, are line personnel. They report to the principal through the assistant principal and are charged with carrying out one aspect of the educational process.

In Figure 4-4, counselors are seen as staff personnel. Their function in this school is to assist line personnel—teachers, assistant principal, and principal—to carry out their duties. The counselors assist through their specialization and through their ability to advise on such matters as individual differences among students.

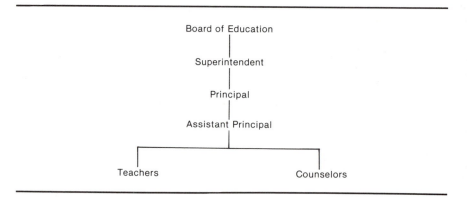

FIGURE 4-3   Counselors as Line Personnel

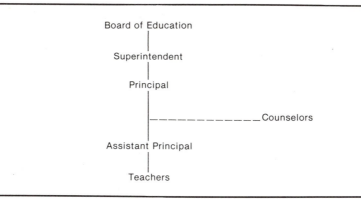

FIGURE 4-4   Counselors as Staff Personnel

Neither of these approaches is necessarily correct, but it is vital that the counselor's view of his or her place in the organization be consistent with the administrator's view. Counselors who are considered line personnel should not be surprised when the assistant principal tries to give them orders, and counselors who are considered staff should not expect to be "promoted" to assistant principals.

This kind of issue is always apparent in school settings. It also appears in a number of other human service agencies because the dual hierarchy is almost always a factor when human service professionals are employed. It is as important to determine whether those professionals are considered line or staff as it is to determine their place within the agency's system of departmentalization.

Dividing activities among groups

In business settings, activities are normally departmentalized using functional departmentation, a division form, or a matrix structure. Functional departmentation involves grouping together all the personnel who share common functions or procedures. This type of departmentation is usually considered efficient because functions are routinized and duplication of effort is avoided. The weakness of the functional form is that individuals tend to be so aware of their own departments that they lose sight of the common purpose of the organization as a whole. Power and authority become overly centralized in the hands of the few top managers who are able to see the "big picture."

In the divisional form of departmentation, individuals with complementary specializations are grouped together. The grouping may be on the basis of product, of customer, or of location. Product departmentation involves all the people contributing to the development of a given product or service; customer departmentation involves all the workers dealing with a specific category or segment of the public; and location departmentation involves decentralizing operations so that smaller organizations are duplicated in each of several geographical areas. The strength of this approach is that individual workers can closely identify with the outcome of their work in terms of the creation of goods or services rather than becoming involved strictly in means, or methods. For small organizations, however, the duplication of effort involved in recreating functions across divisional lines can be costly.

The matrix structure involves a compromise between the functional and divisional forms. Organizations using this structure are functionally divided but use temporary task forces for projects that require the work of several specialists. Each project has its own manager, and personnel receive temporary assignments to work with special projects. The strength of this structure is that it uses the positive aspects of both the other types of departmentation. It tends to be complex and to require strong human relations skills on the part of managers who must share authority with others, but it allows for rapid reorganization in response to immediate needs for change.

The ideas of private sector managers concerning departmentation have not been utilized in human service settings as much as they might be. In fact, the utilization of divisional or purpose-type departmentation might be very useful for the human services. Agencies might be divided in terms of type of client being served, allowing human service workers to share complementary expertise toward the goal of providing effective services. The efficacy of this approach was illustrated in a recent needs assessment workshop where counselors, social workers, psychologists, paraprofessionals, and others were brought together to share their experiences in a number of settings. Greater commonality of purpose was found when all the human service workers familiar with a given population or setting were brought together to dialogue. When workers were brought together by specialization (counselors in one group, psychologists in another), less creativity resulted. Larger agencies might be more effectively divided if they departmentalized by purpose or clientele rather than by professional specializations.

Another type of divisional departmentation—geographic—is also highly appropriate for human service settings. When agencies divide by geographic location, utilizing small, community-based agencies rather than centralized offices, they tend to increase the active participation of both service deliverers and consumers. Effective coordination and sharing of resources among such outreach branches are important because duplication of effort is as uneconomical in the human services as it is in the production-oriented firm.

The matrix structure has a great deal of promise for utilization by human service agencies. Although this structure has been used primarily in very large and complex organizations, it could be adapted to the needs of the small agency. The agency could departmentalize by specialization and overcome the weaknesses of this approach by using interdisciplinary team projects. Whenever a human service professional joins forces with other professional and paraprofessional helpers, consumers, and community members to plan a specific project, a form of matrix structuring is actually being used. At the same time, agencies receiving funding for special projects involving several staff members on a part-time basis are also using a matrix form that, if recognized officially, could be handled more efficiently. The important aspect of departmentalization is that it be used as a way to organize and at the same time to build a human service agency that is ready and able to make creative adaptations to changing consumer needs.

Coordinating efforts

Human service professionals performing administrative tasks have a doubly important responsibility. Their work involves not only coordinating efforts in the interest of efficiency for the organization, but also providing coordinated services for the benefit of individual clients. The concepts of networking and linkage are especially useful for the coordination function.

Networking involves a recognition that human services are part of a helping network that includes mental health facilities, educational institutions, rehabilitation settings, and a wide variety of specialized agencies. In the interests of efficient use of resources, as well as effective delivery of services, the efforts of these services should be coordinated.

> When agencies are small, workers and community members can feel a sense of ownership, a sense that the agency belongs to them. . . . Yet, in every community, there must be some kind of centralized planning. . . . These small, localized agencies can only play a part in the planning that affects their own futures if they join together in cooperative networks. . . . They can recognize gaps in the community's services, plan joint programs when they are appropriate, and share valuable services [Lewis & Lewis, 1977, p. 125].[1]

Networking combines the creativity and flexibility of the small, organic agency with the efficient utilization of resources found in the larger, more mechanistic organization. As a coordinating technique, networking is appropriate both for coalitions of small, independent agencies and for subdivisions of large, complex service organizations.

Closely related to the concept of networking is the idea of *linkage*. Effective coordination requires that consumers of services, as well as deliverers, recognize the connections among departments and separate agencies. Organizing for linkage involves developing procedures that overcome fragmentation in service delivery so that individual clients do not become lost in a tangle of agencies and programs. Linkage efforts can include special coordinating departments, interface task forces among agencies, or client advocates.

[1] From *Community Counseling: A Human Services Approach*, by J. Lewis and M. Lewis. Copyright © 1977 by John Wiley & Sons. Reprinted by permission.

The human service professional's efforts in the organizational sphere should reflect his or her role as client advocate. Management theories and practices, many of which have been developed for private sector organizations, have much to offer. The human service worker must adapt these principles to fit the special contingencies of the human service program or agency. The skill of organizing must be used as a means toward the universal goal of the helping services: enhancing client development.

Discussion questions

1. Chapter 4 discussed several approaches to organizational design, including (1) classical, bureaucratic theories, (2) human relations approaches, (3) contingency theories, (4) open systems theory, and (5) Theory Z. Do you find some of these theories more helpful than others? If you were designing a human service organization, which theories would you be most likely to use?
2. Think of an agency or organization that you found particularly effective in meeting the needs of its clients or members. In general terms, how was that organization designed? To what degree did the design seem to affect the organization's accomplishments?
3. What is the best way to departmentalize human service organizations—by function, purpose, or use of a matrix design? What factors would you take into account in deciding this?

Group activity

Return once more to your previous small groups of three or four and look at the hypothetical agency you planned. Design an organizational structure in order to make the agency operational. Begin this process by writing down your group's answers to the following questions:

1. How should the organization's work be departmentalized?
2. How should work be divided among departments and individuals? Draw an organizational chart that you would use to describe the agency's design.
3. How would you make sure that the work of various individuals and groups was effectively coordinated?

Share your organizational chart with the other groups. Have most of the groups designed similar organizations, or are there major differences among them? What seems to account for the difference?

Cases

See Case 4-1 ("The Community Career Center") and Case 4-2 ("The Umbrella Organization").

References

Argyris, C. *Personality and organization.* New York: Harper & Row, 1957.

Berger, M. Coping with anarchy in organizations. *Annual Yearbook.* La Jolla, Calif.: University Associates, 1981.

Burns, T., & Stalker, G. M. *The management of innovation.* London: Tavistock, 1961.

Cohen, M., & March, J. G. *Leadership and ambiguity: The American college president.* New York: McGraw-Hill, 1975.

Dale, E. *Management: Theory and practice.* New York: McGraw-Hill, 1969.

Fayol, H. *General and industrial management.* London: Sir Isaac Pitman, 1949.

Gerth, H. H., & Mills, C. W. (Eds.). *From Max Weber: Essays in sociology.* New York: Oxford University Press, 1958.

Hall, R. H. *Organizations: Structure and process.* Englewood Cliffs, N.J.: Prentice-Hall, 1972.

Katz, D., & Kahn, R. L. *The social psychology of organizations.* New York: Wiley, 1966.

Kouzes, J. M., & Mico, P. R. Domain theory: An introduction to organizational behavior in human service organizations. *Journal of Applied Behavioral Science, 15*(4), 1979, 449–469.

Lawrence, P. R., & Lorsch, J. *Organization and environment.* Cambridge, Mass.: Harvard University Press, 1967.

Lewis, J., & Lewis, M. *Community counseling: A human services approach.* New York: Wiley, 1977.

Likert, R. *The human organization: Its management and value.* New York: McGraw-Hill, 1967.

McGregor, D. *The human side of enterprise.* New York: McGraw-Hill, 1960.

Mintzberg, H. *The structuring of organizations.* Englewood Cliffs, N.J.: Prentice-Hall, 1979.

Newman, W. H., & Wallender, H. W. Managing not-for-profit enterprises. *Academy of Management Review, 3*(1), 1978, 24–31.

Ouchi, W. G. *Theory Z: How American business can meet the Japanese challenge.* New York: Avon, 1982.

Perrow, C. *Complex organizations: A critical essay.* Glenview, Ill.: Scott Foresman, 1972.

Sofer, C. *Organizations in theory and practice.* New York: Basic Books, 1972.

Stewart, R. *The reality of management.* London: Pan Books, 1968.

Taylor, F. W. *Principles of scientific management.* New York: Harper & Row, 1911.

Wilson, M. *The effective management of volunteer programs.* Boulder, Colo.: Volunteer Management Association, 1976.

Woodward, J. *Industrial organization: Theory and practice.* London: Oxford University Press, 1965.

DEVELOPING HUMAN RESOURCES

In an era of austerity, when funds are severely limited and organizations need to contract in size and cut back program offerings, human service managers are virtually forced to develop clear plans for working toward their agencies' central missions. For many HSOs, such strategic planning represents new and untried ground. In the halcyon days of expanding resources, growth could be allowed to happen without a great deal of forethought.

> During a period of growth, the absence of any clear understanding of purposes, plans, and resources may not threaten the survival of the organization—at least not immediately. Resources are growing. There is no need to deny support to anyone. . . . Next year there will be an additional increment of resources, which can be used to expand those activities that proved worthwhile without having to eliminate the ones that failed [Behn, 1980, pp. 616–617].

When agencies retrench, however, managers need to consider the central purposes of the agency and to ask "How can the resources it has, and can expect to have in the future, be best mobilized and organized to achieve these purposes?" (Behn, 1980, p. 613).

Human service agencies are labor intensive organizations. A sizable portion of each budget goes toward salaries and the other costs of maintaining human, rather than just material, resources. The way these human resources are to be used and enhanced must be decided in a careful, rather than a haphazard, manner.

The concept of *human resource development* provides a context for a broad vision, encompassing the needs of the organization as a whole. It also utilizes a long-term perspective in planning, attempting to deal with both immediate needs and future requirements.

> Human resource development (HRD) is a planned approach to enhance the development and growth of employee skills, abilities, judgment, and maturity to better meet overall organizational and individual employee goals. HRD programs are implemented to develop employee capabilities to carry out job functions more effectively and to meet projected staffing needs [Craft, 1979, p. 103].

To meet their human resource needs in the 1980s and 1990s, human service managers must deal effectively with a number of related issues:

- They must expand human resources by encouraging the participation of volunteers.
- They must maintain their commitment to equal employment opportunity, even in the face of cutbacks.
- They must develop effective and efficient methods for hiring and appraising agency employees.
- They must provide training to enhance the effectiveness of service deliverers.
- They must protect valuable human resources by taking steps to prevent burnout and improve the quality of work life.

Each one of these steps plays an important part in the effective development of human resources.

Encouraging volunteer participation

Utilization of volunteer human service deliverers must be as carefully planned as the hiring of paid employees. When volunteers are recruited and selected to meet needs that clearly relate to the agency mission, they can make a major contribution to each program. Wilson (1980) points out that when an agency has a clear plan concerning the need for volunteers, it is possible to "target recruit" people who have specific skills and interests, rather than to depend on a "shotgun" approach. She suggests that agency personnel attempting to recruit volunteers do the following:

1. Do specific rather than general recruiting whenever possible.
2. Choose audiences whose interests and priorities meet your needs.
3. Determine the skills you need and actively seek them out.
4. Establish a year-round recruitment plan.

5. Use a variety of recruitment techniques, such as newspaper ads, human-interest stories, radio and television spots, posters, billboards, bumper stickers, displays, tours and open houses, newsletters, and person-to-person contact.
6. Utilize the services of voluntary action centers, volunteer bureaus, retired senior volunteer programs, and student volunteer bureaus.
7. Recruit volunteers from all segments of the community.
8. Be enthusiastic! If you, as a recruiter, aren't excited about your agency's programs, then those you attempt to recruit won't be excited [Wilson, 1980, p. 119].

This approach to volunteer recruitment helps build a large pool of potential personpower. At the same time, it focuses on finding volunteers whose skills can be most effectively used because they fit program requirements. A human service manager would never recruit and hire a paid employee without having at least a rough job description in mind. The same should apply to volunteer workers.

Although recruitment programs should try to target potential workers who might have needed competencies and interests, they should never limit themselves to one segment of the community. The people who have the required abilities might be found in other places, among other groups. "Instead of being the privilege of the already privileged, volunteering must become the right of everyone: minorities, youth, seniors, the handicapped, blue-collar workers, business people, the disadvantaged" (Wilson, 1976, p. 118). Recruiters miss important sources of personpower if they try to attract only affluent people who are assumed to have adequate leisure time.

Traditional concepts of volunteerism should also be expanded to include attention to the self-help phenomenon. Helping resources are multiplied when individuals have the opportunity to participate in relationships that make no distinction between helper and helpee. In self-help groups or organizations, people assist others who share common concerns while they receive help. Self-help groups work because they provide support, effective communication, realistic assistance, and understanding. Perhaps most important is the fact that when individuals have the chance to help others, they tend to make major gains in their own lives.

Self-help, by definition, must remain under the control of community members, rather than agency personnel. The appropriate role for human service workers to play is one of support. Professional helpers can work to encourage the formation of needed self-help organizations. Once these organizations have formed their own structures, professionals can provide technical assistance, training, and referrals.

The needs for services are increasing rapidly while the resources available to human service agencies dwindle. It would not be possible to provide help to everyone who needs it by depending on the services of professionals alone.

Volunteers make it possible to stretch available resources, but that represents only one part of their contribution. Self-help may be the treatment of choice for many individuals whose need to become involved with other community members is greater than their need to become clients. When community members help themselves and one another, resources increase geometrically.

Equal employment opportunity

The way community members feel about themselves and their local human service agencies is also affected by the organizations' staffing. When public programs are cut back, women and minorities tend to lose their jobs in disproportionate numbers, primarily because they are likely to have been among the most recently hired agency employees. Although some managers find it difficult to maintain their commitments to affirmative action in the face of economic adversity, equal employment opportunity must be maintained. In the private sector, fairness in hiring, appraising, and promoting women and minorities is often seen almost entirely as a benefit for the employees themselves. In human service agencies, the presence of minority and women service providers and managers is also of major importance for clients. A human service program is limited in its effectiveness if the makeup of its professional staff differs significantly from that of its clientele. Affirmative action programs recognize that equal opportunity affects the agency's services as much as it benefits the target group of employees.

People involved in making decisions about the allocation of human resources need to understand exactly how the intent and effects of their practices might tend to discriminate against women and minorities. Beyond this, managers and supervisors must be aware of the federal and state legislation and guidelines governing fair employment practices. In human service agencies, which are often too small to maintain separate personnel departments, equal employment opportunity must be understood by everyone with decision-making power.

Federal legislation

Title VII of the Civil Rights Act of 1964 prohibits discrimination on the basis of race, color, religion, sex, pregnancy, or national origin. The act covers conditions of employment and hiring and promotion practices. When this federal legislation was passed, it called for an Equal Employment Opportunity Commission that would enforce it. The commission was limited in its powers, however, until passage of the *Equal Employment Opportunity Act of 1972*. This act gave the Equal Employment Opportunity Commission the power to initiate court action against discriminating companies. The 1972 act also provided for coverage of public employees.

The *Equal Pay Act of 1963* requires employers to pay equal wages for equal work. Companies can differentiate pay based on merit or measurable differences in productivity. They cannot have different pay scales for men and women working at jobs with the same demands, responsibility, and level of required skill.

The *Age Discrimination in Employment Act of 1967* prohibits discrimination against employees between the ages of 40 and 70. Individuals protected by this legislation cannot be denied employment or promotion on the basis of age.

The *Pregnancy Discrimination Act of 1978* is actually an amendment to the Civil Rights Act. Employers cannot discriminate against women on the basis of pregnancy if the women are capable of performing their jobs. Pregnant women cannot be forced to resign or take leaves of absence. They are entitled to disability and medical coverage.

The *Rehabilitation Act of 1973* prohibits discrimination against handicapped employees who could perform successfully with reasonable accommodation. The act, which applies to both mentally and physically handicapped individuals, includes sections specifically outlawing discrimination by the federal government or its contractors.

Finally, the *Vietnam Era Veterans Readjustment Act of 1974* requires that equal employment opportunity be provided to Vietnam era veterans by government contractors.

Enforcement of federal legislation

The Civil Rights Act of 1964, along with its later amendments, is enforced by the Equal Employment Opportunity Commission, which maintains offices in a number of cities. An individual who believes that he or she has been a victim of employment discrimination can file a charge with the E.E.O.C. After an investigation of the charges, the commission can seek a conciliation agreement with the employer. If no settlement is reached and if the E.E.O.C. decides that the employer is in violation, a suit can be filed by the commission (if the employer is a private company) or by the United States attorney general (if the employer is a public agency). If the E.E.O.C. does not bring suit, a "right to sue" letter is provided for the individual, who is then free to sue privately.

If the employer is found to have engaged in discriminatory practices, the company may be required to make up for losses suffered by the employee or applicant, often involving payment of back wages. If systematic discrimination has taken place, the employer might need to develop organizationwide remedies, including affirmative action programs.

Executive orders

Executive orders apply to the federal government and to employers having government contracts. Because many human service agencies depend on federal funds, they are affected by these presidential orders.

Executive Order 11246 prohibits employment discrimination on the basis of race, color, religion, or national origin by employers having government contracts. *Executive Order 11375* extends the previous order so that discrimination on the basis of sex is also prohibited.

Executive Order 11478 also outlaws discrimination based on race, color, religion, national origin, or sex, but applies specifically to government agencies themselves.

Executive Order 11141 applies both to public agencies and to government contractors and outlaws employment discrimination based on age.

The executive orders duplicate federal equal opportunity legislation, but they focus specifically on government agencies and contractors and are, in some respects, stronger. The federal government could instigate an investigation without the existence of a specific complaint. Beyond that, agencies with government contracts can be required to submit affirmative action programs.

Affirmative action

Affirmative action programs are designed to remedy discriminatory patterns that have existed in the past. An organization, recognizing that past inequities have brought about an underrepresentation in the work force of women or minorities, can develop a set of goals for hiring and promoting groups that have been the victims of past discrimination. Such goals take into account both the specific problems of the organization and the presence of the protected class of workers in the available labor force. Affirmative action plans are usually based on surveys of the local labor market and the employer's own work force. If inequities are found, the employer develops goals, usually in terms of time guidelines, and decides on the methods to be used in reaching them. The goals might affect either the percentage of targeted groups in the total work force of the company or the number of women and minorities in managerial or professional positions.

Implications for human resource development

It is important that human service managers maintain an awareness of the basic intent of equal employment legislation and affirmative action. The spirit of equal opportunity recognizes that changes in human resource management practices must occur if equity in the workplace is to grow. These changes can take place only if people involved in hiring and appraising employees take time to think through the methods they are using. A great deal of discrimination happens not because decision makers purposely exclude women and minorities, but because unexamined practices result in unintentional exclusion.

Agency policies relating to recruitment, selection, promotion, appraisal, and discharge of employees must be scrupulously fair. Recruiting and selecting workers, as well as appraising their on-the-job performance, must be based on careful analyses of the nature of the work. If hiring is based on requirements concerning personal characteristics, past training, or experience, employers need to be able to justify the real importance of these qualifications while ensuring that applicants are recruited from a variety of sources. When current employees are evaluated, promoted, selected for special training programs, or selected for merit pay increases, decisions must be based on clear and objective criteria. Supervisory recommendations alone cannot be the basis for selection if recommendations are based on subjective and vague standards, if a small percentage of women and minorities is selected through the process, or if hourly employees are not notified of the qualifications necessary for promotion (Halley & Feild, 1978). Performance appraisals must be valid, clear, and related to bona fide job specifications. Otherwise employers have a great deal of difficulty supporting their contentions of fairness.

Commitment to equal employment opportunity requires that criteria related to hiring and appraisals be carefully examined. It may actually provide the impetus for human service decision makers to take steps toward developing objective processes that are needed anyway. If human resource development is to be based on planning and if efficient use of personpower is to become a reality, careful thought about criteria for selection and appraisal is an important first step.

Hiring practices

Selection processes work most effectively when information about job openings is widely disseminated. Wide dissemination helps ensure fairness for potential applicants, but it also helps the agency by expanding the pool of available individuals.

The person chosen from this pool will, ideally, be the one most perfectly suited for the job. This ideal can be met only if decision makers are familiar both with the characteristics of the applicant and with the characteristics needed for good job performance. "If a selection program is to be successful, hiring persons who perform well, the unit requiring the employee needs to specify the characteristics for effective performance on the job. . . . Basically, what is needed is specification of the characteristics of successful employees" (Glueck, 1974, p. 287).

Surprisingly, many managers concentrate their efforts on appraising job applicants' aptitudes and background without paying equal attention to the organization's needs. Especially in situations calling for the hiring of a person to perform a newly developed function, employers need to prepare for the selection process by analyzing potential job tasks and related competencies. Then preliminary screening and interviews can focus on bona fide qualifications.

Russell suggests a series of steps that should form part of the hiring process:

1. Define the job responsibilities and required skills thoroughly and clearly.
2. Review the organizational context of the position and amend the job requirements accordingly.
3. Examine each candidate in light of the specific job and organizational demand, given their work experiences and skills.
4. Look for candidates who fit the job you're offering, not candidates who will settle for it.
5. Know which qualities for the job are most important and which are least important.
6. Know yourself and your style and assess your hiring needs in that context.
7. Match some part of the interview to the actual job conditions.
8. Involve others in the hiring process [Russell, 1982, pp. 24–26].

These steps call for careful analyses of the organization and its needs prior to beginning the recruitment process. If decision makers begin by analyzing the kinds of tasks the workers will be expected to perform, they can list and rank the skills and competencies that the effective employee will need. Each applicant can then be considered with a reasonable degree of objectivity. Giving interviewees the chance to demonstrate relevant competencies and involving more than one person in making the final decision also helps increase realism and objectivity.

Human service organizations that are large enough to go through hiring processes fairly frequently or that keep lists of qualified workers might consider using some form of assessment center. These centers, which are largely used to appraise performance and make decisions about the development of current employees, can also be helpful in predicting job applicants' effectiveness. Assessment centers, by definition, use multiple methods of assessment, including simulations or situational tests that provide opportunities for performance of actual, job-related behaviors. Centers also use multiple assessors, each of whom has been trained to make judgments based on observations of performance. Assessors' independent evaluations are combined to make final assessments of participants.

The assessment center concept was pioneered by industries attempting to assess potential managers or executives. A group of middle management personnel might be brought together in an assessment center to examine their skills in leadership, organizing, decision making, human relations, or other factors considered relevant for managerial performance. Behavior samples might be gleaned from a combination of in-basket exercises, leaderless group discussions, management games, individual presentations, objective tests, projective tests, and interviews (Howard, 1978).

Assessment center methods can be adapted to the needs of human service agencies and used to predict the effectiveness of service deliverers as well as managers. The important point is that "the dimensions, attributes or qualities evaluated by the assessment center are determined by an analysis of relevant job behaviors" (James, 1980). When such analyses have been completed, even small agencies can utilize some of the assessment center ideas by building opportunities for objective behavioral appraisals into the selection process. Such methods can then be carried into the agency's systematic performance appraisal program.

Performance appraisal

Every organization has some kind of performance appraisal system. Whether the system is formal or informal, explicit or implicit, objective or subjective, the organization uses some method to evaluate the way employees do their jobs. This process can have a major impact on the effectiveness of the organization as a whole.

> A properly constructed and maintained performance appraisal system can contribute to employee effectiveness by providing feedback about specific strengths and weaknesses, documenting the fairness of administrative personnel decisions, providing information to guide employee training, development, and placement programs, and enhancing feelings of responsibility on the job. Since organizational effectiveness is strongly influenced by individual effectiveness, it is obvious that a good performance appraisal system can improve the overall effectiveness of the organization [Sauser, 1980, p. 13].

Performance appraisal can serve a great many simultaneous functions, each of which is important to the management of human resources. These functions seem to boil down to two major purposes, which might be in opposition to each other.

> On one hand, employers need objective evaluations of past individual performance for use in making personnel decisions. On the other hand, employers need tools to enable managers to help individuals improve performance, plan future work, develop skills and abilities for career growth, and strengthen the quality of their relationship as manager and employee [Walker, 1980, p. 202].

Walker questions whether it is realistic to think that one performance appraisal system can accomplish both central purposes. The evaluation aspect requires that the appraiser make hard judgments on the basis of past performance; the development approach calls for a joint effort and uses past performance primarily to lay the groundwork for future goals and plans. Because these purposes sometimes conflict, many systems tend to concentrate on one at the expense of the other.

In most human service agencies, performance appraisal systems do need to fulfill both evaluation and development functions because separate appraisal programs would be too expensive. It is not easy to create a system that can accomplish so much, but it is possible, as long as rating mechanisms are practical, objective, and clearly job related and as long as the people who carry out the system have been adequately involved in its development.

Appraisal mechanisms

Any appraisal system depends on the use of some kind of mechanism to form the basis of rating employee performance. The best appraisal mechanisms come closest to evaluating the behaviors that actually distinguish between successful and unsuccessful job performance. Any scales used should be based on objective criteria that have been established through analysis of the jobs being performed. Although this may seem obvious, arbitrary and subjective performance measures are still very much in evidence in human service organizations. The nature of many commonly used evaluation techniques makes unreliability and rater bias common.

Traditional rating scales.   Every human service worker has used evaluation systems based on rating scales. Usually, a list of characteristics is presented and the assessor is asked to rate the employee on each quality listed. Ratings are usually on three-, four-, or five-point scales, from "excellent" to "poor" or "needs improvement," with gradations in between.

The primary problem with such rating scales is that the characteristics listed are often vague and subjective. Assessors are asked to rate employees in terms of their personal characteristics, rather than in terms of specific skills or work-related behaviors. Appraisal of employees' work attitudes, enthusiasm, honesty, dependability, or initiative are common.

Such ratings can be called into question in terms of their fairness. Interrater reliability is low, partly because the characteristics being evaluated are subject to perceptual differences and partly because rater bias is a reality. Biases can include a "halo effect," through which the assessor's total perception of the employee affects each separate rating, or a tendency among some assessors to rate everyone as average, avoiding either positive or negative extremes.

Traditional rating scales are also limited in their practicality. If the purpose of appraisal is to improve performance, the mechanisms used must point the way toward behaviors that need strengthening. If an employee receives low ratings on his or her personal characteristics, there is little that can be done to improve.

Some appraisal systems have attempted to add relevance to rating scale mechanisms by using forced choices, requiring raters to choose one of a pair of statements as being more characteristic of the employee, or by using weighted checklists. These methods are also susceptible to bias on the part of the person making the choices. They are viable only when item weighting is based on secure knowledge about the characteristics that successfully distinguish between effective and ineffective workers.

Rankings and comparisons. The use of group-oriented appraisal mechanisms is less common in human service organizations than in production-oriented companies. When such methods are used, each employee is compared with other employees in comparable positions in accordance with some criterion or criteria. The assessor might rank employees from best to worst or compare each individual in turn to all others.

Rankings and forced distributions help make distinctions among employees when selections must be made for differential compensation or for promotion. Such methods operate implicitly, under the surface, even when no conscious effort is made to tally points or complete rankings.

Such methods hold little promise of effectiveness, however, if performance appraisal is meant to aid employee development. Appraisal can help motivate employees by identifying areas they can build on, by comparing each employee with his or her own goals. Comparisons with other employees do little to help in this area.

Performance tests. Tests of job-related skills are most often based on simulations or demonstrations. Employees are asked to show they have competencies related to effective job performance. This can work only if the process designers have validated the methods used and if the skills being tested lend themselves to objective measurement.

In human service agencies, it might be possible to base performance appraisal, at least in part, on evidence such as video- or audiotapes of therapy sessions or other work with clients. Use of this type of performance test would require that raters agree on what characteristics they wish employees to demonstrate. Even if appraisers could agree on the competencies underlying effective work with clients, the performance test might lend itself more to the purpose of employee development than to evaluation. Human service workers tend to have a number of responsibilities beyond direct service delivery; so other appraisal tools would be needed to supplement the skill test. Use of an assessment center, involving multiple appraisers and several methods, might provide an ideal setting for simulations and demonstrations.

Critical incident techniques. Supervisors are sometimes asked to keep logs of important incidents that demonstrate employees' strengths or weaknesses. Such records provide solid data that can be used to give feedback to employees. The ability to point toward concrete experiences helps appraisers in their efforts to share appraisal results with employees.

The concreteness of the critical incident approach makes it somewhat less subject to rater bias than ratings of personal characteristics. Supervisors using this method do need training in order to be as objective as possible in the selection and recording of incidents. A halo effect can occur, with supervisors finding negative or positive incidents that can support their overall impressions of certain employees.

Some appraisal systems call for supervisors to go beyond the keeping of a simple log to the actual writing of essays concerning employees' strengths and weaknesses. Although such essays might be subjective, they do at least provide more depth than simple rating scales, which can be just as biased. Like the performance test, essays or logs might be most useful as part of a multifaceted appraisal program.

Behaviorally anchored rating scales.   Critical incident records can form part of the process of developing behaviorally anchored rating scales. These scales are different from others in the way they are developed and in their focus on measurable employee behaviors rather than on general traits (Schwab & Heneman, 1978). There are five major steps used in developing behaviorally anchored rating scales, or BARS. First, people who are familiar with the job list specific kinds of incidents that would illustrate effective or ineffective performance. These incidents are then clustered into groups or performance dimensions. In order to provide for accuracy and objectivity, a second group of people familiar with the work matches incidents with performance dimensions, and the work of the two groups is matched. Once incidents and performance dimensions have been selected, the incidents are scaled and a final instrument is developed. The incidents that have been selected now serve as "behavioral anchors" that translate important performance dimensions into concrete, behavioral, measurable terms.

The shortcoming of this approach is that many people must spend long hours developing the instrument, and some human service managers might not want to devote a great deal of time and energy to performance appraisal. Once such an instrument has been developed, however, it might save time and effort by streamlining evaluation. In the long run, more time might be wasted by using inaccurate measures that take supervisors' time but do not provide real assistance in decision making.

The kinds of behaviors involved in human service work might lend themselves to the use of BARS. Clayton and Gatewood (1981) describe the development of an appraisal system used by a social service agency to evaluate coordinators. System designers used both interviews with agency personnel and literature reviews to select a number of performance dimensions that were appropriate for all the coordinator positions. They decided to use the social work job dimensions of direct service, indirect service, programming and directing work for self and others, development for self and others, information processing, and managing work units. It was found that, when coordinators wrote activity statements describing their own jobs, the statements fit the performance dimensions. Once agreement had been reached concerning the clusters of activities that lent behavioral bases to each job dimension, a rating scale could be developed and managers trained in conducting performance appraisal. This "multistage process" seems to have been successful on two counts: the development of the rating scale itself and the involvement of potential system users in the planning process.

Involvement in the appraisal process

In human service settings, performance appraisal is often difficult because widespread agreement concerning appropriate criteria and standards is lacking. Employees perform ambiguous tasks; the outcomes of their work are not always tangible; and their success in working with clients can be affected by many external factors. Criteria that are imposed on the appraisal process can easily be seen as unfair and as unrelated to job effectiveness. Because of the difficulty in measuring the effectiveness of human service workers, it is especially important that all those involved in the appraisal process—employees as well as supervisors—play roles in specifying the performance dimensions that will be measured. As Stein (1979, p. 91) points out, "Where employees have little control over conditions that affect their job performance and where there is little certainty in predicting the outcomes of their actions, it is important for the success of a program that employees accept the measures as valid."

Stein suggests that the only way to ensure that employees will, in fact, accept appraisal measures as valid is to involve them fully in identifying productivity measures. Group techniques, such as brainstorming and priority setting, can be used to identify the outcomes and competencies seen as important and measurable. When the appraisal system is put into effect, this prior involvement in planning can help set a basis for communication between supervisor and supervisee.

Finally, supervisors who will be asked to implement the appraisal program need to receive ongoing training so that they can use rating mechanisms fairly and confidently. If supervisors and employees agree that the strengths and weaknesses being measured are the ones that matter, appraisal can provide guidelines for meeting the training and development needs of human service workers.

Training

Effective use of limited human resources requires that human service workers receive ongoing training to meet the changing needs of community and clients. A major shortcoming of human service programs has been the tendency of service deliverers to continue performing activities for which they have been prepared and with which they feel comfortable, even when client needs dictate different approaches. If human service workers are to be effective, they need to add new behaviors to their repertoires when changing services are mandated. If helpers are asked to change, they must receive the training that can help them maintain their current level of competence.

Training programs need to take into account both individual workers' development needs and the organization's long-range personnel needs. Nadler (1970) distinguishes among three activities that differ from one another and that together form the basis for human resource development in varying organizational settings. The three areas include (1) employee training, which focuses on introducing new behaviors to improve the individual's immediate effectiveness; (2) employee education, which provides broader preparation to help the individual's career mobility; and (3) employee development, which prepares the individual to evolve and grow with the organization. The training focus is on the job; the education focus is on the individual; and the development focus is on the organization.

In human service settings, there is a need both to train individuals in the context of their current work and to educate human service workers—professionals, paraprofessionals, or volunteers—for delivery of innovative services still in the planning stages. Making such distinctions helps in the development of an overall training plan. In reality, however, the basic steps to be followed in implementing training programs are the same, whether the focus is on an individual or a group, on immediate needs or long-term plans.

Assessing learning needs

Both for the sake of appropriate use of resources and for the sake of participant motivation, training programs must be based on careful assessment of real needs. The assessment might be based on the measurement of existing problems in service delivery, on the suggestions of employees or supervisors, or on an awareness that changes in the agency's mission are on the way. In any case, solid recognition of a goal that can be attained through learning of some type must precede the implementation of a training intervention.

Davis and McCallon (1974) suggest that two possible methods for assessing needs can be used: problem analysis or a competency model. In problem analysis, the trainer begins by seeking a statement of the presenting problem, being careful to avoid stating a suggested solution as a problem. Once the problem has been stated accurately, the trainer attempts to refine the problem statement, find evidence to support the existence of the problem, and then identify the needs that must be met. At this point, the key step is to separate learning from nonlearning needs. The trainer is concerned with those needs that can be met through the participation of some individual or group in a learning event. Nonlearning needs require different types of interventions, such as structural reorganizations or changes in planning mechanisms.

The competency model also leads to the development of plans based on identification of learning needs. The difference between the two methods is that although the problem analysis method begins by identifying a shortcoming in the present system, the competency method begins by identifying a desired outcome. The needs assessment then focuses on discovering the present level of competency, specifying needs in terms of the distance between present and desired levels, and identifying the learning needs that must be met.

Developing training objectives

Both the competency approach and problem analysis lead to the same point. Once learning needs have been clearly identified, they can be stated in terms of objectives. In some way, it is expected that trainees will be different after the educational intervention. Their behavior will be changed because they have developed new skills, gained new knowledge, or learned new attitudes. The specific nature of the desired change should be clearly stated before the training program is designed.

Designing the training program

The design of the training program depends on the kinds of objectives being met and the resources available. In most work settings, training can run the gamut from on-the-job instruction and coaching to specially designed workshops for groups, ongoing classroom teaching, individualized programmed instruction, use of audiovisual media, laboratory training, and conferences. Within the confines of the workshop format, which is used very commonly in human service settings, methods can involve lectures or panel discussions, case conferences, demonstrations, use of media, discussions, gaming, role playing, laboratory training, exercises, or simulations. The nature of the activity selected must take into account the availability of both human and inanimate resources, and the program design must be based on the learning objectives that have been set. Knowledge acquisition objectives can sometimes be met through essentially passive learning, such as reading, watching films, listening to lectures, or using programmed materials. Either skill acquisition or attitude change, however, depends on learners' active involvement and should use approaches that encourage individual and group activity (Craft, 1979).

The alternatives for training program design are infinite. Most important, the interventions selected must suit the objectives that have been developed and at the same time meet the needs and orientations of trainers and trainees.

Implementing the training program

If the training methods selected are appropriate to the objectives that have been set, the likelihood for effectiveness is enhanced. It is still important to remember, however, that intervention methods should be appropriate to adult learners' needs. Their motivation depends on their ability to recognize the importance of the training program to their own work effectiveness. They must have been actively involved in selecting training goals. At the same time, they should be assured that the skills and knowledge they are gaining will be recognized and reinforced in the context of their posttraining work. The kind of training program to avoid is one that has little connection with the ongoing work of the agency and its employees. The one to use extensively is the type that seems a natural outgrowth of the needs that have been identified through the appraisal process and that have been recognized by all involved.

Preventing burnout

The development of human resources must take into account the fact that agency employees are valuable and that steps must be taken to protect them, to the degree possible, from some of the work-related stress that can lead to "burnout."

Burnout among professionals in public service organizations involves a negative change in attitude and behavior. It includes a tendency to leave behind idealism and personal concern for clients and to move toward more mechanistic behaviors. "Other changes include increasing discouragement, pessimism, and fatalism about one's work; decline in motivation, effort, and involvement in work; apathy; negativism; frequent irritability and anger with clients and colleagues; preoccupation with one's own comfort and welfare on the job; a tendency to rationalize failure by blaming the clients or 'the system'; and resistance to change, growing rigidity, and loss of creativity" (Cherniss, 1980, p. 6).

Human service agencies cannot afford the loss in productivity involved when an active, enthusiastic professional burns out. This process can never be completely prevented because individual, as well as organizational, characteristics affect susceptibility. Cherniss suggests, however, that a number of positive steps can be taken to lessen organizational stress and prevent burnout.

One approach is to change the way jobs are structured. Many human service professionals find it stressful to work continually at a single type of service, often without feedback or collegial interaction. Changes might be as simple as assigning more varied types of clients to each service deliverer or as complex as developing matrix systems that allow workers to accomplish some major tasks through teamwork. Adaptations must depend on the unique problems of a specific organization, but the key factor is to find ways to break into routine patterns and to increase the intangible rewards that participation in human service delivery can provide.

Attention should also be paid to the supervisory relationships that each human service professional has the opportunity to form. New professionals often need support, information, and some degree of structure because they tend to be concerned about their own competence (Cherniss, 1980). Supervisors can help human service workers make the transition from newcomers to self-sustaining, confident professionals if they devote energy to establishing strong relationships and if they understand their own importance as role models. Supervisors, too, can burn out, and they need feedback, support, and interaction in their own work lives.

The organization as a whole can also provide a more or less stressful work environment, depending on whether all organizational members share a sense of excitement and strong purpose. Human service professionals, para-professionals, and volunteers can often withstand very heavy work loads if they feel they are participating in an effort that will lead to major accom-plishments. Clarity of purpose in an agency helps bring this feeling to the surface.

Human service workers also need to have access to counseling and support groups that can help meet their own emotional needs. Many industrial settings now provide employee assistance programs for workers, and human service agencies might benefit from following this example.

Employee assistance programs, at least as they are used in the private sector, are means of improving productivity. There is a recognition that, in any company, most employees want to be productive. Unfortunately, a num-ber of factors can stand in the way, causing job performance to deteriorate and productivity to decline. These influences—all correlated highly with absenteeism, with loss of motivation, and with errors—include both job-related stress and personal concerns. Alcoholism, drug dependency, emo-tional problems, family conflicts, interpersonal difficulties, and legal and financial issues are all personal matters. They become the concern of the organization, however, when they affect on-the-job behavior.

Employee assistance programs deal with these problems by providing services to employees as part of their job benefits. Components of such programs usually include short-term counseling for employees and their families, assessment and referral services for people who need more intensive treatment, training for supervisors in recognition and referral of problems, and sometimes educational seminars and workshops.

If such programs are appropriate in other settings, they might be consid-ered even more important in human service agencies. The mental health and well-being of service deliverers has a strong and immediate impact on their competence as helpers, and personal problems can cut their effectiveness drastically. Human service agencies may be too small to have their own fully developed employee assistance programs, but they can join forces with other agencies to develop cooperative programs that meet the needs of all employ-ees in the network.

Human service agencies are faced with declines in material resources. They cannot afford to lose the productivity of their most valuable resource: the people who make the programs work.

Discussion questions

1. Many agencies use volunteers because of their helpfulness in strength-ening ties to the community and because of the personnel dollars saved. Although this can be very positive, many people have pointed out that use

of volunteers can cost human service workers their jobs. Should agencies be encouraged to save human resource costs by using volunteers in place of salaried personnel? What would you see as the primary arguments on either side of this question?

2. We favor equal employment opportunity and affirmative action, not just because of their legality, but also because of the importance of having diversity among service deliverers. What other ways do you see for combating racism and sexism in human service organizations?

3. If you were setting up an assessment center to measure the competencies of current or potential human service workers, what types of measurements might you use? What competencies would you be looking for?

4. Suppose you were directing an agency that needed to extend its community outreach programs in order to generate revenues. What would you do if you believed this direction was right but if the professional service deliverers insisted on staying in their offices and waiting for individual clients to come in? Would you try to change the behaviors of these professionals? What steps would you take to train them for new functions?

Group exercise

In groups of about six to eight people, develop a job description for a human service worker in a hypothetical agency. Use this job description as the basis for role-played employment interviews. Take turns playing the parts of interviewer and job applicant, with the other group members observing. When observing, watch for the effects of the job description that has been developed. Is it clear enough to provide guidelines for the interviewer? Think also about suggestions you can make to the interviewer concerning his or her skills in eliciting needed information.

Cases

See Case 5-1 ("Director of Training") and Case 5-2 ("Burnout").

References

Behn, R. Leadership for cut-back management. *Public Administration Review,* 1980, *40,* 613–620.

Cherniss, C. *Professional burnout in human service organizations.* New York: Praeger, 1980.

Clayton, K., & Gatewood, R. The development of a managerial performance appraisal system in a social service agency. *Public Personnel Management Journal,* 1981, *10,* 261–269.

Craft, J. A. Managing human resources. In G. Zaltman (Ed.), *Management principles for nonprofit agencies and organizations.* New York: AMACOM, 1979.

Davis, L. N., & McCallon, E. *Planning, conducting, and evaluating workshops.* Austin, Tex.: Learning Concepts, 1974.

Glueck, W. F. *Personnel: A diagnostic approach.* Dallas: Business Publications, 1974.

Halley, W. H., & Feild, H. S. Equal employment opportunity and its implications for personnel practices. In H. G. Heneman & D. P. Schwab (Eds.), *Perspectives on personnel/human resource management.* Homewood, Ill.: Irwin, 1978.

Howard, A. An assessment of assessment centers. In H. G. Heneman & D. P. Schwab (Eds.), *Perspectives on personnel/human resource management.* Homewood, Ill.: Irwin, 1978.

James, T. *The assessment center method applied to competency assessment of clinical workers in mental health.* Paper presented to Illinois Department of Mental Health & Developmental Disabilities, University of Chicago, May 1980.

Nadler, L. *Developing human resources.* Houston: Gulf Publishing Company, 1970.

Russell, K. Sisterhood is complicated: Hiring and firing feminist-style. *Ms.,* 1982, *10*(7), 24–28.

Sauser, W. I. Evaluating employee performance: Needs, problems and possible solutions. *Public Personnel Management,* 1980, *9*(1), 11–18.

Schwab, D. P., & Heneman, H. G. Behaviorally anchored rating scales. In H. G. Heneman & D. P. Schwab (Eds.), *Perspectives on personnel/human resource management.* Homewood, Ill.: Irwin, 1978.

Stein, J. M. Using group process techniques to develop productivity measures. *Public Personnel Management,* 1979, *8*(2), 89–93.

Walker, J. W. *Human resource planning.* New York: McGraw-Hill, 1980.

Wilson, M. *The effective management of volunteer programs.* Boulder, Colo.: Volunteer Management Associates, 1976.

Wilson, M. Effective volunteer programs. In R. L. Clifton & A. M. Dahms (Eds.), *Grass-roots administration: A handbook for staff and directors of small community-based social-service agencies.* Monterey, Calif.: Brooks/Cole, 1980.

CHAPTER **6**

BUILDING SUPERVISORY RELATIONSHIPS

Most human service professionals find themselves playing at least limited supervisory roles throughout their careers. Sometimes they may act as managerial supervisors, with responsibility and authority for overseeing the work of others. Just as often they may see themselves primarily as professional mentors or coaches, helping enhance the skills and abilities of less experienced service deliverers.

The distinction between managerial and professional supervision may be less important to supervisory effectiveness than the quality of the relationships that the individual supervisor is able to create. A model for supervision can be broad enough to adapt to subtle role differences. Such an all-encompassing model must take into account issues related to the supervisor's leadership style, the supervisee's motivation, the relevance of power and authority, and the special problems inherent in human service settings.

Leadership

If leadership is defined as the process of influencing human behaviors in the interest of achieving particular goals, it is a key factor in supervision. The supervisor is clearly interested in influencing the supervisee's behavior; so some kind of "leadership event" must take place.

"Readily identifiable leadership events exist in empirical reality [and] that leadership is a major variable impacting on human and organizational effectiveness" (Davis & Luthans, 1979, p. 237). Yet the very term *leadership* is often used loosely, and it is difficult to identify the nature of the actual leadership "event." For instance, Burns (1978) distinguishes between two basic forms of leadership. "Transforming leadership" is based on the ideal of unified effort, with leader and follower both working on behalf of goals to which each subscribes. "Transactional leadership," in contrast, does not require a common goal between leader and follower; instead, divergent interests are recognized, and the leadership process becomes a kind of quid pro quo bargain in pursuit of separate but complementary aims.

Leadership in the supervisory context can be either transforming or transactional in nature, depending on the unique interaction between the supervisor's leadership style and the supervisee's motivation.

Traditionally, views of leadership style have focused on making sharp distinctions between opposing forms of relating to followers. Managers have been seen as either job-centered or employee-centered (Likert, 1961), as Theory X versus Theory Y (McGregor, 1960), as task centered versus process centered, as autocratic versus democratic. The notion underlying these categories is that a leader tends to utilize a consistent way of interacting with followers and that this method is based on his or her philosophy and assumptions concerning human behavior. The task-oriented, autocratic, Theory X leader assumes that subordinates need close supervision and that major decisions should be made by the individual in an officially designated leadership position. The primary focus of this leader's behavior is on accomplishment of the task at hand rather than on employee morale or needs. The opposite form of leadership, the employee-centered, democratic, or Theory Y orientation, centers more specifically on the relationship between leader and follower, between manager and subordinate. This leader assumes that followers are capable of participating effectively in decision-making processes and that employee satisfaction is of major importance in an organization.

Of course, no one leader is ever a pure example of either basic approach. Leaders may, however, tend to emphasize one aspect of leadership over another, and this emphasis has major implications both for the way they structure their organizations and for the way they interact with employees or supervisees on a daily basis. Leadership style can affect every aspect of an organization. For this reason, it has been the focus of a number of research studies during the last 30 years, and this has brought an appreciation of the degree of complexity in leadership behavior. The simplistic notion of two opposite behavioral categories has given way to a recognition that many factors can affect the leadership events in even one individual's professional life.

Tannenbaum and Schmidt continuum

Tannenbaum and Schmidt (1958) examine leadership behavior in terms of a continuum from "boss-centered" to "subordinate-centered" leadership. This continuum runs from the autocratic leader, who makes maximum use of his or her authority, to the participative, employee-centered leader, who recognizes a larger area of freedom for nonmanagers.

The authors' classic work of the 1950s has been augmented by increased recognition of the role of environmental factors affecting leadership behavior (Tannenbaum & Schmidt, 1973). The idea of a continuum has been maintained, however, with the recognition that a dichotomy between authoritarian and participative leaders may be less realistic than a continuum with the leader who makes decisions single-handedly at one pole and the manager who allows for group decision making at the other.

Ohio State leadership studies

Another series of studies that has had major developmental influence on the field of leadership is the Ohio State University group of studies (Stogdill & Coons, 1957), which began in the 1940s. These studies identify leadership behavior in terms of two dimensions: initiating structure, which delineates clear organizational patterns and methods, and consideration, which indicates the use of supportive, relationship-oriented behaviors.

The factors of initiating structure and consideration are similar to the more commonly recognized factors of task versus process, or job-centered versus employee-centered, leadership. The Ohio State studies, however, indicate that these dimensions are separate. This means that for the first time a leader could be characterized both by high structure and high consideration or by low structure and low consideration or by any combination of the two characteristics. Instead of being illustrated either by a dichotomy or by a continuum, leadership behaviors could now be plotted on two axes, with a resulting four quadrants: (1) high consideration and low structure; (2) high consideration and high structure; (3) low consideration and high structure; and (4) low consideration and low structure.

The idea of the independent axes of leadership behavior has paved the way for the more current approach and terminology of the "managerial grid."

Blake and Mouton's managerial grid

Blake and Mouton (1978) developed the two-axis model by making a distinction between concern for people and concern for production. Their managerial grid pictures graphically the management styles of leaders who are identified not necessarily by their behaviors, but by their attitudes. Managers who are concerned primarily with output, or task, and less concerned with people are considered 9,1-oriented managers. Those more concerned with people and who have little concern for production are considered 1,9-oriented managers. It is possible to be a 1,1-oriented manager or a 9,9-oriented manager. The two axes are independent; so more concern for one factor does not necessitate less concern for the other, as is shown in Figure 6-1.

On the widely used managerial grid, the figure 9 indicates maximum concern, while the figure 1 denotes minimum concern. Thus, the 1,1 management

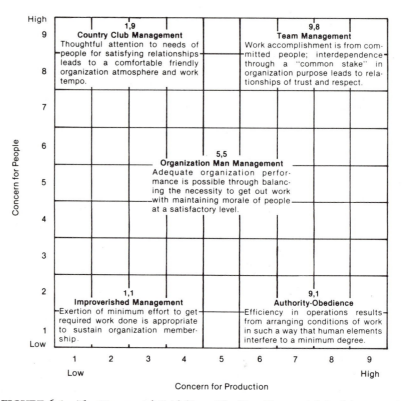

FIGURE 6-1 The Managerial Grid *(From* The New Managerial Grid, *by R. R. Blake and J. S. Mouton, p. 11. Houston: Gulf Publishing Co. Copyright © 1978. Reproduced by permission.)*

style is one in which the manager displays little concern for either people or production. Often called an "impoverished" style, it implies a withdrawal from leadership functions. The 9,1-oriented manager, whose concern for production clearly overrides a concern for people, is a task leader whose leadership depends on strong authority. The 1,9-oriented manager, or "country club" leader, also shows limited respect for employees, providing protection and morale-building support at the expense of the tasks that need to be performed. The 5,5 orientation indicates a compromise, with the leader feeling that concerns for production and for people are mutually exclusive and continually trying to maintain balance. The 9,9-oriented manager sees concern for people and concern for production as complementary. This team-oriented leader sees people as potentially productive and enhances this productivity by building commitment and mutual responsibility. In the Blake and Mouton model, the 9,9 management style is seen as the ideal and one toward which managers can and should strive.

Reddin's effectiveness dimension

A number of writers use the terms *task* versus *relationship* to equate with the managerial grid's concern for production versus concern for people. The leader who stresses the task dimension is primarily oriented toward completion of the job; the relationship-oriented leader pays close attention to interpersonal relations as they affect the organization.

Reddin (1970) discusses the relationships-oriented versus the task-oriented leader, but adds a third dimension: effectiveness, seen in the context of the situation. In some situations, one leadership style may be more effective than another. A leadership style that has been effective in one setting may be ineffective in another. Thus, the leader with a high degree of concern both for task and for relationships is an "executive" when that style is appropriate but a "compromiser" when the dimension of effectiveness is missing. A high relationship–low task leader is a "developer" when effective, a "missionary" when ineffective. This analysis recognizes that leaders need a degree of flexibility, allowing changes in style in differing organizational contexts.

Fiedler's contingency theory

The idea that varying leadership styles may be appropriate in different situations has been studied in depth by Fiedler (1967). Fiedler's "contingency" model indicates that leader effectiveness depends on three situational variables: leader-member relations, task structure, and leader position power. Leader-member relations involve the degree to which the leader is accepted by followers; task structure deals with the degree of specificity of the job at hand; and leader power reflects the actual power that the organization provides for the person in a given position.

Fiedler's research indicates that a task-oriented leader is most effective when conditions for leadership are either very favorable or very unfavorable—that is, when there are extremely good or very poor relationships, very high or very low task structures, and very strong or very weak position power. The employee-oriented or relationship-oriented leader is most effective in situations that are intermediate in favorableness and in degree of task structure.

Hersey and Blanchard's situational leadership model

Hersey and Blanchard (1977) also recognize that the effectiveness of leadership styles depends to a great extent on the situation. Their model is unique in its attention to the variable of follower maturity level, which they see as the most important situational factor.

The Hersey and Blanchard situational model distinguishes between task behavior and relationship behavior on the part of the leader. They contend that either high relationship or high task orientations can be appropriate, depending on the maturity level of the follower or followers. In this model, follower maturity is associated with achievement motivation, with the willingness and the ability to take responsibility, and with the experience and training one brings to the situation. The followers' maturity is measured in terms of the specific task to be performed; so a given follower might be mature in one setting and immature in another. The leader must also take into account both the maturity level of individuals and the maturity level of the group (Moore, 1976). The model is shown in Figure 6-2.

The top of the figure illustrates differing levels of follower maturity, with psychological maturity relating to motivation for achievement and job maturity relating to training and ability. The follower at the lowest level of maturity (M1) is both unable and unwilling to perform the task at hand. The follower at the M2 level is willing but unable. At the next level of maturity, the follower

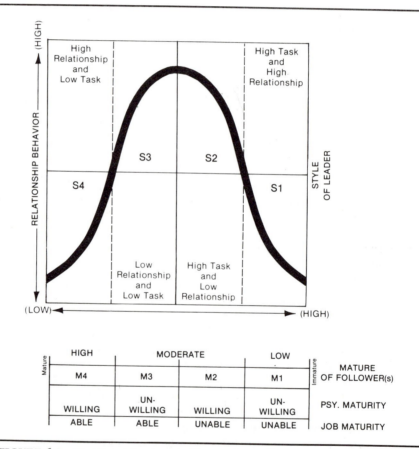

FIGURE 6-2 Situational Leadership Theory *(From "Contracting for Leadership Style: A Process and Instrumentation for Building Effective Work Relationships," by P. Hersey, K.H. Blanchard, and R.K. Hambleton. In P. Hersey and J. Stinson (Eds.),* Perspectives in Leadership Effectiveness. *Copyright © 1980 by The Center for Leadership Studies, Athens Ohio University. Reprinted by permission.)*

has the necessary ability to perform but not the appropriate level of motivation or confidence for working independently. At the highest maturity level, the follower combines both the ability and the willingness to perform the task with a minimum of assistance.

According to the situational leadership model, the leader should adapt his or her style to the followers' needs. A leader dealing with individuals who are "immature" in terms of the job in question should use a high degree of structure or task orientation. As the follower's maturity level increases, less structure and increasing attention to relationships become appropriate. Finally, when followers have reached a high degree of maturity, the leader can decrease both supportiveness and structure. At this point, the leadership process becomes one of delegation.

This model might be especially helpful to supervisors in human service settings, where supervisees may vary greatly in terms of their maturity levels and motivation. Although a person new to an agency might require a high degree of structure, at least temporarily, a seasoned professional might be comfortable only with the kind of independence allowed in the fourth quadrant (S4). It is especially important that the human service professional recognize the individualized nature of motivation and make distinctions both between individual followers and between stages in one supervisee's development.

The leadership style can provide, at best, only a partial explanation of effectiveness. An understanding of various forms of motivation is just as important to the supervision process.

Motivation

The leadership event involves an influencing process. Supervision also requires an understanding of the complex needs that affect individual performance. These needs have been categorized and explained in a number of ways.

Maslow's hierarchy of needs

Maslow's hierarchy of needs (Maslow, 1954) is familiar to human service professionals in the context of personality theory. This concept is also important in the study of motivation in the work place.

According to Maslow, human needs can be identified in terms of a hierarchy, with higher needs coming to the fore after lower needs have been met. The hierarchy of needs includes, from lowest to highest: (1) physiological needs, at the level of basic survival; (2) needs for safety and security; (3) needs for belonging, love, and social interaction; (4) esteem and status needs; and (5) self-actualization needs. Maslow's notion is that the lower needs dominate until they have been reasonably satisfied. When the lower needs have been met, the human being becomes increasingly motivated to satisfy higher needs. Finally, the search for self-actualization, or the realization of individual potential, can begin.

This idea has strong implications for work-related motivation because leadership must involve the identification of those needs that will form the basis for employee performance. Traditionally, attempts to motivate workers were oriented toward the use of economic rewards and the giving or with-holding of job security. This process recognized only the lower-order needs.

Maslow's theory makes it clear that once these lower order needs have been met, they no longer serve as motivators. When economic needs have been met and when some degree of security has been achieved, workers will tend to seek ways to meet higher level needs through their work. When that point has been reached, the supervisee can best be motivated if some method is used to help him or her strive toward self-actualization. The worker at this level can be motivated only if the job itself allows for some degree of creativity, autonomy, and growth toward increased competence.

Herzberg's motivator-hygiene theory

The notion of differing sets of motivating needs is enhanced in the work of Herzberg (1975). Herzberg makes a clear distinction between the factors related to job dissatisfaction and the factors involved in producing job sat-isfaction and motivation. The factors that relate to job dissatisfaction, what Herzberg terms *maintenance factors,* involve such aspects of the work envi-ronment as the fairness of company policies, the quality of supervision, rela-tionships with supervisors and coworkers, salary, job security, and working conditions. These are not motivating factors; their presence or absence deter-mines whether the worker will be dissatisfied with the work setting. The *motivator factors* relate to the job itself and involve the ability of the specific job to offer the worker opportunities to accomplish something significant, to receive recognition for accomplishments, to grow and develop, to gain increased responsibility, and to advance.

According to Herzberg, the maintenance factors simply trigger the worker's pain-avoidance behavior, and the motivator factors relate to the need for growth and advancement. These growth factors are intrinsic to the nature of the job and relate to job satisfaction. Attention to hygiene factors is insufficient to motivate workers. The only way supervisees can be effectively motivated is through attention to the degree to which their work provides chances for growth, development, and increased responsibility. Herzberg's notion is to use the concept of job enrichment, building into each job the maximum opportunity for challenge and advancement.

McClelland's achievement motivation

McClelland (1965) makes clear the fact that not all workers are equally moti-vated by achievement needs. Three distinct motivators can impel individuals in the work setting: the need for achievement, the need for power, and the need for affiliation. Although workers may possess all these needs to some degree, each individual is most strongly motivated by one. Thus, the power-motivated worker, being primarily concerned with influencing others, is most highly motivated in a setting giving him or her the opportunity to meet this need. The person motivated by affiliation needs is most concerned with interpersonal relationships and is most effective in a setting offering supportiveness and opportunities for positive interactions. The achievement-motivated person values personal success and views it in terms of his or her ability to achieve measurable accomplishments. The individual who is motivated by achievement needs sets individual goals that are ambitious but clearly attainable and seeks frequent feedback concerning his or her competency and success.

This approach to motivation has two implications for supervision. First, it makes clear that people with differing motivational sets have contrasting supervision needs. The affiliation-motivated worker is likely to respond to a relationship-oriented style, but an achievement-motivated person can be most effective when he or she has been delegated tasks that allow for individual performance.

A second implication for supervision is that achievement motivation, which may be closely related to high performance on the job, can be developed. In many work settings, training modalities and job redesign have been used to increase individuals' achievement motivation, and this approach might work in human service settings.

Person-task fit

Johnson and Stinson (1980) point out that individual differences among workers are too great to allow for generalizations about what kinds of factors can motivate people to perform effectively. Job enrichment can improve the motivation and attitudes of people interested in growth and personal responsibility, but it would have a negative or nonexistent effect on individuals not impelled by such growth needs.

Johnson and Stinson (1980) distinguish between two basic types of motivational orientations: expressive and instrumental. Individuals with expressive motivation are interested in achievement (McClelland's achievement-motivated individuals) and attempt to obtain self-actualization through their work. Those characterized by the instrumental orientation see a job as a means to an end and are more concerned with external rewards and with what Herzberg would term hygiene factors.

People with alternate types of motivation would react differently both to leadership styles and to job styles. The expressive orientation lends itself to transforming leadership and to effectiveness in jobs allowing for personal discretion and growth. The instrumental orientation implies responsiveness to transactional leadership and to jobs with clear purposes and good working conditions.

The idea of person-task fit is also presented by Morse and Lorsch (1975), who adapt the notion of contingency theory in organizational structure to questions relating to individual motivation. The common factor Morse and Lorsch (1975, p. 387) identify is that of the need for competency.

> All people have a need to feel competent; in this one way they are similar. But in many other dimensions of personality, individuals differ, and these differences will determine how a particular person achieves a sense of competence. . . . We must not only seek a fit between organization and task, but also between task and people and between people and organization.

The competency need shared by all can be met in a variety of ways. How it will be met depends both on the individual's other needs, such as the need for affiliation or for power, and the organization's other needs, such as the need to adapt structures to environments. The motivational process becomes one of balancing organizational, task, and individual needs so that one worker's tasks both allow for his or her sense of competence and fit the nature of the work to be done by the organization as a whole.

Expectancy theory

Expectancy theory is a general model of motivation developed by Vroom (1965). As this widely used theory is described by Davis (1972, p. 60),

> A person's motivation toward an action at a particular time is determined by the anticipated values of all the outcomes (positive and negative) of the action, multiplied by the strength of a person's expectation that the action will lead to the outcome sought. In other words, motivation is the product of the anticipated values from an action and the perceived probability that these values will be achieved by the action. The anticipated value is called "valence," and it is defined as the strength of a person's preference for one outcome in relation to others. The perceived probability is called "expectancy," and it is defined as the strength of belief that a particular act will be followed by a particular outcome. Motivation is defined as the strength of drive toward action [and] is expressed in the following formula:
> Valence × expectancy = motivation.[1]

Workers, then, are motivated when they perceive that their work will lead to valued outcomes (rewards) and that this outcome is likely to occur. Thus, leadership would involve increasing rewards and/or strengthening the relationship between work and desired outcome. Like the person-task fit model, this theory allows for vast individual differences in terms of motivating factors.

---

[1] From *Human Behavior at Work,* by K. Davis. Copyright © 1972 by McGraw-Hill, Inc. Reprinted by permission.

Expectancy theory provides the basis for the path-goal theory of leadership (House & Mitchell, 1980), which has recently become widely recognized. The work of House and Mitchell recognizes that the individual's behavior in the work setting is based on the degree to which the job is seen as leading to desired outcomes. Thus, leaders are effective when they make satisfaction of their followers' needs contingent on effective performance and when they help ensure this performance by providing help and support when necessary. Thus, the "strategic functions of the leader" include the following:

> (1) recognizing and/or arousing subordinates' needs for outcomes over which the leader has some control, (2) increasing personal payoffs to subordinates for work goal attainment, (3) making the path to those payoffs easier to travel by coaching and direction, (4) helping subordinates clarify expectancies, (5) reducing frustrating barriers, and (6) increasing the opportunities for personal satisfaction, contingent on effective performance [House & Mitchell, 1980, p. 84].

This process is difficult because it involves recognizing that individuals may differ markedly in terms of the outcomes that they see as valuable. The leader must be able to identify which factors are motivating for each worker. As Pinder (1977, p. 386) points out, "the supervisor is expected to conduct a rigorous and accurate survey of employee needs and values, and manipulate the task setting and reward system accordingly in order to maximize employee motivation." This degree of individualization is complex, but one way to make it possible is to attach it to the system of Management By Objectives.

Management by objectives as a motivator

Although Management By Objectives (MBO) may be thought of primarily as a planning tool (see Chapter 2), it also has strong implications for individual motivation. When an organization uses MBO, those who have responsibility for the overall plan set general objectives. Additional levels of objectives are then set so that each department or work unit also has a set of objectives designed to work toward the general goals of the organization. Individuals participate with their immediate supervisors in setting objectives for their own participation in the overall design. These objectives then form the basis upon which their performance is evaluated.

Some students of motivation processes have noted that the act of being involved in the setting of individual objectives has positive effects on the individual's commitment and work attitudes. McConkey (1975, p. 95), discussing human service managers, points out that

> All available evidence indicates that managers are more highly committed and motivated when they have definite objectives to work toward, when they know where they're going, when they receive feedback on their performance, when they are judged on results, and when they are rewarded on the basis of results.

These ideas have a familiar ring because they come close to describing the kinds of factors that achievement-motivated individuals tend to value: opportunities for individual excellence, ongoing feedback, and rewards based on accomplishments. McConkey adds that MBO has positive effects on the individual because of its usefulness in providing for greater self-management and self-supervision, clarity of expectations, better time management, greater commitment toward a specific end, better communication, and greater job satisfaction and respect.

The use of individual contracting mechanisms inherent in MBO can also be combined with other leadership and motivational methods. Hersey, Blanchard, & Hambleton (1980) suggest that, in the process of Management By Objectives, the leader can also contract for leadership style by determining, in a joint planning session, how much help and support the individual needs in order to meet the objectives that have been set. In the same context, the strengths of the path-goal theory could be put to use. The agreement that forms the basis of MBO can also be broadened to involve a mutual understanding of the kinds of outcome rewards that might be attached to successful meeting of objectives, as well as the degree of support needed to "clear the path" to success.

Behavior modification

Most approaches to motivation assume that behavior is affected by complex internal processes. Behaviorism, however, examines only concrete, measurable behaviors. "According to behaviorism, the *consequences* of behavior, not any supposed inner mental or emotional goings-on, shape and determine particular ways of behaving" (Hampton, Summer, & Webber, 1978, p. 543). If the supervisor assumes that behavior is motivated primarily by its effects, he or she will attempt to shape positive behaviors and skills by reinforcing behaviors as they occur.

Luthans and Kreitner (1975) suggest that "organizational behavior modification" can provide a system through which positive reinforcement, or reward, is made contingent on improvements in work-related performance. The supervisor and supervisee would work together to define specific target behaviors. The individual's interests, concerns, and abilities would be taken into account as reinforcers for specific behaviors were selected. As the individual's work effectiveness improved, he or she would receive positive reinforcers. The supervisor would also try to make the work environment favorable for skill development. Ideally, as the supervisee became more effective and confident, he or she would have complete control over the reinforcement schedule, with little outside help needed. The behavior modification approach might be used more directly with new or inexperienced workers or with those grappling with a specific difficulty. Experienced professionals could become "self-supervisors" or "self-modifiers."

Power and authority

Most analyses of the supervisory relationship assume that, given a degree of supervisee motivation to succeed in a job or profession, the supervisor has the power to influence behavior. In fact, some supervisors are more influential than others, depending on the kind and amount of power they hold in the organizational context. The interactions among power, authority, and leadership are complex, and they can have significant impact on the supervision process.

Kadushin (1976) provides a particularly helpful distinction between authority and power, pointing out that "authority . . . is the sanctioned use of power, the expected and validated possession of power" (p. 93), but "power is the ability to implement the rights of authority" (p. 94). An individual's title or position in an organization may give him or her the right to influence others' behavior, the right to provide leadership. The degree to which influence actually does occur is a function of the individual's power and of other people's perception of that power.

An individual's power to direct or influence others comes from a variety of sources. Most observers of power relationships still find useful the categories suggested by French and Raven (1959): coercive power, legitimate or positional power, expert power, reward power, and referent power. Hersey and Blanchard (1982) add to this list information power and connection power. In a supervisory situation, the use of *coercive* power is based on the supervisor's ability to control punishments, such as poor job assignments, low compensation, or disciplinary action. *Legitimate* or *positional* power involves acceptance of the supervisor's right to influence the supervisee's work by virtue of his or her official position in a hierarchical organization. *Expert* power depends on the supervisee's respect for the expertise and knowledge that the specific supervisor brings to the work setting. *Reward* power finds its source in the supervisor's ability to provide positive rewards as incentives for defined behaviors. *Referent* power depends not on the external trappings of power, but on the personal relationship between supervisor and supervisee, on the degree to which the supervisee respects and identifies with the supervisor. *Information* power draws on the supervisor's access to valuable information. *Connection* power becomes a reality when the supervisor is perceived as having close contact with other influential people.

These sources of power can be categorized as stemming either from the supervisor's personal capabilities or from his or her position in the organization. *Personal* power, which finds its sources in the supervisor's expertise and relationships, depends on the supervisee's willingness to accept the leadership being offered. It is far from automatic. *Organizationally based* power implies a degree of control over the resources and rewards that can be made available to supervisees. It depends on the supervisor's formal position in the organization, but it can also be affected by his or her place in the informal network of relationships.

Uniquely organizational sources of power ... consist ... of three "lines":

1. *Lines of supply* ... Managers have the capacity to bring in the things that their own organizational domain needs.
2. *Lines of information* ... To be effective, managers need to be "in the know" in both the formal and the informal sense.
3. *Lines of support* ... Managers need the backing of other important figures in the organization whose tacit approval becomes another resource ... [Kanter, 1979, p. 66].

Hersey and Blanchard (1982, pp. 107–108) point out that position power tends to flow downward in an organization, as a function of the degree to which a supervisor's superiors are willing to delegate it, while personal power flows upward, from followers. Yet the two sources of power affect each other. Authority and resources will tend to be delegated to supervisors who are seen as having won the respect of their supervisees, and "the ability to get cooperation from subordinates is strongly defined by the manager's clout upward" (Kanter, 1979, p. 66).

Whether a supervisor's power is personally or organizationally based, it must be perceived as real by the supervisee if the relationship itself is to prove influential. Some supervisees will respond to position power alone, however, and others will respond only to certain types of personal power. Supervisors do want to influence supervisees' behavior, attitudes, and effectiveness, and the supervisory relationship is the vehicle through which this process takes place. The form of the relationship must take into account the source of supervisory power. If supervisees are inexperienced, insecure, or at the beginning of the training process—if they are what situational leadership theorists would term immature—they might at first respond to supervisors who clearly control the rewards and punishments that the system has to offer. More experienced and professional human service workers tend to gain only from supervisory relationships based on their respect for the expertise of a supervisor who is willing to maintain an egalitarian affiliation. Ideally, the supervisory relationship can develop and change over time, as the supervisee is actively encouraged to take increasing control over his or her learning.

In human service settings, issues of power are often especially difficult because supervisors tend to be wary of overcontrolling others' efforts. Professionals want to be mentors but might feel uncomfortable about evaluating and influencing other workers' progress toward effectiveness. The supervisory relationship must recognize the existence of power while taking into account the unique aspects of the human service environment.

Problems of supervision in human service settings

In human service settings, appropriate leadership styles are difficult to maintain because objectives are often unclear, effectiveness of performance is difficult to measure, and both supervisors and supervisees experience frequent conflict between their identities as professionals and their responsibilities as members of organizations. Supervisors are faced with a variety of needs as they work with professionals, with paraprofessionals, and with volunteers. At the same time, they often find the transition from independent practitioner to manager and motivator of others difficult to make.

Human service professionals as supervisors

Managerial functions can be carried out effectively by human service professionals if their clinical training is supplemented by the development of leadership skills. In discussing mental health administration, Whittington (1973, p. 84) points out that agencies can be "best administered by competent mental health professionals with special training and experience in administrative theory and practice" so that patient and professional goals maintain their transcendence over business and political goals.

This can be just as true for other types of human service agencies, provided that professionals are able to balance their organizational and professional roles. Research by Luecke (1973) seems to indicate that they can.

Luecke (1973, p. 86) asserts that organizational leaders who are also professionals are expected to "retain some degree of professional perspective, characterized by allegiance to the interests, values, standards and goals of their particular profession; and, at the same time, have some degree of the organizational perspective of commitment to their organization's specific goals, concern for its stability and growth, and interest in its operational procedures." His research indicates that the effective leader does not choose between emphasis on the professional perspective and emphasis on the organization. Instead, effective leaders combine high degrees of both perspectives. These effective leaders are termed *synthesizers* and contrasted with *idealists,* who have high professional perspectives and low organizational perspectives; *operators,* whose concern for organizational matters overrides their professional commitments; and *caretakers,* who combine low organizational perspectives with low professional orientations.

Yet the transition from service provider to synthesizer is by no means easy. The professional must move from the position of being nonjudgmental with clients to one of being an evaluator of workers (Ewalt, 1980), from a stance of encouraging clients to take total responsibility for their own goals to one of motivating other human service workers to strive toward the meeting of mutually accepted objectives. These sometimes subtle differences often lead to ineffective supervision, with the individual either placing total focus on relationship behavior at the expense of the tasks to be performed or, recognizing that accustomed behaviors are not workable in this new situation, focusing total attention on the task in an authoritarian style. These difficulties in finding a comfortable leadership style are exacerbated by the problems inherent in human service organizations: that appraisal of the quality of work is difficult and that those being supervised are often professionals who themselves have little interest in conforming to organizationally defined expectations.

Supervising professionals

Kouzes and Mico (1979) identify the "service domain" in human service organizations as including those who provide services to clients and who see themselves as being in control of the nature and quality of those services.

> Those who provide services to clients of HSOs also see themselves as having rights to control what they define as their professional domain. After years of schooling, professionals consider themselves capable of self-governance and believe they have the expertise to respond to the needs and demands of their clients. . . . "Quality of care" and "professional standards" are the preferred criteria for measuring success [Kouzes & Mico, 1979, p. 457].

In some respects, this attitude of professional human service workers is helpful to agency management. It means that employees come to their jobs with a high degree of motivation that is intrinsic to the work. They do not require a great deal of externally based motivation. They are, in effect, workers who can be defined both as achievement motivated and as possessing high task maturity.

Yet emphasis on utilizing professional standards as the primary criteria for effectiveness has negative aspects for the supervisory process. Workers tend to value means over ends; so it becomes difficult to change established behaviors in order to fit changing agency missions (Newman & Wallender, 1978). At worst, "clinicians are prima donnas who resist being managed, perhaps because they fervently believe that their method of training and legitimacy are their products, not the degree to which they are effective in producing results" (Carver, 1979, p. 3).

The human service professional's emphasis on the means of service delivery is joined by personal values that work against conformity to externally imposed policies. The human service professional, like Whittington's (1973, p. 63) typical mental health worker, "comes prepared to see the organization as his enemy, and to view it also as the enemy of the patient. For mental health personnel, more often than not, are private people, dedicated to the attainment of individual freedom for themselves and for their clients." The key to effective supervision of professionals is to build on the strength of motivation that is present in workers who have been attracted to the helping professions while building an involvement and mutuality in working toward outcomes that meet client needs. Effective supervision of professionals also seems to require that the supervisor be an individual who is seen as having a high degree of expertise in the professional specialty.

> The most desirable situation ... is one where the formal power and functional power are congruent. This is the situation when the person accorded positional authority and the power of the office to reward and punish is, by virtue of his [*sic*] human relations skill and knowledge of the job, also capable of demonstrating the power of expertise and of developing referent power [Kadushin, 1976, p. 98].

If the supervisor is not experienced in the kind of helping being carried out by the supervisee, he or she might need to focus on using supervision for the development of common organizational goals rather than for enhancing the supervisee's treatment skills.

The focus of the supervisory process might also depend on the supervisee's orientation. Cherniss (1980) presents a typology of four "career orientations" found in professionals working in public service settings. The *social activists'* primary objective is to bring about broad social and institutional change through their work. *Careerists* are more concerned with prestige and career advancement, with the extrinsic rewards of a job. *Artisans* are concerned with the quality of their work, as they judge it themselves, and with their senses of accomplishment and growth. *Self-investors* are more concerned with their lives outside the work setting than with using their careers as the central focus of their lives.

Apparently, the professionals' long-range satisfaction and effectiveness can depend on the degree of fit between their career orientations and the setting in which they work. Supervision of professionals might also need to take into account the differing orientations that supervisees bring with them. What would be seen as reinforcing or supportive by a careerist would seem irrelevant to a social activist or artisan.

Supervising paraprofessionals

Paraprofessionals also bring a variety of orientations and motivations to the work setting. The main differences between professionals and paraprofessionals lie in the degree of prior training. Professionals normally have completed university-based training that emphasized theory and research and practical applications. Their training has usually included supervised experience and an orientation toward the professional field. They come to the work setting with previously developed notions about what kinds of services they are prepared to give and what types of technology they will use.

Paraprofessionals are often just as serious about their careers and just as clear about the kinds of services they are prepared to give. Usually, however, their academic work has been of shorter duration, with great emphasis on practical experiences and on-the-job training. There is a high degree of variation concerning level of prior training; so no assumptions about level of expertise can be made. One paraprofessional might be highly skilled in service delivery; another might come to an agency needing virtually all his or her training to be provided by the supervisor.

Many human service paraprofessionals have been recruited from the local community by the agency itself. Their lack of specific training in human services may be balanced by their familiarity with the community.

> Some indigenous helpers may be especially effective because (a) they may have an ability to develop and utilize ties with a variety of informal resources, and/or (b) their knowledge of the norms and values of a particular community may allow them to structure helping transactions in ways that are more comfortable and credible for consumers [Mitchell & Hurley, 1981, p. 282].

Although paraprofessionals can bring great benefits to the human service organizations that employ them, they often "remain on the bottom of the pecking order, with little status and low salaries and very little in the way of prospects" (Bloom, 1977, p. 22).

The effective supervisor of paraprofessionals is able to recognize and build on his or her supervisees' strengths. Too often, paraprofessionals are pushed to conform to a professionally based model that fails to appreciate their knowledge and skills, which professionals unfamiliar with the local culture may lack. They have been "faced with the task of accommodating themselves to a professionally dominated system that devalued their worth and curtailed their autonomy" (Mitchell & Hurley, 1981, p. 282).

Sometimes paraprofessionals are brought into an agency with the idea that they will be able to have a major impact on the lives of their neighbors and then, little by little, are shown that their contribution is less valued than the work of the more traditionally trained professionals. In such circumstances, they cannot be expected to remain highly motivated. Supervision of paraprofessionals requires supervisors to work closely with their supervisees to develop roles and functions that build on their real strengths, to provide coaching that will fill in any gaps in their skills, and to identify realistic career paths.

Supervising volunteers

Volunteers, too, bring special benefits to human service agencies, often helping build bridges between organizations and their communities. Most human service managers recognize the importance of involving volunteers in their programs. Yet one often hears complaints from supervisors about how difficult it is to maintain high motivation among unpaid workers and how inconvenient the high turnover rate among volunteers can be. Such supervisors sense their own lack of control over the work of individuals who are not considered "employees."

The problem with that line of reasoning is that it incorrectly assumes that the paycheck is the primary motivator of human service workers. Motivation is complex. It is inseparable from the individual's personality, needs, and desires. Professionals are driven by what Maslow would call *self-actualization needs* and what Herzberg would term *motivators* as often as they are spurred by basic survival needs or hygiene factors. There is no reason to believe that volunteers' motivations are any different. Each volunteer is present in the agency because he or she has had some initial level of motivation, whether it was a desire to achieve recognition, a wish to serve others, a drive to be part of an important endeavor, a need to feel competent, a hope for positive learning experiences, or a wish to meet other people. If volunteers seem to lose this motivation over time, it might be because their work in the agency has not met the unique needs that brought them there. If supervisors are concerned about maintaining a high degree of worker involvement, they need to consider the individual motivations of their supervisees, whether those supervisees are paid or unpaid. Volunteers, like paid human service workers, need to be recognized as important members of the agency's staff, rather than as troublesome adjuncts. They need to have assurance that their own needs can be met while they are helping meet the needs of others. They need supportive and concerned supervisors who are willing to make the efforts needed to build effective supervisory relationships.

The supervisory dyad

The process of supervision has several complementary goals. The supervisor's responsibilities include:

- Providing encouragement and support for the supervisee
- Building motivation
- Increasing the mutuality of individual and organizational goals
- Enhancing the supervisee's competence in service delivery

All these responsibilities serve the same overall purpose: helping supervisees help clients more effectively.

The basis for meeting these goals is the supervisory relationship. The supervisor and supervisee form a working pair, or dyad, and supervision can be successful only if the dyad itself is successful.

The nature of the supervisory relationship depends on the specific situation, especially on the supervisee's needs and developmental level. It is unrealistic to think that one supervisor could form the same kind of relationship with each of his or her supervisees. In fact, the relationship with one supervisee changes over time as the supervisee grows in competence and independence.

In the context of the dyadic interaction, the two participants should select together both the objectives toward which the individual is expected to strive in his or her work and the goals of the supervisory process itself. It is important to have clarity concerning both the supervisee's work objectives and the supervisor's role in providing support and assistance.

It is especially helpful to think of the supervisee's needs in terms of the Hersey and Blanchard model of maturity in motivation and ability. The supervision needs of a "high-maturity" supervisee can be expected to differ significantly from those of an individual who needs active assistance either in the development of ability to perform or in the enhancement of willingness to learn.

In human service settings, the equivalent of the less mature worker is simply one who does not have a fully developed set of goals, methods, and motivations for meeting client needs. The major factor is not the supervisee's length of time on the job or years of training, but rather his or her readiness to function independently. A specific supervisee may need additional task supervision in order to gain competency in a new area, or he or she may simply prefer a close working relationship with the supervisor. Whether the level of maturity is defined in terms of abilities or personal needs, the supervisor's goal should be to help the worker move steadily toward higher levels of maturity and thus toward increased autonomy.

Clear differences between dependent and independent supervisees are frequently found in human service settings.

> Supervisees who feel uncertain about their competence to do the job will press for greater direction and more precise delegation from supervisors than will their more confident peers. Supervisees who feel a strong need for independence, who are ready to risk mistakes and who need less structure will encourage the supervisor to delegate tasks in a general way [Kadushin, 1976, pp. 47–48].

A supportive supervisory relationship can form the basis for moving the individual from a stance of dependence to one of independence.

The idea of a step-by-step progression toward increased effectiveness is often used in the supervision of beginning helpers. Boyd (1978) discusses the supervision of counselors in terms of three stages: an initial stage, designed to establish a working relationship, to decrease anxiety, and to begin self-assessment; an intermediate stage, involving self-appraisal, identification of skill deficiencies, goal setting, and active training; and a terminal stage, when the supervisee learns to use his or her own judgment, to develop a personal style, and to move toward autonomous self-management. What Boyd terms the *terminal stage* might more appropriately be called a stage of high maturity.

If supervision proceeds through developmental stages, the nature of the relationship itself changes as the supervisee grows. Littrell, Lee-Borden, and Lorenz (1979) suggest that, in earlier stages, the supervisor may act as a counselor or teacher, taking an active role in selecting goals and managing the supervisory process. Later the supervisee takes primary responsibility for identifying areas for exploration while the supervisor acts as a consultant. Finally, the supervisee reaches the stage termed *self-supervision,* with active supervision no longer necessary.

Throughout the supervision process, the supervisor and supervisee work together to specify objectives, to clarify the criteria against which progress will be measured, and to identify movement from one stage to the next. The supervisor must also specify his or her own contributions to the relationship, ensuring that the degree of personal support and task-oriented training needed will be offered. The supervisory contract involves recognizing both the supervisee's work objectives and the supervisor's contribution toward meeting them. As the worker becomes increasingly competent, the relationship may move away from a high task orientation, to a more supportive interaction, and finally to increased delegation and autonomy.

In the context of human service settings, many workers who are at a high level of maturity can be considered professionals. Because of their professional training and identification, they have skill and knowledge in performing their jobs. They might be motivated by high-level needs, such as the desire for growth, for personal responsibility, and for self-actualization. Such workers are motivated by expressive needs. Often they can be thought of as "cosmopolitan" in their outlook.

Davis (1972) distinguishes between employees who are "cosmopolitan" in their outlook, meaning that they are more concerned with professional recognition than with recognition by their current employer, and those who are "local" in orientation, implying that they are more concerned with their status and role in their own organizations. Cosmopolitans respond to different incentives than do those motivated by local concerns; yet most managerial theories tend to assume local orientations to be the norm. In human service agencies, this is far from the case.

> The cosmopolitan is oriented beyond the organization to his [*sic*] occupation and to recognition in it. His frame of reference for judging his progress is not so much his rank in the organization . . . but rather his rank in the professional community. He is as much interested in what his professional peers think of his work as what his manager thinks of it. Looking outward beyond his employer and having his own professional standards, the cosmopolitan is more independent and resentful of close supervision, deadlines, and paperwork. The organization is merely the vehicle which permits him to pursue his professional goals [Davis, 1972, p. 346].[2]

The cosmopolitan orientation is common among human service professionals, who often feel that their primary identification is with their profession

[2]From *Human Behavior at Work,* by K. Davis. Copyright © 1972 by McGraw-Hill, Inc. Reprinted by permission.

rather than with their employing agency. Such professionals rarely respond well to very active supervision. They tend to see themselves functioning most effectively when work is delegated, in a low task–low relationship supervisory style. Thus, supervisors who are ineffective with mature professionals are those who attempt to provide strong, task-oriented leadership based on position power. Those who are effective with highly motivated, cosmopolitan workers are those who recognize that the strength of motivation that is already present should be utilized positively and who are able to be influential through referent or expert power. Instead of attempting to change cosmopolitan professionals to meet the expectations one might have of a more locally oriented supervisee, the supervisor should accept and encourage the motivating forces that work for the person conscious of his or her professionalism. A high degree of autonomy in actually carrying out work—in selecting the means through which goals will be met—must be allowed, with creativity and innovativeness being encouraged.

Skilled supervision is needed in the joint selection of goals, in the attempt to find commonality between the supervisee's individual needs and the agency or program mission. There is a thin line between the cosmopolitan whose motivating force is a drive toward professional excellence and the prima donna who is more concerned with using professional methods than with achieving the ends that are most valuable to clients.

When dealing with a professionally competent supervisee, the supervisor should place a high priority on seeking a set of goals and objectives that are acceptable to both parties of the supervisory dyad. These goals must be based upon a recognition of changing client needs, with both supervisor and supervisee attempting to determine what amount and kind of services the specific worker can reasonably be expected to provide. The degree to which additional training or support is needed should also be specified. Most important, there should be an acceptance by the supervisor that, once agreement about goals and objectives has been reached, the mature supervisee should be allowed to work in an autonomous fashion.

Yet autonomy does not mean isolation. Throughout the supervisory process, the relationship between supervisor and supervisee remains important. Although the need for active intervention may lessen, the supervisory dyad thrives in an atmosphere of trust and supportiveness. The supervisee in a human service setting is not just learning to perform tasks, but is learning to use the self as an instrument for helping others. That process implies a need for continual growth and nondefensiveness.

> The ultimate goal of supervision is not simply a more knowledgeable
> and skilled technician but rather a more human self-actualizing person.
> Supervision should provide an extending experience in which the
> supervisee can blend professional knowledge and personal qualities. . . .
> While part of supervision is instructional, it goes beyond instruction to

focus upon the person or self of the supervisee [Moses & Hardin, 1978, p. 444].

In human service organizations, workers should be, and usually are, motivated by high needs for achievement and effectiveness, by expressive, rather than instrumental, orientations. Their continued motivation, whether they are professionals, paraprofessionals, or volunteers, depends on the degree to which their jobs can be enriched and the degree of involvement they feel in the ongoing work of the program.

Democratic supervision

The goals of providing encouragement, building motivation, and increasing the commonality of individual and program goals cannot be met solely through a collection of dyads. Instead, supervisors must find ways to involve workers, as a group, in planning and problem-solving processes.

This need is brought about partially because of the unique nature of human service workers themselves. Because they are often motivated by idealistic needs, they tend to work most effectively toward goals in which they feel a sense of ownership. Because their work entails personal involvement, as well as task completion, they must be committed to what they are doing. The human services, almost by definition, do not lend themselves to mechanistic task performance.

The nature of human service organizations also lends itself to collegial and democratic approaches to management. The goals toward which HSOs work are often unclear and certainly subject to a variety of interpretations. At the same time, there are many possibilities in terms of methods—tried and untried—that can be used to serve client needs. If there is to be an attempt to work toward client goals, rather than to emphasize performance of accustomed services, the ideas of many people are needed. Workers who are very familiar with client needs can help reach innovative solutions to long-standing problems.

In effect, what Blake and Mouton (1978) would call a 9,9 manager is an appropriate participant in the human service scene. Such an individual recognizes that one cannot choose between concern for people and concern for production. Instead, he or she knows that all the people who will be affected by a decision should have a part in making it. All the people whose commitment will be needed in carrying out a new solution should be involved in the problem-solving process. All the people whose individual objectives will lead to the meeting of organizational goals should be part of the goal-setting process. In the human services, where people are production, this approach is even more appropriate than it is in other settings.

Human service professionals are often very familiar with principles of group dynamics, but they may have difficulty applying them when they serve in supervisory capacities in their own agency settings. A few basic guidelines can help in the process.

First, when a group of colleagues is expected to develop a plan or solve a problem, be sure to clarify beforehand what constraints might be present. Groups in human service settings often spend endless hours developing novel solutions, only to learn later that their ideas cannot be implemented because of budgetary constraints, little-known federal regulations, specifics in the agency's bylaws, or opposition of a powerful board member. After this happens several times, workers' commitment to involve themselves in agency governance lessens, and a low degree of energy is available to the task.

Second, clarify the purpose of a meeting or task force. Sometimes there is misunderstanding concerning the purpose of a procedure, whether it involves a face-to-face meeting, a series of task force projects, or individual interviews and questionnaires. The people who are asked to give input need to know whether the process they are involved in is meant to provide useful advice to a problem solver or whether they, as a group, will be asked to solve the problem or submit the plan of action. A meeting, like an agency plan, must be seen as a means to some specific end.

Third, clarify the procedures to be used. Just as participants must be aware of the goals toward which they are working, they must also be privy to the process being used. Clarity concerning procedural questions is especially important in human service settings, where clear-cut guidelines are often lacking and where participants can be expected to be reasonably expert in using a variety of processes. Many human service workers know how to use such approaches as brainstorming and priority setting with clients but fail to use such useful tools in the context of their own meetings.

Fourth, pay attention to process variables. A major concern in democratic supervision is the blending of concern for task with concern for people or relationships. As workers join in a mutual search for effective solutions, they need to stop and check the process of their own interactions. This awareness of human interactions is an important part of the leadership process and one that cannot be left to chance.

Fifth, choose carefully who is to be involved in each problem-solving process. The human service professional as leader often makes the error of involving too many or too few people in a problem-solving or planning process. It is well worth the time spent to identify, as specifically as possible, who will be affected by a particular decision and then to involve all the people listed in the decision-making process. At the same time, there is a need to recognize the differences between major and minor problems and to use human resources wisely. A large number of people, including volunteers, should be involved in setting broad agency goals; a small number of people should be involved in setting the specific objectives of one individual or work unit. A large number of people should be involved in seeking the solution to a major problem; a small number should work actively on the elimination of a minor annoyance.

In the long run, it is up to the supervisor to recognize that human service workers bring a variety of needs and motivations to the work setting and that they can meet those needs most effectively if they are actively involved in controlling the quality of their own work lives.

Discussion questions

1. Think about the best and the worst leader or supervisor you can remember. What does leadership theory tell you that helps you understand what went on in each situation?
2. Think about a situation in which you and your coworkers or fellow students were highly motivated and effective. What motivation theories help you account for what went on?
3. How would you describe yourself as a leader or supervisor? Which leadership theories most help you understand your own style? Do you tend to supervise the way you like to be supervised, or do you assume that other people have different needs and motivations?
4. What do you see as the most important characteristics of an effective supervisory relationship?

Group exercise

As a total group, take turns role playing the following situations. The rest of the group should be prepared to discuss alternative ways of dealing with the same situations.

1. The supervisee is a volunteer in a human service agency. Although his or her work with clients is excellent, this supervisee has been undependable. The supervisor counts on this volunteer but never knows whether he or she will show up on a given day as promised.

2. The supervisee is a professional therapist who has been working in an agency for many years. Because of changes in the agency's total mission, the supervisor hopes that the supervisee can be encouraged to move toward doing preventive work with families and groups. The supervisee does not want to change.

3. The supervisee is a counselor who has effective helping skills but who does not seem to have an overall theory of helping or confidence in his or her work. He or she keeps asking the supervisor to suggest specific techniques that can be used with all clients. The supervisor feels that there is no simple technique that works for everyone all the time. He or she hopes that this

counselor will develop professionally and clarify his or her goals for client service.

4. Generate some situations from your own experience and role play the supervisory process.

Cases

See Cases 6-1 ("The Token Economy") and 6-2 ("A Test of Supervisory Skills").

References

Blake, R. R., & Mouton, J. S. *The new managerial grid.* Houston: Gulf Publishing Company, 1978.

Bloom, B. L. *Community mental health: A general introduction.* Monterey, Calif.: Brooks/Cole, 1977.

Boyd, J. D. Integrative approaches to counselor supervision. In J. D. Boyd (Ed.), *Counselor supervision.* Muncie, Ind.: Accelerated Development, 1978.

Burns, J. M. *Leadership.* New York: Harper & Row, 1978.

Carver, J. Mental health administration: A management perversion. Paper presented at the annual meeting of the Association of Mental Health Administrators, September 8, 1979.

Cherniss, C. *Professional burnout in human service organizations.* New York: Praeger, 1980.

Davis, K. *Human behavior at work* (4th ed.). New York: McGraw-Hill, 1972.

Davis, T. R. V., & Luthans, F. Leadership reexamined: A behavioral approach. *Academy of Management Review,* 1979, *4,* 237–248.

Ewalt, P. L. From clinician to manager. In S. L. White (Ed.), *Middle management in mental health.* San Francisco: Jossey-Bass, 1980.

Fiedler, F. E. *A theory of leadership effectiveness.* New York: McGraw-Hill, 1967.

French, J. R. P., & Raven, B. The bases of social power. In D. Cartwright (Ed.), *Studies in social power.* Ann Arbor: University of Michigan, 1959.

Hampton, D. R., Summer, C. E., & Webber, R. A. *Organizational behavior and the practice of management.* Glenview, Ill.: Scott, Foresman, 1978.

Hersey, P., & Blanchard, K. H. *Management of organizational behavior: Utilizing human resources* (3rd ed.). Englewood Cliffs, N. J.: Prentice-Hall, 1977.

Hersey, P., & Blanchard, K. H. *Management of organizational behavior: Utilizing human resources* (4th ed.). Englewood Cliffs, N. J.: Prentice-Hall, 1982.

Hersey, P., Blanchard, K. H., & Hambleton, R. K. Contracting for leadership style: A process and instrumentation for building effective work relationships. In P. Hersey & J. Stinson (Eds.), *Perspectives in leader effectiveness.* Athens: Ohio University, Center for Leadership Studies, 1980.

Herzberg, F. One more time: How do you motivate employees? In Harvard Business Review (Ed.), *On management.* New York: Harper & Row, 1975.

House, R. J., & Mitchell, R. T. Path-goal theory of leadership. In P. Hersey & J. Stinson (Eds.), *Perspectives in leader effectiveness.* Athens: Ohio University, Center for Leadership Studies, 1980.

Johnson, T. W., & Stinson, J. Person-task fit and leadership strategies. In P. Hersey & J. Stinson (Eds.), *Perspectives in leader effectiveness.* Athens: Ohio University, Center for Leadership Studies, 1980.

Kadushin, A. *Supervision in social work.* New York: Columbia University Press, 1976.

Kanter, R. M. Power failure in management circuits. *Harvard Business Review,* July–August 1979, pp. 65–75.

Kouzes, J. M., & Mico, P. R. Domain theory: An introduction to organizational behavior in human service organizations. *Journal of Applied Behavioral Sciences,* 1979, *15*(4), 449–469.

Likert, R. *New patterns of management.* New York: McGraw-Hill, 1961.

Littrell, J. M., Lee-Borden, N., & Lorenz, J. A developmental framework for counseling supervision. *Counselor Education and Supervision,* 1979, *19,* 129–136.

Lord, R. G. Functional leadership behavior: Measurement and relation to social power and leadership perceptions. *Administrative Science Quarterly,* 1977, *22,* 114–133.

Luecke, D. S. The professional as organizational leader. *Administrative Science Quarterly,* 1973, *18,* 86–94.

Luthans, F., & Kreitner, R. *Organizational behavior modification.* Glenview, Ill.: Scott, Foresman, 1975.

Maslow, A. H. *Motivation and personality.* New York: Harper & Row, 1954.

McClelland, D. Achievement motivation can be developed. *Harvard Business Review,* 1965, *43,* 6–8, 10, 12, 14, 16, 20, 22, 24.

McConkey, D. D. *MBO for nonprofit organizations.* New York: AMACOM, 1975.

McGregor, D. M. *The human side of enterprise.* New York: McGraw-Hill, 1960.

Mitchell, R. E., & Hurley, D. J. Collaboration with natural helping networks: Lessons from studying paraprofessionals. In B. H. Gottlieb (Ed.), *Social networks and social support.* Beverly Hills, Calif.: Sage, 1981.

Moore, L. I. The FMI: Dimensions of follower maturity. *Group and Organization Studies,* 1976, *1*(2), 203–222.

Morse, J. J., & Lorsch, J. W. Beyond theory y. In Harvard Business Review (Ed.), *On management.* New York: Harper & Row, 1975.

Moses, H. A., & Hardin, J. T. A relationship approach to counselor supervision in agency settings. In J. D. Boyd (Ed.), *Counselor supervision.* Muncie, Ind.: Accelerated Development, 1978.

Newman, W. H., & Wallender, H. W. Managing not-for-profit enterprises. *Academy of Management Review,* 1978, *3*(1), 24–31.

Pinder, C. C. Concerning the application of human motivation theories in organizational settings. *Academy of Management Review,* 1977, *2*(3), 384–397.

Reddin, W. J. *Managerial effectiveness.* New York: McGraw-Hill, 1970.

Stogdill, R. M., & Coons, A. E. *Leader behavior, its description and measurement.* Columbus: Ohio State University Press, 1957.

Tannenbaum, R., & Schmidt, W. H. How to choose a leadership pattern. *Harvard Business Review,* 1958, *36,* 95–101.

Tannenbaum, R., & Schmidt, W. H. How to choose a leadership pattern. *Harvard Business Review,* 1973, *51,* 162–164, 168, 170, 173, 175, 178–183.

Vroom, V. H. *Work and motivation.* New York: Wiley, 1965.

Whittington, H. G. People make programs: Personnel management. In S. Feldman (Ed.), *The administration of mental health services.* Springfield, Ill.: Thomas, 1973.

CHAPTER 7

EVALUATING HUMAN SERVICE PROGRAMS

Planning, organizing, and implementing human service programs are only worth the effort and resources they consume if the programs prove useful. Ultimately, evaluation is needed to let us know whether services have taken place as expected and whether they have accomplished what they were meant to accomplish. This kind of information can provide the basis for making sensible decisions concerning current or projected programs.

Program evaluation is

1. A process of making reasonable judgments about program effort, effectiveness, efficiency, and adequacy
2. Based on systematic data collection and analysis
3. Designed for use in program management, external accountability, and future planning
4. Focused especially on accessibility, acceptability, awareness, availability, comprehensiveness, continuity, integration, and cost of services [Attkisson & Broskowski, 1978, p. 24].

Evaluation is an eminently practical endeavor, designed with as much technical care as possible but oriented toward immediate improvement of program quality. Although research designs can play an important part in this process, program evaluation does differ from research to a certain extent.

Research, in comparison to evaluation, tends to be more theory oriented and discipline bound, exerts greater control over the activity, produces more results that may not be immediately applicable, is more sophisticated in complexity and exactness of design, involves less judgment of the researcher, and is more concerned with explanation and prediction of phenomena. Conversely, evaluation is more mission oriented, may be less subject to control, is more concerned with providing information for decision-makers, tends to be less rigorous or sophisticated, and is concerned primarily with explanation of events and their relationship to established goals and objectives [Burck, 1978, p. 179].

Human service evaluation, if it is to be of value, must be seen as an integral part of the management cycle and must be closely involved with the kinds of decisions that are made in agencies every day. Its results must be disseminated to and understood by the people most concerned with program functioning, including community members, funding sources, and service deliverers, as well as administrators. It can be practical only if it is seen as practical by individuals who have an impact on service planning and delivery.

Purposes of evaluation

Evaluators may use research techniques, but they apply them to the needs of specific agencies. Evaluation can be used to aid in administrative decision making, to improve currently operating programs, to provide for accountability, to build increased support for effective programs, and, in some instances, to make generalizations about the connections between specific activities and their effects.

Administrative decision making

Evaluative procedures can provide information about activities being carried out by the agency, as well as data describing the impact of these activities on clients.

Information about current activities can help decision makers deal with immediate issues concerning resource allocations, staffing patterns, and provision of services to individual clients or target populations. At the same time, data concerning the outcomes of services can lead the way toward more rational decisions about continuation or expansion of effective programs and contraction or elimination of less effective services. Decisions concerning the development of new programs or the selection of alternate forms of service can also be made, not necessarily on the basis of evaluation alone, but with evaluative data making a significant contribution.

Improvement of current programs

A basic thrust of evaluation is toward the comparison of programs with the standards and criteria developed during the planning stage. Evaluation can serve as a tool to improve program quality if it provides data that help contrast current operations or conditions with objectives. Activities performed as part of an agency's operations can be compared or contrasted with standardized norms, such as professional or legal mandates, or with the agency's own plans, policies, and guidelines. Evaluation of service outcomes means that results can be compared with measured community needs, leading to an assessment of the program's adequacy. With systematically collected data on hand, agency personnel can make improvements either in the nature of the services or in the ways they are delivered. Although evaluation does not necessarily identify the direction an agency should take, its systematic application does point out discrepancies between current and planned situations. Without it, quality control cannot take place.

Accountability

Most human service programs are required to submit yearly evaluation reports for the scrutiny of funding sources or public agencies, and many specially funded projects are required to spend set percentages of their total budgets on evaluation. Beyond this, however, agencies are also accountable to their communities. The "accountability model" Windle and Neigher (1978, p. 97) describe stresses this component of evaluation. The accountability model takes the position that a program

> should be evaluated by the public and/or those who support it. Such evaluation can have at least three purposes: (1) to let the public or other supporters make wise decisions concerning support, (2) to motivate the public and other supporters to greater program support by involving them in the goals and activities of the program, and (3) to motivate the program staff to greater public service and efficiency by their awareness that their activities are being monitored.

Dissemination of evaluation reports describing the agency's activities and their effects can help reinforce program accountability. People concerned with agency performance can gain knowledge about the results of services, and this information undoubtedly increases community members' impact on policies and programs.

Building increased support

Closely related to accountability is the "advocacy model" (Windle & Neigher, 1978), which assumes that agencies, in the context of their accountability, must compete for scarce resources. Evaluation can enhance an agency's position by providing the means for demonstrating—even publicizing—an agency's effectiveness.

> The staffs of human service programs are often called upon to justify the
> program and their own jobs at budget time. . . . If it can be shown that
> the program is effectively meeting a community need and it appears that
> the services provided exceed what should be expected from available
> resources, a major part of the justification has been accomplished.
> Telling your story well and developing appropriate political support will
> complete the justification and aid in getting a positive response [Caines,
> Lewis, & Bates, 1978, p. 14].

Evaluation provides information that helps the agency gain political support,
along with community involvement. Evaluative data and analyses can have
great impact on the agency's well-being if they are disseminated to potential
supporters and funding sources, as well as to agency staff.

Establishing cause-and-effect relationships

Much of what is termed *program evaluation* today consists of routine monitoring of agency activities. Sometimes, however, experimental designs are
used to develop knowledge about the relationships between interventions
and desired outcomes. Controlled experiments help determine whether clearly
defined activities can lead to measurable client changes. Although such research-
oriented studies cannot normally be expected to take place with great frequency in small agencies that have limited resources, they do play a major
part in establishing the effectiveness of innovative approaches. Program planners need to be able to make judgments concerning the effects of specific
kinds of services. Information concerning such cause-and-effect relationships
can be gained through a combination of activities, including reviewing research
completed in other settings, carrying out ongoing internal evaluations, and
utilizing the services of researchers to implement special studies of program
innovations.

The scope of human service evaluation

Human service evaluation can take many forms. The approach used in any
one setting is likely to be a function of several variables, including (1) the
resources and expertise available for use in evaluations, (2) the purposes for
which evaluation results will be used, and (3) the orientations and philosophies guiding agency decision makers. Figure 7-1 illustrates something of the
scope of possible orientations to evaluation, as seen by Hagedorn, Beck, Neuberg, and Werlin (1979, p. 5).

Figure 7-1 shows that the variations among program evaluation approaches
can best be explained in terms of contrasting interests, varying degrees of
commitment to systematic research, and divergent views of the role of objectivity in evaluation.

Viewing the spectrum from left to right, one sees first an approach to
evaluation that places high value on data gathering as an internal, manage-

PROGRAM EVALUATION ACTIVITY	Administrative judgment based on immersion in the living data of the program being evaluated, and buttressed by documented answers to specific, sometimes rather trivial-seeming, questions	Conclusions drawn from routine monitoring of explicit program data arranged in preselected categories, processed, analyzed and displayed to enable implicit or explicit comparison with norms or with other experience	Analyses, conclusions, and recommendations based on recurring studies of routinely and periodically reported data	Analyses and interpretations of recurring studies augmented by specific one-time investigations	One-time studies requiring special care in data-gathering procedures; methods used and questioned asked are mainly related to managerial utility of results	Quasi-experiments and carefully controlled research studies, with clear and specific management focus	Research studies with broad management implications; but the surest predictable payout will be research results: validated rules of thumb which may or may not turn out to be applicable in the setting where the study was done
EVALUATION THEORY	Intuitive judgmental integration of data, some of which data may be kept relatively implicit	Interpretation of trends and variances in the data clarifies and verifies necessary corrections	Complex analytical interpretations of regularly recurring data series leads to advice and recommendations	Ingenious use of specially gathered information to resolve uncertainties resulting from trends in recurring data or otherwise	Complex analytical interpretation plus anticipatory testing of emergent trends, crises, new patterns produces useful advice for management	Scientific backup to help in defense of management action; reduces management uncertainties	Resolution of scientific issues that may or may not impact directly on the management problem first impelling interest in the subject; the usefulness of truth
OPERATIONAL THEORY: WHAT EVALUATION "DOES" FOR MANAGEMENT	Using feedback to guide the influencing of interactions between the program and other entities			"Knowledge is power"			Increase the confidence level that management has in particular diagnoses and remedies by demonstrating cause and effect relationships
GENERALIZABILITY	Slightly generalizable if at all			Generalizability occasionally possible			Moderate to high level of generalizability

FIGURE 7-1 A Spectrum of Program Evaluation Activities (*From A Working Manual of Simple Program Evaluation Techniques for Community Mental Health Centers, by H. J. Hagedorn, K. J. Beck, S. F. Neuberg, and S. H. Werlin. National Institute of Mental Health, Washington, D.C.: U.S. Government Printing Office, 1979.*)

ment-oriented activity. This intuitive orientation downgrades the role of objective, external evaluators. The program administrator using this approach would utilize evaluation primarily as a means for making better decisions. Evaluation would take place only when specific information was needed.

The second approach, which might be termed *monitoring,* depends on internal evaluation as a routine, ongoing activity. This orientation tends to assist more in the assessment of activities, or processes, than in the measurement of results, or products. With its focus on comparison of program data with norms or standards, this range of evaluative activities is most helpful for management decision making or quality control.

The third and fourth orientations are more balanced in emphasis, with attention paid both to ongoing, internal data collection and to special studies, augmented by research expertise as needed. Research studies might be carried out, but their purpose would be to answer questions posed from within the agency rather than to search for generalizable truths. Objectivity would be valued as a means for finding more useful answers rather than as an end in itself.

The fifth and sixth approaches involve the use of one-time studies or experiments as needed. The use of outcome studies would help demonstrate the effectiveness of the agency's activities or clarify the relative efficacy of alternate intervention strategies. Managers would therefore tend to use these studies either to aid in decision making (the fifth orientation) or to increase the level of support for the agency's endeavors (the sixth orientation). The ability to present concrete data based on research studies would be seen as a way to enhance the agency's capacity to gain political and economic support.

An agency utilizing the seventh type of evaluation activity would need either to use external consultants or to protect the objectivity of a highly skilled internal evaluator. This orientation stresses the use of research studies to test hypotheses concerning specific causal relationships. The ultimate purpose of such an approach would be to make valid generalizations about the effects of interventions. Such truths might actually be more useful as generalizations than as immediate helps to administrative decision making.

Human service programs vary tremendously in their orientations to evaluation, running the gamut from simple program monitoring to controlled experiments studying client outcomes. Regardless of their use of resources, their depth, or their concern for objectivity, however, evaluation efforts need to be reasonably comprehensive if they are to serve any of their stated purposes. Evaluation should provide, at a minimum, basic information concerning program *processes and outcomes.*

Process evaluation

Process evaluation involves assessing agency activities to determine whether programs are actually operating in accordance with plans and expectations. As Rossi, Freeman, and Wright (1979, p. 38) point out, "There is no point being concerned about the impact or outcome of a particular project unless it did indeed take place, and . . . was received by the appropriate participants." Perhaps surprisingly,

> A large proportion of programs that fail to show impacts are really failures to deliver the interventions in ways specified. Actually, there are three potential failures: first, no treatment is delivered at all (or not enough); second, the wrong treatment is delivered; and third, the treatment is unstandardized, uncontrolled, or varies across target populations. In each instance, the need to monitor the actual delivery of services and identify faults and deficiencies is essential [Rossi et al., 1979, p. 132].

Although few administrators would accuse themselves of delivering "non-programs," anyone with responsibility for human service delivery should recognize that even subtle differences between planned and implemented services can have major effects on program results. Process evaluation provides a means for determining whether members of target populations were reached in the numbers projected and whether specified services were provided in the degree and with the quality expected. Process evaluation also leads the way toward efficiency assessment by helping specify exactly how agency resources, especially human resources, were used.

This type of evaluation normally takes the form of a comparison with identified standards for program implementation. This process depends on the existence of clearly defined, measurable program objectives. It also depends on the presence of an information system that can provide answers to the basic process evaluation question: Exactly what services were provided, by whom, for whom, and how many, in what time period, at what cost? When this information is used to compare accomplishments with objectives, guidelines for needed program improvements become clear, comparison of alternate methodologies becomes feasible, and accountability becomes a reality.

Outcome evaluation

Outcome evaluation also depends on clearly specified objectives. The objectives, however, are stated in terms of expected results rather than in terms of projected activities. "Outcome evaluation . . . does not ask whether the services were delivered, but rather attempts to assess their verifiable impact" (Zigler & Trickett, 1979, p. 280). The basic question underlying outcome evaluation must be "To what degree have clients or the community changed as a result of the program's interventions?"

Community impact might be measured in terms of changes in the incidence of a targeted problem. Client change would probably be evaluated in terms of level of functioning before and after receipt of services. Whether services are designed to affect clients' adjustment, skills, knowledge, or behaviors, some type of assessment tool must be used to determine whether change in the desired direction has taken place. Outcome evaluation depends on the routine use of such measures as ratings by service providers, surveys of client satisfaction, gauges of behavior change, and standardized or specially designed instruments.

If program administrators wish to make confident statements about the effects of services, they must also use studies that distinguish between treatment results and chance occurrences. Positive changes in clients can take place as a result of maturation, experiences that are unrelated to the agency's services, or just chance. Sometimes what appear to be changes are actually results of the measurement tool's unreliability or even the effects of measurement itself. Accurate outcome evaluation must use statistical or experimental designs that can control for these contaminating influences. Definitive statements concerning program outcomes depend on the evaluator's ability to make a reasonable estimate of the degree to which measured outcomes can be attributed to the service being evaluated. Most human service agencies use routine monitoring devices to assess all clients' development and add controlled outcome studies with smaller samples of clients, especially when special interventions are being tested.

Efficiency evaluation

The data gathered through process and outcome evaluations are sometimes adapted to the needs of an efficiency evaluation. As Zigler and Trickett (1979, p. 280) point out, human service agencies are invariably subjected to the question, "What is being accomplished as a result of the expenditure of hundreds of millions of dollars?" Efficiency evaluations are meant to connect costs and outcomes.

The core question involved in an efficiency evaluation is, "Can the same program results be achieved *either* by reducing the amount of program effort *or* by choosing other, less costly alternatives (different kinds of efforts)?" (Tripodi, Fellin, & Epstein, 1978, p. 46). The concept of "program effort" involves the amount and kind of activity carried out by service deliverers as well as the total costs of resource utilization. Level of effort is thus measured as part of the process evaluation. Program effectiveness is determined most accurately through the outcome evaluation. With these data on hand, the next step is to decide whether the level of effort, or cost, of a program was appropriate, given the results that were attained. Administrators or policymakers might compare two programs by examining the results of process and outcome evaluations. They might then decide to select the less costly of the two efforts for continuation, if effectiveness seemed to be equal. Efficiency does not involve simple cost cutting; it involves recognizing that alternate methods might differ in the amount of resources used to arrive at the same end. Making these kinds of determinations requires the use of the most accurate possible information and analysis. It requires careful implementation of evaluative procedures.

Implementing the process evaluation

Successful implementation of a process evaluation requires careful collection and analysis of information that can verify the program's success in meeting operating objectives. The existence of specific, measurable objectives and of a comprehensive data-collection system must precede the implementation of evaluative procedures.

Specifying goals and objectives

Process evaluation depends on the evaluator's ability to assess the differences between objectives and actual accomplishments. Objectives, therefore, must be well defined and measurable.

The first step in developing measurable objectives is to determine the program's goals. Each goal specifies some condition that program operations will help bring into being. Although a goal is not itself necessarily quantifiable, it must be clearly enough defined so that it can be divided into quantifiable objectives. Measuring the attainment of each objective then helps determine whether the goal has been met.

In a hypothetical example utilized by Caines et al. (1978), a community information and referral agency has conducted a needs assessment and estimated that approximately 2000 alcoholics below the poverty level live in the community and are not receiving services. The program goal is *all poverty-level alcoholics in this community will be referred to appropriate financial, rehabilitative, and family services in three years.*

It is necessary first to define each term used in the goal. In our example, planners must specify what is meant by *community,* what is meant by *alcoholic,* how *poverty level* is defined, and what services are to be considered *appropriate.*

Once terms are defined in ways that are agreeable to all participants, the goal can be analyzed by determining what activities must take place within what time span if the goal is to be attained. In this example, the objectives for the first part of the initial fiscal year include:

1. *Identification of all poverty alcoholics in the community within three months*
2. *Identification of all appropriate services in the community within three months*
3. *Establishment of facilities and equipment to provide referral services within two months*
4. *Employment and training of referral and administrative staff within two months*
5. *Finalizing of operational program within three months*
6. *Establishing liaison with all referral agencies within four months*

The existence of these time-oriented objectives means that process evaluation efforts can take place on a continuing basis rather than awaiting the developing of an annual report. For example, at the end of month 4, objective 6 might be examined as follows:

Objective: Establishing liaison with all referral agencies within four months

Evaluation: Coordination operations with 30% of identified referral agencies have not been completed

Evaluation: Referral of alcoholics and their families for medical and financial assistance cannot be done

Evaluation: Alcoholics unable to utilize family services due to financial problems

It is apparent that, in this situation, referral liaisons with family service agencies have been completed but linkages with medical and financial resources have not been established. Because of this, goal attainment for the entire program is in jeopardy.

Timely recognition of the problem area can point the way toward changes in program operations and toward immediately needed actions. If evaluation were not completed on a continuing basis or if objectives were not clear and measurable, the nature of the problem might not be apparent when failure to attain the overall goal was discovered.

The objectives leading to goal attainment can be considered measurable only if they contain clear criteria and standards that let the evaluator know whether objectives have been met. The *criterion* is what is to be measured; the *standard* involves the desirable quantity or quality of the criterion. One objective might include several criteria for accomplishment; each criterion must have a standard that the evaluator can use as a measurement. To continue our example, one of the objectives listed is *Identification of all appropriate services in the community within three months.* One of the criteria, services, includes several standards: "all," "appropriate," and "in the community." The other criterion, time, involves the standard "three months." The evaluator can determine whether the objective has been met by examining each criterion in terms of previously established standards for accomplishment. It is readily apparent whether the services have been identified within the three-month time limit set as a standard.

Many human service workers find it difficult to specify goal-related objectives in terms of relevant criteria and standards. One way to accomplish this task effectively is to analyze program goals by asking, "Exactly what is this program designed to do, for whom, how many, and when?" (Caines et al., 1978, p. 39). The answer to this question brings with it the identification of the factors that must be analyzed. For instance, the initial goal of our example was *All poverty-level alcoholics in this community will be referred to appro-*

priate financial, rehabilitative, and family services in three years. This goal might be "factored" as follows:

Program Designed To	Provide referrals to other agencies
For Whom	Poverty alcoholics
How Many	All in community
When	In three years

Each of the factors identified lends itself to the development of criteria and standards that can be utilized to build measurable objectives. Each operating objective can also be factored, with criteria and standards identified. For instance, our hypothetical agency might determine that in order to accomplish their overall goal, service deliverers would need to refer 20% of the poverty alcoholics in the community to appropriate services within one year. The format would appear as in Table 7-1.

Table 7-1 shows that the question, "Exactly what is this program designed to do, for whom, how many, and when?" has been answered in such a way that evaluators can determine whether the objective has been met. In this situation, then, the goal has been analyzed so that the criteria and standards to be met by operating objectives are clear. At the same time, each objective has been analyzed so that relevant data can be collected on an ongoing basis. When this system works smoothly, accomplishment of all objectives can be assumed to bring accomplishment of the program goal. At the same time, the nature of the objectives is such that their accomplishment is readily measurable. With quantifiable objectives in place, administrators can ensure that the information needed for evaluation is readily available.

The management information system

The data required for evaluation can be identified through examination of the criteria listed as part of the planning process. Each criterion points the way toward information that will be needed to assess agency progress in

TABLE 7-1   Criteria and Standards for Referral Program

Factor	Criterion	Standard
Referral services	Quantity	All
Poverty alcoholics	Income	Federal standard
	Alcoholism	Medical standard
	Adults	Over 18
Alcoholics in community	Community	Boundaries
	Number	20%
Schedule	Time in years	One

meeting desired standards. For example, one of the criteria of our hypothetical agency involved client income, with the standard being that clients could be defined as being at or below the federally stated poverty level. Information concerning income must thus be obtained from each client. Otherwise the service deliverers and evaluators have no way of knowing whether the specified target population is being reached. If the correct number of clients is being served but these clients have high incomes, the agency's goal is not being met. Client information is needed to determine whether the targeted consumer group is being served, just as service delivery information is needed to determine whether the correct treatments are being offered.

Once information requirements have been specified, agency personnel need to determine the appropriate source for these data. Most agencies use forms that identify client characteristics and/or the nature of services delivered. Evaluation data requirements should be taken into account when such forms are designed. Then a method for handling evaluation data can be built into the routine agency operations, allowing the collection of evaluation data to become part of the agency's everyday operating procedures. Evaluators can determine what person or functional unit within an agency can most easily record needed information, to whom the information should be reported, and who should be responsible for analyzing the information.

Process evaluation is greatly simplified in agencies that have integrated management information systems. Such systems are not only computer based but can involve "any system of people, equipment, documents, procedures, and communications which gathers, stores, processes and presents information for the purpose of assisting managers with a variety of managerial functions" (Hagedorn et al., 1979, p. 73). The information that can be provided by an effectively planned management information system, or MIS, includes:

- Information related to the community, such as demographic information, data on social and economic characteristics, identification of underserved populations, and listings of external services and resources
- Information concerning individual clients, groups of clients, and the client population as a whole, including such data as presenting problem, history, type of service received, length of service, socioeconomic and family characteristics, employment, and even measurements of satisfaction and service outcome
- Service information, including types of service provided by units within the agency, number of clients served, number of admissions and discharges in a given time period, and specification of service-related activities
- Staff information, including time spent in varying activities, number of clients served, volume of services, and differences among separate programs within the agency

• Resource-allocation information, including total costs, costs for specific types of services, and data needed for financial reporting

With the exception of the external community information, all these data can be obtained through normal agency operations. Regardless of how complex or expensive the system might be, however, it can store only what planners have selected as useful information.

Similarly, MIS output can involve only the kind of information recipients have requested. The management information system can be planned so that both regular reports and special requested information can be routinely distributed to targeted individuals and groups. For instance, a computer-based information system described by Sorensen and Elpers (1978, pp. 143–144) generates regular reports to the state and county, to the federal government, to agency management, to line staff, and to sections of the information services division. These reports are provided on the basis of the type of information each office needs as well as required frequency. Thus, agency management receives broad information concerning "admissions, movements, treatments, and location of treatments by individual clinics and other treatment settings," and line staff receive specially tailored, weekly lists of currently open cases. Both monthly and annual reports are automatically provided for funding sources at the county, state, and federal levels. Computerized systems can also provide aids to "management by exception," such as lists of clients missing appointments or dropping out before treatment has been completed (Elpers & Chapman, 1978).

Not all agencies have the resources or the desire to install computerized systems. An agency's MIS can be purely manual and limited to the use of papers and files; it can be based on use of computer service bureaus; or it can utilize a leased or owned computer. The key to system effectiveness is the degree to which it meets the agency's unique planning, management, and evaluation needs. Agency personnel need to identify as specifically as possible the kinds of data needed, the source of these data, and the frequency with which they should be distributed. Beyond this, planning for effective gathering and disseminating of information involves working out the type of system that is most appropriate for the agency's functions, size, and degree of complexity. The same kinds of planning processes are needed for a small agency using one client data form as for the large institution with a full-fledged information department.

Process evaluation strategies

Process evaluation depends on the active involvement of all human service workers in an agency because they are all required to set objectives, to meet those objectives, and to gather data on a continual basis. The effective agency must be able to retrieve evaluative information as part of its normal procedures so that progress toward meeting objectives becomes clear far in advance of the times when summary reports are required.

It is inappropriate to think of evaluation as a separate function, performed by experts and unrelated to the work of the agency's programs. Evaluation needs to be built in at all planning and implementation stages.

There is also a need, however, to step back from service delivery on occasion and examine progress objectively. Although evaluative information should inform managerial decisions at all times, there are also times when more objective and stringent approaches should be used. Whether evaluations are performed by internal evaluation teams or by outside consultants, specialized information may need to be gathered, and all data should be analyzed with a view to making concrete recommendations for change.

Information gathering.   The evaluation team can use a variety of methods to gather new data or to place existing information in revised contexts. Rossi, Freeman, and Wright (1979) suggest that the data sources most helpful for monitoring agency activities include direct observation by the evaluator, use of service records, data from service providers, and information gathered from program participants.

Data gathered through direct observation are useful in terms of objectivity because evaluators are freed from the concern that information might be colored by the subjectivity of service deliverers or consumers. There is also the danger, however, that observation might, in itself, bring about changes in the activities being carried out. Direct observation can prove useful if systematic methods are used, but it is more helpful in some types of situations than in others. For instance, unobtrusive observation can be more appropriate in the context of a public educational program than in the case of a private counseling session. Use of audio- or videotapes of selected service delivery episodes can prove to be a more effective adaptation of observational data gathering than in vivo observations would be.

Use of service records can be helpful for analyzing the nature of the consumer population, as well as for examining the number and nature of service delivery units. Such records as daily, weekly, or monthly activity reports can provide the basis for the development of program statistics concerning number of individuals served, types of services provided, or other aspects of program processes. Client data forms can also be used to determine the degree to which service consumers are members of the population originally targeted for services.

Although service records that form the bulk of the agency's stored information also provide most of the information needed for evaluation, they are not always adequate for intensive assessments. The evaluation team often finds it useful to gather data directly from service deliverers, either through questionnaires or interviews. Such procedures can provide deeper or more subtle information than that provided through routine forms, especially because differences in service deliverers' perceptions of program goals can be recognized. Intensive interviews can also point the way toward instances in which services are not delivered in standard ways by different individuals within programs.

Accurate information concerning service delivery can also be obtained through contacts with service consumers. Sometimes samples of entire communities can be surveyed to determine whether information concerning the program is being disseminated adequately and to the targeted consumer group. Interviews with or questionnaires distributed to actual agency clients can help determine consumer perceptions of services, especially if they differ from provider notions of the same activities. Information about consumer satisfaction with services is normally collected on a routine basis, and these data, too, can prove important for the purposes of comprehensive evaluation.

The varying types of information available to the evaluation team should be compared to verify their accuracy. The accuracy of stored information can be ensured if staff members receive training in recordkeeping skills (Lewis, 1972) and if samples of forms are routinely checked. Existing and specially gathered information can then form the basis for evaluative analysis.

Analysis.   The process evaluation can use most effectively the analytic approaches identified as monitoring strategies, including social accounting, administrative audits, and time and motion studies (Tripodi et al., 1978).

Social accounting involves the development and use of program statistics to determine what services were provided for what number and type of consumer. Essentially, it involves examining stored information, checking on accuracy, and possibly making suggestions concerning the actual procedures used for gathering and using data. The result of analysis should be a descriptive report that allows the reader to form an accurate picture of the agency and its activities as well as of community members and their use of services.

Administrative audits compare agency activities with goals, policies, or standards. Through analysis of information concerning program structures and services, evaluators can determine the degree to which the program meets desired norms. The administrative audit also helps point up strengths and weaknesses of program structures because estimates can be made of the degree to which functions and responsibilities of staff members accomplish goals and adhere to plans.

Time and motion studies also provide detailed examinations of the activities performed by human service deliverers, support staff, and administrators, with emphasis placed on analyzing the time allotted and used for various types of services. Analysis of time use, especially in service delivery units, can help point toward more effective use of resources in the interest of meeting agency goals. Often, failures to meet objectives can be diagnosed through such analyses.

The process evaluation can use a variety of data sources and analytic strategies. Its basic purpose is to determine what services were delivered, to whom, and whether they were performed in accordance with the schedule set as part of the planning process. It is just as important to determine whether the services that were planned and delivered had the desired effect on the community. For this purpose, an outcome evaluation should be used.

Implementing the outcome evaluation

As Krowinski and Fitt (1976, p. 25) point out, "Activities, i.e., intervention techniques including individual and group therapy, vocational counseling, consultation, psychopharmacological therapy, education, etc., should be viewed as vehicles through which objectives can be achieved. . . . The assessment of each activity's ability to achieve defined objectives can result in service by prescription rather than whim." A comprehensive evaluation must include attention both to activities performed and to the results of those activities. Measurement of both means and ends can lead to appropriate use of the agency's resources because the effectiveness of varying methods can be estimated, if not established. The purpose of the outcome evaluation is to measure, to the degree possible, the results of program interventions.

Routine outcome measurements

Outcome objectives, like process objectives, should be specific and measurable. The existence of concrete objectives allows for ongoing evaluation as client outcomes are routinely monitored. If measurements are inexpensive and convenient to use, they can be utilized even by small agencies with limited resources. The results of services for all consumers can be measured as part of the normal program operations.

Use of unique measurements.   According to Nickson (1978, p. 75), Galileo points the way toward the idea that it is important to "count what is countable, measure what is measurable, and what is not measurable make measurable." Human service workers, often lacking standardized instruments that relate specifically to their objectives, must work out new ways of assessing effectiveness. If objectives are clear, criteria and standards for success can be developed to relate to them. A training program can measure trainees' skills, with a specific level selected as an appropriate standard. A treatment program for alcoholics can measure its success in terms of long-term client sobriety; a corrections program can measure recidivism rates; and a mental health program can assess rehospitalization rates. It is not always simple to determine methods for quantifying outcome objectives and selecting appropriate criteria and standards. Desired client changes often seem impossible to measure, especially when communitywide, indirect services are offered, when it may be necessary to measure outcomes indirectly, through assessment of variables assumed to be closely related to desired outcomes. Regardless of the difficulty, it is worth the effort to search for creative ways of measuring the real goals of services rather than to revise objectives so that they describe easily quantifiable but less valued ends. "A crude measure of the right concept is far more effective in directing organizational activity than a precise measure of the wrong one" (Carver, 1979, p. 6).

Assessments of client functioning.   A number of standardized instruments are available to serve diagnostic or specialized purposes. Agencies serving clients with varying problems find it helpful to use measurements that are easily interpreted and that can assess clients' general levels of functioning. Such instruments are readily adaptable to varying purposes because they can be used both to assist in working with individual clients and to evaluate the effectiveness of program thrusts with entire groups or categories of consumers. Flexible instruments can be used with each client before and after intervention. Standards can vary in terms of consumers' pretreatment functioning; so the objectives for one client group might differ, in terms of realistically expected outcome, from the objectives for another.

Hargreaves and Attkisson (1978) recommend that, especially for the purposes of a mental health agency, global ratings of client functioning can be helpful. The Global Assessment Scale (Endicott, Spitzer, Fleiss, & Cohen, 1976) uses a 0 to 100-point range to differentiate among gradations from the individual needing constant supervision to the symptom-free client who is managing his or her life well. Although this scale depends on the perceptions of the service deliverer, the fact that it uses many levels makes it helpful for recognizing subtle changes and for making distinctions among varying client groups.

Krowinski and Fitt (1976) also stress the importance of having separate objectives for different groups, depending on current level of functioning. They suggest that the Functional Baseline Scale can distinguish among groups both in terms of level and in terms of type of functioning to be measured. The instrument includes three subscales: a skill task/vocational functioning scale, a social functioning scale, and an emotional functioning scale, as well as a composite overall functioning scale. With each scale based on eight points, the measurement can detect changes among greatly varying target populations.

A particularly interesting assessment tool is the Human Service Scale (Rehabilitation Research Institute, 1973), based on the notion of measuring the extent to which client needs are satisfied. The scale measures seven areas of need satisfaction: physiological needs, emotional needs, economic security needs, family needs, social needs, economic self-esteem needs, and vocational self-actualization needs. The Human Service Scale can be used diagnostically to determine what client needs are not being met. The instrument also serves the evaluative purpose of assessing the degree to which changes have taken place, either in specific life areas or in overall need satisfaction.

Many such assessments of client functioning are available and in widespread use. Their effectiveness in human service agencies depends on the care with which they are selected and the regularity and assiduousness with which they are used.

Goal attainment scaling.   Kiresuk and Lund (1978) use goal attainment scaling (G.A.S.) for both clinical and organizational evaluation. This process involves the development of specific evaluation criteria for each client, based on his or her treatment goals. Evaluation is based not on a dichotomy between success or failure in reaching goals, but on a five-point scale, with the target goal at the center of the range, the most favorable expected outcome at one end, and the least favorable at the other end. The client's progress toward attaining each goal is measured, resulting in a score related to each goal, as well as a summary goal attainment score that weighs the average of scores on each individual scale.

One benefit of this approach is that widely varying outcomes can be compared. Systematic evaluation does not require that all clients' goals have commonalities. The same is true when G.A.S. is used for evaluating an agency as a whole. Although each program or service might be oriented toward a different goal, the success of goal attainment across programs can be measured, and the scores of a number of individuals can be combined to estimate a program score.

Measures of client perceptions.   Most agencies also use measures of client satisfaction, asking consumers to evaluate the services they have received. Such measures can be useful only if they are obtained on a regular basis, both from people who have dropped out of treatment programs and from people who have completed them. Consumers may be asked to rate their overall satisfaction with services or to respond separately to individual aspects of program delivery. Normally, such measures are based on questionnaires using four- or five-point rating scales.

Clients may also be asked to evaluate their own well-being before and after receiving services. Such evaluations provide an additional way of examining treatment outcomes. Each client's perceptions of his or her own functioning can be combined with standardized measures and with service deliverers' perceptions, resulting in a more accurate picture of the individual's progress.

All these routine monitoring devices help measure changes in human service clients. They do not provide information concerning the degree to which these changes can be attributed to service interventions. Actual estimates of program effectiveness, especially when one type of intervention is being compared with another, depend on the use of more carefully controlled evaluation methods.

Experimental designs

Experimental designs are used to examine the effects of specific interventions on clearly defined outcomes. In the context of program evaluation, such designs are needed not necessarily for the purpose of making generalizations to other populations, but simply to enhance the certainty that services are causally related to the results being measured. Epstein and Tripodi (1977, p. 117) point out that evaluations "are seriously affected by problems of *internal validity,* that is, the extent to which it can be inferred that: program interventions do affect particular outcomes; evaluation instruments do accurately describe and measure interventions and outcomes; and the evaluation process itself does not influence program outcomes." Many constraints prevent agencies from using true experimental designs. Such designs could be used more frequently than they are, however, if agency workers and administrators recognized their utility in controlling for extraneous factors that impinge on postintervention measurements.

A number of factors converge to make simple outcome monitoring an inadequate method for measuring program impact. Although outcome measures alone allow evaluators to recognize whether change has taken place, such methods do not demonstrate that the human service intervention caused the effect. Experimental designs help do this by comparing groups of people who have received the service in question with control groups that have not received the same intervention. True experimental designs require random selection of experimental and control groups, carefully controlled interventions, and scrupulously examined outcome measures.

Randomization.   Experimental studies are based on the use of experimental and control groups that have been randomly selected. Each individual member of the target population must have an equal chance of being selected for the experimental group, which is to receive the service being tested, or for the control group, which will receive a different intervention or no intervention. When the experimental and control groups have been randomly selected, the evaluator knows that any differences between the groups are the result of chance.

With randomly selected groups in place, the evaluator knows that the groups are as equivalent as possible. Differences between the groups that appear in measurements taken after the delivery of services can then be seen to relate to the intervention or to chance variations that can be dealt with statistically.

Many human service workers find it difficult to allocate clients randomly to experimental or control groups because this process requires that services be withheld from some strictly on the basis of chance. Many agencies are obliged to provide services to all clients who present themselves, or at least to those most in need of assistance. Yet self-selected experimental groups certainly tend to differ from otherwise comparable groups of people who have not volunteered to receive services, and selecting the most needy among voluntary participants jeopardizes the study by the likelihood that people at extreme ends of the measurement scale will move toward the mean.

Sometimes it is possible to use randomization, even in the context of a working agency, by providing differing services to the experimental and control groups, rather than by withholding services altogether. If the intervention involves a reasonably short span of time, a crossover design can be used, with the control group receiving services after postintervention measurements have been completed. This design eliminates the possibility of doing follow-up comparisons, just as it fails to work if the time on the waiting list for control group members is inordinately long. In some instances, however, this approach does allow for both an experimental design and an ethical provision of equal services.

Measurement.   Experimental studies often use measurements taken both before and after the presentation of the program. Again, the effectiveness of this approach depends on the existence of an equivalent control group that has also received the pretest and posttest. Without the existence of the control group, there is no way to determine whether differences measured before and after the intervention were the result of variations in the measurement itself or group changes unrelated to the service being provided. The existence of the randomly selected groups controls for the presence of extraneous variables.

The use of a pretest sometimes can influence the attitudes or behaviors of the individuals being tested. For this reason, many evaluators prefer to use a posttest-only design. After the intervention has taken place, both the experimental group and the control group are measured in terms of the variable being tested. This works under the assumption that randomization has brought into being two equivalent groups and that, because the two groups are considered equivalent, differences following the experiment can be said to relate to the intervention itself.

Intervention.   In an experimental study, the intervention being tested must be carefully controlled. When experimental designs are used in human service agencies, the situation is usually one in which an innovative service is being tried out. It is especially important that service deliverers be thoroughly trained in the provision of the service so that there are no major differences either among workers or among methods used with different clients within the experimental group.

Criteria.   The criteria to be used in judging the impact of the experiment must also be selected with great care. Use of an experimental design means that differences in outcome measurements between groups, if they are beyond what would be expected on the basis of chance, can be said to result from the intervention. Thus, the measurements themselves must relate to the real objective of the program and must be as valid and reliable, in themselves, as possible. In most instances, evaluators using experimental designs for internal program evaluation can find validated instruments with histories of usage in other settings.

Depending on the specific situation, any one of a number of statistical approaches can be used to analyze the data collected. Well before implementation of the study, decisions concerning both outcome measurements and statistical methods should be made. Although data, once collected, may point toward the use of additional statistical tests, the basic approach to analysis must be integrally involved with the initial planning of the intervention.

Research ethics.   Beyond the question of ethics in assigning individuals to experimental or control groups is the question of ethics in the actual conducting of the experiment. Several basic tenets of research ethics apply as strongly to field-based evaluative studies. Social research must not cause harm to participants, regardless of whether long-range benefits to society are likely to occur as a result of the study. The question of whether the study might prove harmful to participants is not left in the hands of the researcher alone. All potential members of both the experimental and the control groups must be given sufficient information about the research to allow them to make informed judgments about their participation. Although it is sometimes difficult in institutional settings to ensure that participation is completely voluntary, this is the desired norm for research studies. Closely allied with the voluntary nature of participation is the requirement that subjects be aware of the degree to which information they share concerning themselves will remain confidential.

The carefully controlled, randomized experiment can be difficult to implement in human service agencies, especially when its expense is considered. This does not mean that careful evaluation cannot take place. Rather, adaptations to the needs of practicing human service programs can be made in the form of quasi-experimental designs.

Quasi-experimental designs

Pure experimental designs involve the use of randomly selected experimental and control groups. Studies that attempt to control as carefully as possible for a number of variables but that do not meet the stringent definition of experimental design are termed *quasi-experimental*. They include the use of nonequivalent control groups, time-series designs, and multiple time-series designs.

Nonequivalent control groups.   Studies using nonequivalent control groups use essentially the same methodologies as the pretest, posttest experimental design. The only difference, albeit an important one, is that the experimental and control groups are not randomly selected.

Sometimes, in actual human service settings, it is not possible to identify the potential members of a target population and to select the experimental group randomly from among that aggregate. Evaluators may use, for the purpose of control, a group that has been carefully selected and that is seen as similar to the experimental group on the major variables most closely related to the study.

The groups in question might be intact groups already in existence before the implementation of the study. For instance, an intervention in a prison location might be conducted in one cell bloc, with prisoners in another cell bloc being considered the control group. In such a setting, randomization might not be possible. The study might still provide accurate data, however, if prisoners in the two locations were similar in such relevant variables as age, number of years in prison, and seriousness of crime.

Another alternative is to match individuals in the treatment group with counterparts in the control group. Relevant variables, such as age, sex, intelligence, or socioeconomic class, might be considered as the basis for comparison. For instance, students in separate school classrooms might be matched, with an educational innovation applied for members of the experimental group. "Although this study design is not as good as one in which students are assigned randomly, it is nonetheless an improvement over assessing the experimental group's performance without any comparison. That's what makes these designs quasi-*experiments* instead of just fooling around" (Babbie, 1979, p. 301).

This approach can work well in situations when a special, innovative service is being added to a traditional service that continues to be offered to the control group. Use of a pretest, as well as a posttest, is important when control groups are constructed, rather than randomly selected, because the equivalence of the two groups cannot be assumed. With this in mind, the evaluator can utilize this quasi-experimental approach to make reasonably good judgments concerning the efficacy of an intervention.

Time-series designs, like studies based on nonequivalent control groups, also share some of the strengths of true experiments.

Time-series designs.   Use of a time-series design depends on extremely clear and specific objectives and intervention activities. It is exceptionally helpful for examining changes in individuals' measurable behaviors as treatment is provided and withheld.

The time-series design can be used to evaluate the effectiveness of an intervention either with an individual or with a group. Instead of using one pretest, the evaluator identifies the objectives of the service or intervention and identifies a measure that indicates progress. Then this measure is taken several times, at regular intervals, before the start of the intervention. These measurements are recorded to provide a baseline that demonstrates the state of the individual or group before the intervention has begun as well as any upward or downward trends that might already be in motion.

When the intervention is begun, it must be standardized, clearly defined, and operable at a clearly specified time. While the treatment continues, measurements are taken, again at regular intervals. When treatment stops, the taking of measures goes on at the same specified rates. The results of the measurements are graphed so that a visual inspection indicates whether abrupt changes have taken place with the beginning or ending of treatment. Ideally, the design calls for treatment to be performed, ended, and then performed again after a specified interval, allowing evaluators to determine whether measures return to their original levels when treatment is discontinued.

This approach to evaluation is most useful when changes in clients' behavior are sought. It is less helpful when objectives are based on changes in the results of standardized tests or other instruments because these tools do not lend themselves to repeated use with the same individual.

In situations calling for measuring objectives that relate to observable client behaviors, this approach is, in some ways, more useful than traditional experimental designs. It shares, with goal attainment scaling, the ability to be used effectively in the evaluation of an intervention used with an individual. Experimental designs are oriented more toward measuring the central tendencies of groups. In addition, this method might more nearly approach reality in its use of multiple measures.

> These methods . . . share the underlying assumption that human beings change continuously and that one must observe change as a process rather than as a single movement from pretreatment . . . to posttreatment. . . . A single observation, whether it is a test score, a count of specific behaviors, or the client's self-report, may tell us what is happening at a given moment but does not give us any information about the *direction* in which the client is changing [Anton, 1978, p. 121].

The time-series design, as usually implemented, may not lend itself to generalizations about the effectiveness of given interventions on universal populations. It can, however, be very useful in evaluations for immediate usage in human service settings.

Multiple time-series designs.   The time-series design, termed an *interrupted time-series design* when the program intervention is used to interrupt the series of measurements, does not really account for factors that might influence results. In an effort to control for factors such as measurement problems or non-service-related events, evaluators often use a multiple time-series design. The methods used for the basic time-series design are duplicated, but measurements are applied both to an experimental group and to a control group. Observations or measurements are used simultaneously with each group, providing a degree of additional certainty concerning generalizations to be made about the intervention. This approach can even be used to deal with individuals, rather than groups, with measurements taken of the behaviors of a treated and a nontreated individual.

Multiple base lines.   The basic time-series approach can be adapted to use with several types of behavior of the same individual. Whether behavior is observed in different situations or differing behaviors are measured, the approach allows for more specificity in examining the connections between the individual and the environment, as well as between the individual and the intervention.

Such quasi-experimental designs might hold a great deal of promise both for being reasonably easy to implement in the nonlaboratory setting of the agency and for helping analyze the effects of varying services on individual clients. As Goldman (1978, p. 15) points out, "To *understand individuals,* and to be able to apply those understandings in helping efforts with individuals, it is necessary to *study individuals.*"

The purpose of evaluation is to help improve the ways agencies serve individuals and communities. Although it is important to use methods that are as rigorous as possible, it is also imperative to understand that evaluation is a means to an end rather than an end in itself. An elegantly designed evaluative research study is of little use if it is not recognized as important by the people who have a stake in an agency's efforts. Evaluation efforts involve a number of groups, including not only professional evaluators, but funding sources, administrators and policymakers, service deliverers, and community members. These varying role groups serve both as producers and as consumers of evaluations, and they can have tremendous impact on the process if they see themselves as owning it.

Producers and consumers of evaluations

Wildavsky (1972, p. 509) describes the ideal of the self-evaluating organization, saying that

> The ideal organization would be self-evaluating. It would continuously monitor its own activities so as to determine whether it was meeting its goals or even whether these goals should continue to prevail. When evaluation suggested that a change in goals or programs to achieve them was desirable, these proposals would be taken seriously.

This view is seen as somewhat unrealistic by Wildavsky himself, who suggests that human beings are unlikely to take such rational and selfless views of their organizations. In fact, however, the self-evaluating agency might enter the realm of possibility through the combined efforts of researchers, administrators, service providers, and consumers.

Professional evaluators

A sizable proportion of the evaluation that takes place in human service organizations is performed by professional evaluators, researchers who use their skills either within the evaluation and research departments of large agencies or as external consultants offering specialized assistance. Whether evaluators are employed by the organization or contracted as consultants, they are expected to bring objectivity to the evaluation process. Their presence brings to the evaluation task a degree of rigor and technical excellence that could not be attempted by less research-oriented human service providers.

The technical virtuosity that professional evaluators offer has both negative and positive implications. At its worst, the evaluation researchers' contribution can sometimes be irrelevant to the ongoing agency work. Evaluators may produce reports that, although accurate, are too esoteric to be readily understood or used by the people who decide among programs or allocate resources. Evaluators who are overly detached from agency decision making often lose their chance to have impact on services.

Another negative aspect of the use of external consultants as evaluators is agency workers' tendency to place evaluative responsibility totally in the consultants' hands. Evaluation can work effectively only if attention is paid to goal attainment and data collection on an ongoing basis. If no one but the expert evaluator takes responsibility for assessment of progress toward goals, workers see evaluation as unfamiliar, threatening, and potentially unpleasant.

Effective evaluators use their technical expertise not to impose evaluation on unwilling audiences, but to work closely with others in developing feasible designs. If consultants work with internal evaluation committees, they can help administrators, service deliverers, and consumers clarify their goals, expectations, and questions. Then the studies that are designed can meet recognized needs. The external evaluator's objectivity and internal agency workers' active involvement bring the best of both worlds to the evaluation process.

Funding sources

Funding sources, particularly organizations providing grants to human service projects, have had a positive impact on evaluation in recent years. Human service agencies are often required to evaluate projects as part of their accountability to funding sources. Grant applications are expected to include discussions of evaluation designs, and these sections are carefully scrutinized before funding decisions are made.

Funding sources could have even more positive impact if attention were focused more on evaluation content rather than simply form. Funders should not expect that the dollar amount spent on evaluation consultants necessarily coincides with the quality of the research, nor should they accept simple process monitoring as sufficient. Rather, funding sources should press for more effective evaluation of program impact, both on direct consumers and on communities. The response to this stress on results might well be the design of more creative outcome evaluations than are presently in use.

Policymakers and administrators

Policymakers and administrators are among the primary users of evaluation because they make decisions concerning the lives and deaths of human service programs. Decision makers need evaluation data to inform them concerning alternatives, just as evaluators need decision makers in order to make their work meaningful. Yet the linkages between administrators and evaluators are often tenuous. Agency managers, as well as board members, can make evaluation work more effectively for them if they try to identify the real information needs of their agencies. Evaluations do not have to be fishing expeditions. They can be clear-cut attempts to answer the real questions decision makers pose. If administrators and objective evaluators work together to formulate research questions, the resulting answers can prove both readable and helpful.

Human service providers

The deliverers of services have often tended to be left out of the evaluation process, and in some settings they actually feel victimized by it. They are asked to keep accurate records and fill out numerous forms, but they are not involved in deciding what kinds of data are really needed. They are asked to cooperate with consultants making one-time visits to their agencies, but they are not told exactly what these consultants are evaluating. They are asked to make sudden, special efforts to pull together information for use by evaluators, but they are not encouraged to assess their progress toward goal attainment on a regular basis. Many human service workers feel that evaluation is a negative aspect of agency operations, serving only to point up shortcomings in their work, and they tend to provide information in such a way that their own programs are protected.

Human service providers could play a much more active and useful role in evaluation if they were encouraged to design and utilize evaluation processes, using consultants simply as technical assistants. Service deliverers are familiar with changing consumer needs, with the relative effectiveness of varying approaches, and with the agency itself. If they form the heart of the evaluation committee, they can ensure that the real goals of their programs, the objectives being evaluated, and the work actually being done form part of the same whole.

Consumers and community members

Consumers and other community members need to be involved in planning and evaluating, from initial goal setting through developing evaluation designs and assessments of agency effectiveness. Consumers are in a good position to be aware of the strengths and weaknesses of service delivery systems and of the degree to which observed community needs are being met. Just as important is the fact that the power of service deliverers and consumers should be more equitably balanced in human service systems. Zinober, Dinkel, Landsberg, and Windle (1980) point out that professionals, service managers, and even evaluators have vested interests in the maintenance of human service programs and that value judgments concerning program goals and effectiveness should be made not just by agency employees, but by citizens who can assure that community values are taken into account.

Citizens might mount their own evaluation efforts or participate, along with human service workers, on internal evaluation committees. Regardless of the form their participation takes, citizens have a major role to play in deciding how, why, and for whom human services should be provided.

Human service agencies are accountable to the communities they serve. Their purpose is to work toward goals that both helpers and consumers understand and cherish. The function of administration is to make this ideal a reality.

Discussion questions

1. Think of a human service organization with which you are familiar. What kinds of outcomes would you hope this organization could bring about? Are there ways to measure the outcomes you have in mind?
2. Continuing to consider the same human service organization, think about the kinds of information decision makers would need to plan and implement programs.
3. Do you think it is possible to make evaluation nonthreatening for the people who work in human service agencies? What steps would you take, if you were an agency manager, to build evaluation into ongoing processes?

Group exercise

Work in small groups of no more than six people. Imagine that you are the staff members of a human service agency serving alcoholics. The group has decided to use a new methodology for working with clients. Previously, each alcoholic client was seen on an individual basis. Now the group is considering a change to a family-oriented service. Services would be offered both to the client and to his or her family. Design a general methodology you would use to evaluate the new program and compare it with the old approach.

Cases

See Cases 7-1 ("Evaluating the Consultation and Education Department"), 7-2 ("Evaluating a Family Intervention"), and 7-3 ("Evaluation Emergency").

References

Anton, J. L. Studying individual change. In L. Goldman (Ed.), *Research methods for counselors: Practical approaches in field settings.* New York: Wiley, 1978.

Attkisson, C. C., & Broskowski, A. Evaluation and the emerging human service concept. In C. C. Attkisson, W. A. Hargreaves, M. J. Horowitz, & J. E. Sorensen (Eds.), *Evaluation of human service programs.* New York: Academic Press, 1978.

Attkisson, C. C., Hargreaves, W. A., Horowitz, M. J., & Sorensen, J. E. Evaluation: Current strengths and future directions. In C. C. Attkisson, W. A. Hargreaves, M. J. Horowitz, & J. E. Sorensen (Eds.), *Evaluation of human service programs.* New York: Academic Press, 1978.

Babbie, E. R. *The practice of social research* (2nd ed.). Belmont, Calif.: Wadsworth, 1979.

Burck, H. D. Evaluating programs: Models and strategies. In L. Goldman (Ed.), *Research methods for counselors: Practical approaches in field settings.* New York: Wiley, 1978.

Caines, K., Lewis, J. A., & Bates, L. E. *A manual for self-evaluation of human service agencies.* San Francisco: University of San Francisco Press, 1978.

Carver, J. Mental health administration: A management perversion. Paper presented at the annual meeting of the Association of Mental Health Administrators, September 8, 1979.

Elpers, J. R., & Chapman, R. L. Basis of the information system design and implementation process. In C. C. Attkisson, W. A. Hargreaves, M. J. Horowitz, & J. E. Sorensen (Eds.), *Evaluation of human service programs.* New York: Academic Press, 1978.

Endicott, J., Spitzer, R. L., Fleiss, J. L., & Cohen, J. The global assessment scale: A procedure for measuring overall severity of psychiatric disturbances. *Archives of General Psychiatry,* 1976, *33,* 766–771.

Epstein, I., & Tripodi, T. *Research techniques for program planning, monitoring, and evaluation.* New York: Columbia University Press, 1977.

Goldman, L. Introduction and point of view. In L. Goldman (Ed.), *Research methods for counselors: Practical approaches in field settings.* New York: Wiley, 1978.

Hagedorn, H. J., Beck, K. J., Neuberg, S. F., & Werlin, S. H. *A working manual of simple program evaluation techniques for community mental health centers.* (National Institute of Mental Health, Contract No. 278-75-0031 [MH].) Washington, D.C.: U.S. Government Printing Office, 1979.

Hargreaves, W. A., & Attkisson, C. A. Evaluating program outcomes. In C. C. Attkisson, W. A. Hargreaves, M. J. Horowitz, & J. E. Sorensen (Eds.), *Evaluation of human service programs.* New York: Academic Press, 1978.

Kiresuk, T. J., & Lund, S. H. Goal attainment scaling. In C. C. Attkisson, W. A. Hargreaves, M. J. Horowitz, & J. E. Sorensen (Eds.), *Evaluation of human service programs.* New York: Academic Press, 1978.

Krowinski, W. J., & Fitt, D. Y. A model for evaluating mental health programs: The functional baseline system. *Administration in Mental Health,* 1976, *6,* 22–41.

Lewis, M. *A common core curriculum for human service workers.* Chicago: Chicago Consortium of Colleges and Universities, 1972.

Nickson, R. W. *How to be a successful manager.* London: Thorstons, 1978.

Rehabilitation Research Institute, University of Wisconsin. *Human Service Scale.* Madison: Human Service Systems, 1973.

Rossi, P. H., Freeman, H. E., & Wright, S. R. *Evaluation: A systematic approach.* Beverly Hills, Calif.: Sage, 1979.

Sorensen, J. E., & Elpers, J. R. Developing information systems for human service organizations. In C. C. Attkisson, W. A. Hargreaves, M. J. Horowitz, & J. E. Sorensen (Eds.), *Evaluation of human service programs.* New York: Academic Press, 1978.

Tripodi, T., Fellin, P., & Epstein, I. *Differential social program evaluation.* Itasca, Ill.: Peacock, 1978.

Wildavsky, A. The self-evaluating organization. *Public Administration Review,* 1972, *32,* 509–520.

Windle, C., & Neigher, W. Ethical problems in program evaluation: Advice for trapped evaluators. *Evaluation and Program Planning,* 1978, *1,* 97–108.

Zigler, E., & Trickett, P. K. The role of national social policy in promoting social competence in children. In M. W. Kent & J. E. Rolf (Eds.), *Primary prevention of psychopathology* (Vol. 3: *Social competence in children*). Hanover, N.H.: University Press of New England, 1979.

Zinober, J. W., Dinkel, N. R., Landsberg, G., & Windle, C. Another role for citizens: Three variations of citizen evaluation review. *Community Mental Health Journal,* 1980, *16,* 317–330.

CHAPTER **8**

CONSULTING WITH THE HUMAN SERVICE NETWORK

Consultation in the human services involves helping individuals or organizations improve their effectiveness. Usually, the process has a dual aim: assisting consultees as they deal with immediate problems and helping them enhance their long-term capabilities for problem solving. Consultation may focus either on service delivery or on organizational issues. In either instance, it is characterized by a relationship that is voluntary, professional, and essentially egalitarian.

Each human service professional who plays a part in program management also finds himself or herself involved as part of a consultation network, sometimes playing the role of consultant, and just as often needing to select and utilize other consultants. In fact, keeping that network of consultants running smoothly is an important administrative task.

> A coordinated network of helping organizations has a never-ending supply of human resources. . . . Instead of identifying a small group of "experts" to serve as consultants to a large group of potential "consultees," agency workers can recognize that every one of them has expertise to share, and that every one of them might, at some time, need to ask someone else for assistance. What results is "cross-consultation" among cooperating equals [Lewis & Lewis, 1977, p. 181].

Like management, consulting has as its ultimate goal the enhancement of effectiveness in service delivery. Consultation differs from administration or management primarily because the consultant has no supervisory responsibility for the consultee's actions. His or her input into the relationship is advisory or collaborative.

Beyond this, the consultant's role is highly variable, depending on the nature of the consultant's theoretical approach, the consulting relationship, the setting, and the kind of problem being presented. A number of writers have presented typologies that help clarify and categorize the variety of consulting approaches. A knowledge of these models can help in developing a methodology appropriate to human service settings.

Consultation models

As writers in the field attempt to define and clarify the consulting process, they tend to make distinctions among varying approaches, primarily in terms of the nature of the relationship between consultant and consultee or in terms of the target or strategy of the intervention. Although some approaches have been developed for application either to profit-making or to nonprofit organizations, others are designed specifically for human service settings.

Caplan's mental health consultation

Caplan's (1970, pp. 19–20) definition of mental health consultation involves

> a process of interaction between two professional persons—the consultant, who is a specialist, and the consultee, who invokes the consultant's help in regard to a current work problem with which he [*sic*] is having some difficulty and which he has decided is within the other's area of specialized competence. The work problem involves the management or treatment of one or more clients of the consultee, or the planning or implementation of a program to cater to such clients ... the consultant engages in the activity not only in order to help the consultee with his current work problem in relation to a specific client or program but also in order to add to the consultee's knowledge and to lessen areas of misunderstanding, so that he may be able in the future to deal more effectively on his own with this category of problem.

This definition, which applies either to consulting with individuals or to consulting with groups, forms the basis for Caplan's differentiation of mental health consultation into four basic types: client-centered case consultation, consultee-centered case consultation, program-centered administrative consultation, and consultee-centered administrative consultation.

Client-centered case consultation.   In this situation, the consultant directs his or her primary attention not to the consultee, but to the client in question. The consultant communicates direct advice to the consultee concerning an appropriate treatment plan for the consultee's client. This may help the consultee work more effectively with similar clients in the future, but this goal is not addressed directly.

Consultee-centered case consultation.   Again, the consultant helps the consultee work more effectively with a specific client or group of clients. Attention, however, is more sharply focused on the consultee, helping him or her deal directly with such obstacles as lack of knowledge, lack of skill, lack of self-confidence, or lack of objectivity. Even in this instance, however, focus is on the consultee's professional development, rather than on his or her personal development.

Program-centered administrative consultation.   Caplan recognizes that mental health professionals are often called on not just to consult about individual cases, but to assist in program development. When such consultation is program centered, the consultant prescribes effective courses of action to be followed in program development or implementation.

Consultee-centered administrative consultation.   When administrative consultation is focused on the consultee, its primary purpose is to assist the organization by enhancing its effectiveness in planning, organizing, and implementing programs. Organizations, like individuals, can be plagued by such problems as lack of knowledge, skills, self-confidence, or objectivity. Additionally, the consultant may need to help in the recognition of such group difficulties as poor leadership or ineffective communication.

Caplan's frequently cited model illustrates that human service professionals may be called on to consult through use of varying strategies, with their focus being as likely to deal with administrative variables as with the specifics of service delivery. His consultee-centered administrative consultation has much in common with the process consultation Schein describes.

Schein's content-versus-process model

Schein (1978) makes a clear distinction between the consultant's role as a content expert who can solve immediate problems and his or her role as a process facilitator who attempts to enhance others' abilities to solve their own problems independently. He describes three consultation models, each with its own underlying assumptions.

Purchase of expertise model.   In this situation, the consultee has little involvement in the process. The consultant is hired to perform a specific task or solve an identified problem. This approach is workable only if the client, or consultee, has clearly and correctly diagnosed the problem and if the consultant can arrive at an acceptable solution.

Doctor-patient model.   In this model, the consultee (termed the *client*) asks the consultant both to diagnose and to solve an organizational problem. The approach assumes that the client has provided all necessary diagnostic information and that the organization is willing to accept the "prescription." This situation leaves the consultee somewhat dependent upon the consultant and often stops short of planning for the maintenance of organizational "health" after the consultant leaves.

Process consultation.   This approach, which Schein tends to recommend for most situations, involves the consultee in all stages of problem solving, with the consultant acting as a facilitator who can help in the development of effective problem-solving processes. The assumption here is that active involvement will increase the consultee's problem-solving skills, thus providing more long-term benefit, and that the consultee will benefit from being involved in diagnosing the situation. According to Schein (1978, p. 342), "most problems that are nontechnical, that involve one or more other persons, that have group or organizational components, that involve values, attitudes, assumptions and cultural elements, and which involve the client's own feelings fall into this category."

Although Schein has made a major contribution toward the development of process consultation as a model, he recognizes that consultants need to be comfortable with all types of approaches, fitting their strategies to the consultee's needs. Often, however, specific consultants become identified in terms of strategies that they utilize effectively, with the result that their diagnoses tend to lean toward one model rather than another.

Conceptual overview of Dworkin and Dworkin

Dworkin and Dworkin (1975) identify four consultation models that differ in terms of definitions of consultation, self-perceptions of the consultant, target populations, motivation of client systems, entry, goals, and other dimensions. The models identified include consultee-centered case consultation (Caplan, 1970); group process orientation, as exemplified by Lippitt (1971); social action, as implemented by followers of Alinsky (1972); and an ecological model (Kelly, 1970). The distinctions among these four approaches are illustrated in Table 8-1.

As Table 8-1 indicates, the four approaches differ markedly in terms of the underlying definitions of the consulting process, its targets, and its goals. The consultee-centered approach is seen as a process of interaction between two professionals, designed to increase the skills, knowledge, and understanding of the consultee in the delivery of effective help. The group process approach, having much in common with Schein's process consultation, utilizes the consultant as a facilitator, helping bring about organizational change and mobilize the problem-solving resources of the client system. The social action approach, in contrast, sees the consultant as an organizer and strategist, attempting to

TABLE 8-1 The Consultation Process: Four Models

Dimensions	Consultee-centered	Group process	Social action	Ecological
Definition of consultation	Process of interaction between two professionals: consultant and consultee	Voluntary relationship between a helper and a help-needing system	Relationship between a community and indigenous community leaders	Relationship between a professional team and an ecosystem
Self-perception of the consultant	Professional Expert Model Resource	Resource Model Facilitator Participant-observer	Community organizer Strategist	Planner Team member Researcher
Target population	Professional caregivers	Social system or subsystem	Indigenous community leaders	Ecosystem (interrelated systems and subsystems)
Motivation of client system	Anxiety Conflict Crisis	Organizational problem: Internal-external pressure "Images of potentiality"	Unmet basic human needs	Crisis initiated by maladaptation or malfunction of a social system
Entry	Sanctioned, invited short or long term	Invited or self-initiated short or long term	Invited or uninvited long term	Invited long term
Goals	Increased skills, understanding, knowledge, objectivity, mastery of feelings, crisis resolution	Organizational change Mobilization of creative resources Internal consultants	Transfer of power base Fulfillment of basic human needs	Awareness of system functioning Increased coping and adaptive mechanisms

Source: "A Conceptual Overview of Selected Consultation Models," by A. L. Dworkin and E. P. Dworkin. In *American Journal of Community Psychology*, 1975, 3, 157. Copyright © 1975 by Plenum Publishing Corporation. Reprinted by permission.

change the power structure within a community and enhance the well-being of the less powerful segment. The ecological model sees the consultant as a scientist and researcher who attempts to bring about change by diagnosing malfunctions in the social system and seeking effective interventions for improving system functioning.

Each of these consulting models is an independent system, and adherents of each would tend to perceive difficulties in different ways. Yet consultant flexibility remains important. "The selection of a consultation model depends on several criteria including the consultants' training, experience, personal style, and choice of a client system. It is important that the consultant clearly understand the spoken and unspoken goals of the client system prior to selecting a consultation model" (Dworkin & Dworkin, 1975, p. 158).

Tichy's four-category scheme

Tichy (1974) recognizes the need for consultants to broaden the range of the change technologies they are ready to use and to accept consulting contracts only when their expertise and tools are appropriate to the tasks at hand. His four-category typology was used in a study of the degree of congruence among values, cognitions, and actions of consultants adhering to differing change models. The four models identified in Tichy's scheme are (1) outside pressure, (2) people change technology, (3) organizational development, and (4) analysis for the top. These distinctions are made purely in terms of change strategies. The outside pressure strategy involves what Dworkin and Dworkin termed *social action,* with the change agent utilizing political pressure originating outside the system that is considered the target of change. In contrast, the people change technology includes consultation methods that attempt to change individuals within the client system. Such approaches as job enrichment, management development, behavior modification, need-achievement consulting, and other technologies designed to improve organizational effectiveness through individual change are included in this category. Organizational development, akin to Caplan's consultee-centered administrative consultation, to Schein's process consultation, and to Dworkin and Dworkin's group process model, attempts to enhance the work climate within an organization and to make individual needs and organizational goals more congruent. In analysis for the top, consultants use research, analysis, and policy studies to provide advice for the client, who is seen to be the person with control of power and resources within the organization.

Tichy has identified a number of conflicts in values and cognitions as they interact with the change agent's activities. He recognizes the need for the consultant to identify very clearly, prior to entry, the strategies he or she intends to use and the goals toward which these strategies can work efficiently. The kind of specificity Tichy encourages is attempted in another classification scheme: the Consulcube.

The Consulcube of Blake and Mouton

Blake and Mouton (1976) attempt, in their Consulcube, to identify consultation approaches in terms of focal issues, kinds of intervention, and units of change. This typology is illustrated graphically through their well-known Consulcube model, shown in Figure 8-1.

The Consulcube categorizes interventions in such a way that each cell represents a specific type of activity, helping describe the intervention, the type of issue being resolved, and the target of the change process. For example, an intervention categorized as A_1 is acceptant in nature, focused on individual change, and deals with issues of power and authority. A consulting intervention termed B_2 attempts to bring about change in a group, using an acceptant mode of intervention to deal with issues related to morale and cohesion. This detailed scheme assumes that most consultations can be described in terms of breaking behavioral cycles that have become long-standing patterns.

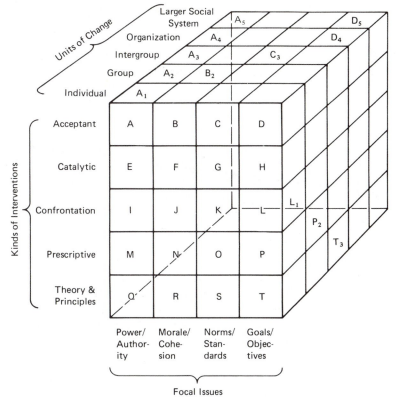

FIGURE 8-1   The Consulcube℠ *(From* Consultation, *by R. R. Blake and J. S. Mouton. Copyright © 1976 by Addison-Wesley Publishing Company. Reprinted by permission.)*

Types of interventions.   Blake and Mouton assume there are only five basic types of interventions used to bring about change or break behavioral cycles: *acceptant* interventions, which help the client change by providing a secure environment; *catalytic* interventions, which provide new data or help change perceptions of existing information; *confrontation* strategies, which challenge the client to reexamine his or her behaviors; *prescriptive* interventions, which call on the consultant to diagnose and solve the presenting problem; and *theory and principles* interventions, which help the client analyze problems from new frames of reference. These basic types of intervention are used in all situations calling for change, with the consultant selecting one on the basis of the consultee's needs.

Units of change.   The Consulcube also distinguishes among differing units of change. The consultant may provide assistance at the level of individual, group, intergroup, organization, or larger social system. The important point is that the consultee, or client, must be clearly identified.

Focal issues.   Perhaps the most controversial aspect of the Consulcube is the categorization of focal issues, for Blake and Mouton imply that human problems tend to revolve around four basic focal issues or problems causing immediate difficulty. These issues include questions related to power and authority, to morale and cohesion, to standards or norms, and to goals and objectives.

According to Blake and Mouton (1976, p. 329), the need for a very detailed classification of consulting interventions is justified by the fact that "consultant effectiveness depends on the consultant's ability to identify correctly the focal issue, to introduce the kind of intervention the situation objectively requires, and to deal with the real client."

Like the Consulcube, Berger's overview of change strategies includes both individual and organizational interventions.

Berger's strategies for change

According to Berger (1980), strategies for change can include individual, technostructural, process, or political interventions. When strategies oriented toward the individual are utilized, the primary focus is on the participant's knowledge, attitudes, skills, or feelings. The intervention used may include direct information, counseling, reinforcement, or even placement of the individual in a workshop or training session. Basically, however, the consultant style relates to a purchase of expertise or doctor-patient modality because the consultant prescribes appropriate experience for his or her client.

The technostructural consultant sees top management as the client and source of change, with the primary focus being on the organization's structure and on the way the organization uses technology. Typical interventions include

job redesign, reorganization, and suggested changes in policies and procedures. Again, the consultant's technical expertise is important.

The process orientation sees an individual, a team, or an organization as
the client and uses interventions such as team building, organizational problem solving, and other group dynamics technology. The consultant style often
utilizes the role of facilitator or catalyst, and the basis of success is interpersonal competence rather than technical expertise.

Berger's political strategy orientation sees the system and environment as
the source of change. The primary focus is on the use of power tactics,
coalitions, and recognition of varying groups' perceptions of self-interest.
Either direct or indirect coercion might be used.

Berger does not distinguish between individuals and organizations as "targets" of the change process. Rather, individual change is seen as one of several
alternate strategies that may, in turn, affect organizational effectiveness. Thus,
it can be compared with Tichy's people change technology.

Berger's technostructural strategy, with success based on the consultant's
technical expertise, can be contrasted with his process interventions, which
depend on the consultant's expertise in facilitating organizational problem
solving. What Berger terms *political* strategies work toward accomplishment
of a very specific objective. The idea that a consultant might, in some circumstances, act as an advocate for one alternative is also present in the
advocate role Lippitt and Lippitt identify.

Multiple roles identified by Lippitt and Lippitt

Lippitt and Lippitt (1978) identify eight consultant roles in terms of a directive
to nondirective continuum. In Figure 8-2, it can be seen that they identify
level of consultant activity in problem solving as a way of distinguishing among
roles of consultant and client.

Figure 8-2 shows a number of possible consultant roles, based primarily
on the degree of activity of the consultant and the consultee, or client. The
advocate takes a good deal of the responsibility for problem solution, to the
point that a particular solution is advocated. The informational expert also
takes primary responsibility for the consulting process, through the provision
of specific information that can lead to a resolution. These approaches are
in sharp contrast with the roles described in the left-hand columns, showing
the consultant as a facilitator who leaves the ultimate problem solution to
the client.

Lippitt and Lippitt, like the other writers we have discussed, recognize that
the consultant always has a choice of many possible roles. Which is selected
depends on an interaction among the situation, the consultee's needs, and
the consultant's skills.

In the final analysis, the approach consultants take depends to a great
extent on their views of what factors tend to bring about change in people's
attitudes and behaviors.

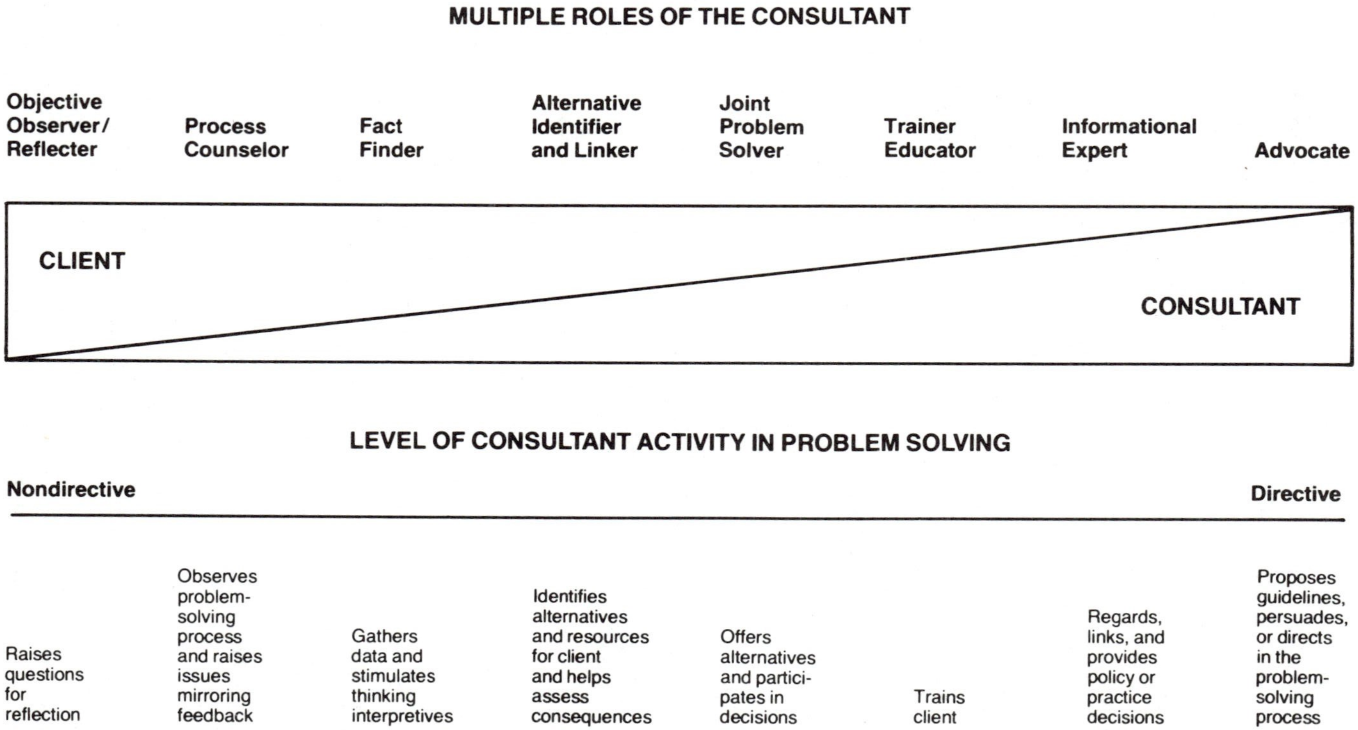

MULTIPLE ROLES OF THE CONSULTANT

CLIENT

CONSULTANT

Objective Observer/ Reflecter	Process Counselor	Fact Finder	Alternative Identifier and Linker	Joint Problem Solver	Trainer Educator	Informational Expert	Advocate

LEVEL OF CONSULTANT ACTIVITY IN PROBLEM SOLVING

Nondirective ———————————————————————————————— Directive

Raises questions for reflection	Observes problem-solving process and raises issues mirroring feedback	Gathers data and stimulates thinking interpretives	Identifies alternatives and resources for client and helps assess consequences	Offers alternatives and partici-pates in decisions	Trains client	Regards, links, and provides policy or practice decisions	Proposes guidelines, persuades, or directs in the problem-solving process

FIGURE 8-2 Consultant Roles and Activities *(Reprinted from: Gordon L. Lippitt & Ronald Lippitt,* The Consulting Process in Action. *San Diego, Calif.: University Associates, 1978. Used with permission.)*

Strategies for effecting change in human systems

Chin and Benne (1969) identify three major types of strategies that can be utilized to bring about change in human systems. Any kind of intervention can be identified as an empirical-rational strategy, a normative-reeducative strategy, or a power-coercive strategy.

Empirical-rational strategies.   These strategies work on the assumption that people will adopt proposed changes if they can be rationally justified through research, analysis, and clarification. The consultant roles that accept the importance of technical expertise in problem resolution tend to fall under this category. Schein's purchase of expertise model, the technostructural approach, the ecological approach, analysis for the top, and both the prescriptive and the theory and principles interventions of the consulcube all share an assumption that systems can be changed through the dissemination of valid information. Thus, they share an orientation toward change as a result of increased rational understanding and self-interest.

Normative-reeducative strategies.   These approaches depend on the notion that

> Change ... will occur only as the persons involved are brought to change their normative orientations to old patterns and develop commitments to new ones. And changes in normative orientations involve changes in attitudes, values, skills, and significant relationships, not just changes in knowledge, information, or intellectual rationales for action and practices [Chin & Benne, 1969, p. 32].

Thus, normative-reeducative strategies are involved in consultant roles that depend on long-term improvement in the problem-solving capabilities of a system and on the facilitation of creative and cooperative relationships among team members. Schein's process model, group process and organizational development approaches, and the consulcube's acceptant intervention all fall into this category. Each assumes that change must await alterations in values, attitudes, and perceptions.

Power-coercive strategies.   These strategies, often overlooked in consultation typologies, assume that change can be implemented most effectively through political and economic sanctions. The consultant using this approach might be interested in such methods as nonviolent resistance; use of political institutions, such as the courts; or building new power bases to oppose concentration of power and resources in the hands of a few. These approaches, identified by Dworkin and Dworkin as social action, by Tichy as outside pressure, and by Berger as political strategies, depend on the identification of clear objectives that are accepted as valid by both the consultant and the consultee.

Regardless of the objectives being sought, all consultants must choose from among the many alternate roles and methodologies based both on their assumptions about human change and on the nature of the situation in which they are working. With the models of consultation providing general definitions of the process, one can develop consultant roles designed specifically for the human service consultation network.

Consultation roles for human service settings

The human service professional, especially when he or she has moved into an administrative role, finds that consultation with others becomes a major area of involvement. In human service settings, the consultant is most likely to provide assistance through *internal consultation,* within his or her own work setting; through *networking,* or collaboration with helpers in other settings; and through *community organization,* or enhancement of the problem-solving capacities of community groups.

Internal consultation

Because of their human relations skills, human service professionals are often called upon to act as consultants to others within their own work settings. Such consultation may focus either on assisting other helpers to gain more effectiveness in service delivery or on enhancing the climate of the agency as a whole through organizational development.

Assisting other helpers.   Consultation often involves a dyadic collaboration, with the consultant assisting a consultee to solve problems related to service delivery. Thus, school counselors help teachers become more aware of the mental health needs of children in their classrooms; college student personnel workers help dormitory staff members provide more effective crisis intervention; mental health workers help professionals with similar specializations view their clients with greater objectivity; coordinators help coach individuals being developed as managers.

The norm when helpers assist other helpers is to use a consultee-centered approach, with its focus on the enhancement of long-term consultee capabilities. In most cases, the purpose of the consultation is to help the consultee gain greater skill or objectivity in working with problems that might be seen again. The consultant might share specific information concerning the needs of certain client groups or the likely effects of selected behaviors. Rarely, however, is an expertise-based provision of a solution presented in a vacuum.

As Dinkmeyer and Carlson (1973, p. 167) point out in a discussion of consultation in educational settings,

> Written reports describing the results of child diagnoses and suggesting specific recommendations developed without dialogue with the teacher will not effect change, but only accumulate reports. Nomothetic

solutions developed to describe how to handle the average child and concerned with the average teacher are no longer efficacious, if they ever were.

Instead, Dinkmeyer and Carlson (1973, p. 180) suggest that the consultant "must avoid playing the role of the specialist who is geared to providing answers" and should focus on communication designed to "elicit feelings, develop self-understanding, extend knowledge, and facilitate action."

This does not mean that the consultant's purpose is to help the consultee deal with personal issues. The consulting process assumes that an outside party, whether a client or an organization, is going to be the primary beneficiary of the collaboration. The consultant's role within his or her work setting is normally devoted to improving long-term effectiveness both of individuals and of total agencies. Thus, whether the consultant is working in an educational setting or a community agency, he or she helps coworkers by facilitating the exploration of problems, by encouraging the active search for alternatives, and by collaborating in the development of concrete plans for action in problem resolution.

This approach to dealing with individuals shares much with Schein's process consultation, although the latter was developed primarily with organizations, rather than individuals, in mind. In both, stress is placed more on improving problem-solving abilities than on providing immediate solutions to current problems. In both, consultant and consultee are seen as collaborators, sharing responsibility for the outcome of the process.

Organizational development. Although both case consultation and management development focus on bringing about growth and change in individuals, organizational development (O.D.) brings about planned change in whole systems. Using process consultation as its "critical ingredient" (Goodstein, 1978), organizational development attempts to change the norms by which an organization works, especially in terms of the integration between individual needs and organizational goals. Making a clear distinction between management development and O.D., Burke and Schmidt (1979, p. 201) state,

> The strategy for change in management development is to improve the individual manager's knowledge and skill and, in some cases, to modify his attitudes. Typical interventions are those of an educational nature. . . . The strategy for change in O.D. is to develop a process which will help the organization to diagnose its problems, plan ways to solve them, and implement these plans. . . . The strategy is to change the organization's culture from one of dealing with problems "as we have always done" to a culture that (1) takes full advantage of the human resources the organization has available, and (2) allows for a process to develop which will insure that the organization can plan and implement needed change at all levels.

In order to change the way an organization solves its problems, the consultant may use any one of a vast number of interventions, with the most common including: (1) *group process interventions,* such as team building, laboratory training, or observation and feedback concerning group dynamics; (2) *intergroup process interventions,* including conflict resolution strategies, intergroup confrontation meetings, and joint problem-solving sessions; (3) *training programs,* designed to enhance organizational skills and using innovative educational strategies such as simulation and gaming; (4) *survey feedback,* or the gathering and sharing of diagnostic data about the organization and its current norms and processes; (5) *action research,* which involves broad participation in the development of change strategies based on structured research and behavioral science technologies; and (6) *changes in the organizational structure* based on group agreement about suggested alterations.

The key to defining an intervention as O.D. is not the specific strategy used, but the democratic involvement of the organization members who might be affected by a change. All strategic planning is done under the assumption that the organization must be enabled to deal effectively with future needs. This assumes that the organization and its members must gain purposeful control over the change process.

Another key to categorizing a consulting process as O.D. is the use of an informed set of planned procedures. For instance, the Grid O.D. model (Blake & Mouton, 1969) is used by many consultants. It consists of a rigidly followed set of six phases, from study of the basic model through testing of the behavioral dynamics within the specific organization, study of the interactions among units, "top team" studies of the properties of an ideal corporate model, implementation of tactics for change, and measurement of changes from pre–phase one to post–phase five.

Although not all interventionists use comparable "packaged" models, O.D. consultants, if they are effective, depend on following clearly laid out procedures that include problem identification, contract setting, diagnosis, planning, intervention, and evaluation.

In many situations, the diagnostic process leads not to training or group process interventions, but to changes in organization structure. "A problem that persists in spite of personnel changes is likely to be structural in nature . . . the recurrence of similar symptoms after a behavioral change may also signal the presence of an underlying structural deficiency" (Aplin, 1978, p. 409).

Thus, an organization that is structured to allow overspecialization, underspecialization, too much or too little flexibility, or an inappropriate division of labor may encourage the development of problems that are seen as behavioral or interpersonal in nature. Aplin (1978, p. 410) suggests that changes in organizational structure may be effective because of the following:

1. *Scope* ... structural change can affect all aspects of the organization.
2. *Rapidity of Change* ... change can be introduced relatively rapidly to top management.
3. *Greater Predictability.* Basic reinforcement theories, organization theory, and O.D. practice enable the change agent to estimate the probable consequences of the change.
4. *Organizational Acceptance of Change* ... Structural changes are consistent with their operating styles and are generally understood by practitioners.
5. *Succession Doesn't Destroy Change Effort.*
6. *Cost Is Low.*

Although structural changes may, in many instances, have broader impact than process interventions, the ideal situation is one in which technostructural adjustments are part of a broader O.D. process. If the members of an organization are actively involved in problem diagnosis, they are likely to be as actively involved in supporting the implementation of structural solutions. An external consultant may be asked to provide a suggested plan from the vantage point of his or her organizational expertise. Internal consultation is more likely to provide an opportunity to integrate structural changes into a long-term planned change process.

Change models for internal consultants.   Whether they are working with individuals or with organizations, consultants use power-coercive, rational-empirical, or normative-reeducative strategies. Having the status of internal consultant, however, has a strong effect on strategy selection.

There are occasional situations in which power-coercive strategies (social action, political strategies, outside pressure, or advocacy) may be used within an organization. Although power may be available to an internal consultant through his or her expertise, resource control, stature, or group support (Pettigrew, 1974; Schein, 1977), these approaches are limited in their usefulness. They are most appropriate when a specific innovation is seen as highly important to the long-term benefit of service consumers and when entrenched power structures would need to be affected in order for any positive change to occur. They are less useful when attitudinal change is sought and, in human service settings, inappropriate as a means for enforcing changes sought by individuals who already control organizational resources.

Rational-empirical strategies are used when consultees seek specific information or advice that can help them reach goals that they, themselves, have set. This implies a purchase of expertise model of the consultant role, which is more often found in the use of contracted, external consultants than in the utilization of internal human resources. Human service professionals are often helpful in analyzing organizational environments (the ecosystem approach) or in diagnosing client needs (client-centered case consultation or the medical model). Normally, these tasks are done in the context of long-term, collaborative, process interventions.

For human service worker/consultants assisting others within their own agencies, normative-reeducative strategies tend to be used effectively because

1. Consultants are able to form the kind of long-term relationships that help the collaborative process.
2. Consultants' ultimate goals are normally to enhance service delivery, not just by solving immediate problems, but by recognizing and planning for future needs.
3. Within their own agencies, human service professionals are likely to be recognized for their facilitative skills even more than for their specific expertise.
4. Educational processes are a strong component of the human service professional's expertise and orientation.

Networking

Human service professionals are often asked to consult with individuals or organizations on short-term or continuing contracted bases. The focus of the networking concept of consultation, however, is on the human service worker who consults with other agencies or institutions not as an individual under a special, paid contract, but as a representative of his or her own organization. Increasingly, consultation with helpers in other agencies is being seen as part of the normal work load of human service professionals, whether their primary duties are administrative or service related. This has been influenced, in part, by the fact that limited resources do not allow each agency to be entirely self-sufficient.

Sarason, Carroll, Maton, Cohen, & Lorentz (1977, p. 21) point out that agencies have always tended to assume that demands for additional services could be met only through obtaining more money or hiring more internal staff.

> Additional resources are needed, but it requires money to obtain them or to be the basis for an exchange of resources. As a consequence, agencies spend a good deal of time trying to get more money, in effect competing with each other for these additional financial resources. And that stance makes it inordinately difficult, and in practice almost impossible, to do three related things: to confront (if only as a possibility) that resources are and will be limited; to examine critically the accepted relationship between problems and solution; and to figure out possible ways in which agencies can learn to exchange resources in mutually beneficial ways and without finances being a prerequisite for discussion or the basis for exchange.

Cross-consultation among agencies involves a recognition that scarce resources can be used more effectively if they are shared than if they are split through intense competition. Thus, the consulting network allows both for sharing information and expertise and for collaborating in the development of linkages that can enhance the resources of the helping network as a whole.

Information sharing. The sharing of information and expertise largely revolves around the use of consultants with helping specializations. Such consultants provide assistance for helpers who have different areas of specialization. For instance, mental health professionals routinely assist such diverse service providers as school personnel, police officers, correctional workers, family service workers, and counselors. Yet, in dealing with special situations, they must also seek assistance from these same workers in return. Substance abuse counselors often act as consultants to educational institutions and as consultees to health care providers. These roles are reversed when the counselor needs assistance in setting up an educational program or when the health care provider requires specialized information concerning patient needs. In all these situations, there is a need to recognize that, by definition, consultation is not hierarchical. It is a responsibility of all human service professionals to recognize when they need help from others and when they should give it and to maintain the linkages that can keep the network running smoothly.

Linkage development. Closely related to consultation is the act of providing linkages among members of the helping network. In recent years, human service professionals have begun to recognize that cooperation tends to increase, rather than decrease, the availability of financial and other resources.

> If agencies do not form cooperative networks, they find themselves simply competing against one another for limited funds. When they do join together, they recognize gaps in the community's services, plan joint programs when they are appropriate, and share valuable resources. Most important, agencies working together have the power to influence the decision making of governmental bodies and established social planning agencies [Lewis & Lewis, 1977, p. 125].

As human service professionals work to join separate programs and agencies into coherent organizations, they concentrate their efforts both on building mechanisms for effective communication and cooperation and on strengthening the network's power base.

Consultation models for networking. The models of change used in the networking process tend to include most of the basic approaches to consulting.

The sharing of information around helping specializations tends to fall into the category of empirical-rational strategies because it works under the assumption that effectiveness will follow the receipt of accurate information.

The consultant might use what Blake and Mouton would label *catalytic* or *theory and principles* interventions to help a consultee analyze problems differently. In this situation, what is happening is, if not purchase of expertise, then certainly borrowing of expertise.

Human service professionals also use reeducative strategies in the context of cross-consultation. Acceptant interventions often show that the consultee's problem is lack of confidence or objectivity, rather than lack of knowledge, as he or she has identified it. Use of consultee-centered case consultation is also more common than client-centered case consultation because it is more efficient. The sharing of information, expertise, and skill is usually considered a short-term measure, with the consultee learning enough from the inter-action to be able to work more effectively on an independent basis in the future. A major strength of process-based, as opposed to expertise-based, interventions is that they encourage the consultee's ongoing independence.

Process consultation also plays a major role in the development of the network itself. The building of a network does, in fact, provide a model of a normative-reeducative strategy because its first aim is to replace competition with cooperation, isolation with relatedness. Ultimately, however, the purpose of building cooperative structures is to change the power alignment within the community. When the separate agencies begin to work as an organization, they become able, for the first time, to use such power-coercive strategies as community organizing, lobbying, and challenging current allocations of resources. These activities are a major component of community consultation as well.

Community organization

Rothman (1974) identifies three basic orientations to the field of community organization: locality development, social planning, and social action. These three modalities parallel the models for change used by human service con-sultants and so help clarify the ways in which organizational consulting pro-cedures can be adapted to community settings.

Locality development. Locality development, like organizational development, is based on a normative-reeducative model. The consultant using this approach assumes that the various community segments have com-mon interests and can learn to identify them. As these groups are brought together, they can become actively involved in solving their own problems. The role of the consultant is to act as a process facilitator, using such tactics as leading small problem-solving groups, planning and implementing inter-group meetings, or providing training in problem solving and communica-tion. Community self-help is seen as a primary goal, with the consultant concentrating on developing the community as the kind of environment where people can collaborate on problem identification and resolution. A broad cross-section of the community becomes involved once the organizer has set appropriate mechanisms in motion.

A human service professional might use this approach to deal with entire communities or to enhance the problem-solving capabilities of a community segment affected by the agency's services. Process-oriented community organization mechanisms would be used:

1. To encourage the development of self-help groups for service consumers
2. To enhance community involvement in the work of the agency or institution
3. To build more effective support systems for individual community members
4. To generate creative solutions both to current problems and to long-range issues
5. To enhance the problem-solving capacities of the community
6. As a first step in readying a community group for social action

Social planning.   A social planning approach assumes that there are specific social problems that can be solved through empirical-rational means. The social planner tends to use a purchase of expertise or analysis for the top consulting strategy, using his or her talents as researcher, analyst, and problem solver. The consultant using this approach acts as a fact gatherer and makes substantive recommendations concerning problem resolutions.

Human service professionals tend to use this approach when they are asked to carry out needs assessments, to implement empirical studies, or to make recommendations based on their knowledge of social or psychological systems. These tasks may be performed on behalf of governmental agencies, civic leaders, or community groups. Such content-oriented consultation might be carried out:

1. When community groups have set clear goals for themselves and require only technical assistance
2. When identifiable ecosystem changes might be important to the well-being of agency clients
3. When agency plans will be affected by the results of local research
4. When those sponsoring the planning process have the power, resources, and commitment needed to implement changes

Social action.   Social action approaches assume that there may be, within a community, a group that is entitled to a more equitable share of available resources and power. The social action consultant thus sees himself or herself as accountable to this segment of the community. Although the consultant might, at times, work to develop local leadership or to provide technical assistance, the ultimate goal of the consultative process is to bring about shifts of power. The power-coercive strategies—what Tichy might term *outside pressure* or Lippitt and Lippitt might call *advocacy*—are designed to help one group increase its power and potency at the expense of another. The consultant does not act as leader, but as an organizer, facilitating the development of indigenous leaders and assisting in the planning and implementing of political strategies. For the purposes of consultation in human service settings, this approach is appropriate only when the consultee is a relatively powerless segment within a community. Power-coercive strategies might be used within a human service setting:

1. To increase community responsiveness to the needs of community members
2. To enhance feelings of potency and self-esteem among community members who were unable to affect their environment as individuals
3. To improve environmental influences impinging on human development
4. To develop responsive local leaders
5. To encourage the use of resources for services actually desired by consumers

Consultation in human service settings can take on many characteristics, depending on the local situation and on the way the consultant perceives the focal issues or problems. Yet the very fact that there are many roles and many models to choose from makes it all the more important that consultants attempt to follow clearly defined steps or procedures. Perhaps surprisingly, consultants who see their roles and objectives in very different terms tend to agree on the steps to be followed in managing the consulting process.

Steps in the consulting process

Lippitt and Lippitt (1978) identify several major phases in the consulting process, including:

Phase I. Contact and entry

Phase II. Formulating a contract and establishing a helping relationship

Phase III. Problem identification and diagnostic analysis

Phase IV. Goal setting and planning

Phase V. Taking action and cycling feedback

Phase VI. Contract completion: continuity, support, and termination

Although there are differences among theorists concerning the precise nature and labeling of the phases to be followed, there is widespread agreement that

the most important aspect to remember when using consultation
as a methodology for problem solving with individuals, groups,

organizations, or communities is to state clearly one's definition of consultation, the modes that seem most appropriate for the problem situation, and to clarify the process stages that the consultant and consultee will follow.... It is important to reach agreement on each stage before moving into the next stage [Kurpius, 1978, p. 338].

This clarity at all stages of the process is especially important in human service settings, where contacts are often informal and where internal consultation proceeds without the benefit of a written contract. Sometimes coworkers help one another without clearly specifying that the process is one of consultation. Yet these contacts are most effective and most satisfying if they include clear agreement on goals, strategies, and evaluation methods.

Contact and entry
When the consulting process begins, both the consultant and the consultee need the opportunity to explore together their definitions of the problems or issues being faced. Often, as more information is gathered, this definition changes. At this point, however, the parties to the consultation should make some preassessment of the problem, their commitment to work toward its resolution, and their ability to work together.

Establishment of the helping relationship
Whether a formal contract is used or not, the consultant and the consultee should develop some explicit agreement about the purpose of the consultation. At this point, general goals can be identified, with these goals ultimately forming the basis for evaluation of the process as a whole. Even in the most informal situation, the consultant should use this opportunity to specify his or her own skills, plans, and projected time lines.

Problem identification/diagnosis
Once general goals have been identified, the consultant and the consultee are ready to begin the diagnostic process. The methods used and the degree of involvement of the consultee depend in large part on the model being used. Whether the consultee is active or passive in the procedure, however, he or she must be aware of the steps being taken and the purpose of each.

Goal setting and planning
With assessment information now available, the consultant and consultee can reexamine their initial problem definitions and set more specific goals and objectives. At this point, the nature of the intervention to be used is specified, and a clear picture of consultant and consultee responsibilities is drawn.

Action and feedback
Depending on the consulting model being used, action is taken by the consultant (in the instance of a purchase-of-expertise or doctor-patient model)

or by the consultant and consultee working together (in the instance of a process-oriented model). Once activities have been set in motion, the consultant ensures that continual evaluation serves as a monitor of the success of each intervention.

Continuity, support, and termination

When interventions have been completed and evaluated, the consultant and consultee must plan together the steps that will be taken to maintain the change with or without the continued involvement of the consultant. Ultimately, the consultation process can be seen as successful only if the consultee—individual or organization—has learned to solve a problem or meet a goal more effectively.

Discussion questions

1. If you were asked to consult with an individual concerning his or her effectiveness as a human service worker, what kind of role or approach would you take? Which models (Caplan, Schein, Dworkin and Dworkin, Tichy, the consulcube, Berger's strategies, Lippitt's continuum) are most helpful to you in developing your thinking?
2. If you were asked to consult with an organization attempting to improve its overall effectiveness, what kind of role would you play? Which models seem most helpful to you in thinking about yourself as an organizational consultant?
3. Think about a situation in which you would want to bring about a major change in the policy and practices of an organization. Would you tend to use empirical-rational strategies, normative-reeducative strategies, or power-coercive strategies? What factors would you take into account in deciding which approach to use?

Group exercise

Organize yourselves into groups of three. One person in the trio should act as a consultee, using a real or hypothetical work situation on which you might need help. The second person should act as the consultant, attempting to be as helpful as possible in a brief period of time (about 15 minutes). The third person should act as an observer, giving feedback to the consultant after the role play. If time allows, repeat the exercise with each person trying out a new role.

Within the group, discuss the consulting process as you saw it in action. What kind of approach did the consultant tend to take? Was enough basic information gathered at the start? Did the consultant focus on the content of the problem or on the problem-solving process? How helpful was the consultation? If you were faced with a similar situation, what steps would you take?

Cases

See Case 8-1 ("Consulting with the Association for Physically Handicapped Children") and Case 8-2 ("Consulting with the Peppermint County School District").

References

Alinsky, S. *Rules for radicals.* New York: Random House, 1972.

Aplin, J. C. Structural change versus behavioral change. *Personnel and Guidance Journal,* 1978, *56,* 407–411.

Berger, M. *Strategies for change.* Unpublished manuscript, 1980.

Blake, R. R., & Mouton, J. S. *Building a dynamic corporation through grid o.d.* Reading, Mass.: Addison-Wesley, 1969.

Blake, R. R., & Mouton, J. S. *Consultation.* Reading, Mass.: Addison-Wesley, 1976.

Burke, W. W., & Schmidt, W. H. Primary target for change: The manager or the organization. In C. R. Bell & L. Nadler (Eds.), *The client-consultant handbook.* Houston: Gulf Publishing Company, 1979.

Caplan, G. *The theory and practice of mental health consultation.* New York: Basic Books, 1970.

Chin, R., & Benne, K. D. General strategies for effecting change in human systems. In W. G. Bennis, K. D. Benne, & R. Chin (Eds.), *The planning of change.* New York: Holt, Rinehart & Winston, 1969.

Dinkmeyer, D., & Carlson, J. *Consulting: Facilitating human potential and change processes.* Columbus, Ohio: Merrill, 1973.

Dworkin, A. L., & Dworkin, E. P. A conceptual overview of selected consultation models. *American Journal of Community Psychology,* 1975, *3,* 151–159.

Goodstein, L. D. *Consulting with human service systems.* Reading, Mass.: Addison-Wesley, 1978.

Kelly, J. The quest for valid preventive interventions. In C. D. Spielberger (Ed.), *Current topics in clinical and community psychology* (Vol. 2). New York: Academic Press, 1970.

Kurpius, D. Consultation theory and process: An integrated model. *Personnel and Guidance Journal,* 1978, *56,* 335–338.

Lewis, J., & Lewis, M. *Community counseling: A human services approach.* New York: Wiley, 1977.

Lippitt, G., & Lippitt, R. *The consulting process in action.* San Diego: University Associates, 1978.

Lippitt, R. On finding, using, and being a consultant. *Social Science Education Consortium Newsletter,* 1971, *11,* 1–2.

Pettigrew, A. M. Toward a political theory of organizational intervention. *Human Relations,* 1974, *28,* 191–208.

Rothman, J. Three models of community organization practice. In F. M. Cox, J. L. Erlich, J. Rothman, & J. E. Tropman (Eds.), *Strategies of community organization.* Itasca, Ill.: Peacock, 1974.

Sarason, S. B., Carroll, C., Maton, K., Cohen, S., & Lorentz, E. *Human services and resource networks.* San Francisco: Jossey-Bass, 1977.

Schein, E. H. The role of the consultant: Content expert or process facilitator? *Personnel and Guidance Journal,* 1978, *56,* 339–343.

Schein, V. E. Political strategies for implementing organizational change. *Group and Organizational Studies,* 1977, *2,* 42–48.

Tichy, N. M. Agents of planned social change: Congruence of values, cognitions, and actions. *Administrative Science Quarterly,* 1974, *19,* 164–182.

HUMAN SERVICE CASEBOOK

Case 1-1 Deinstitutionalization

For several years, an important force in mental health programs has been "deinstitutionalization." Many people who were formerly patients in large state hospitals have been leaving them to be placed in smaller, community-based facilities. The ideal of deinstitutionalization is that people with chronic mental health problems can gradually be integrated back into the community, rather than being "warehoused" in out-of-the-way facilities.

Window on the World (W.O.W.) is one of the new agencies that has arisen in response to deinstitutionalization efforts. Window on the World was designed to act as a halfway house for people recently released from the nearby state hospital. Although the funding for W.O.W. comes from a number of sources, the primary source involves third-party payments from the state vocational rehabilitation agency and the state and local departments of social service. Essentially, these other agencies pay room, board, and fees on behalf of the clients they place in the halfway house.

The W.O.W. facility is clean and well kept. Staff members have real concern for the clients, and efforts are made to keep the surroundings comfortable. Yet some of the staff members have begun to question the treatment plans for individual patients.

In one such recent situation, John Billings, a staff member, asked to see Harmon Fisk, the executive director, about one of the patients.

"I'd like to talk to you about Gail Drew," he began. "I'm positive she's ready to get on her feet and start moving. If we could just cut back on her medication, I think we might really see an improvement in this case. She might even be ready to be placed in a part-time training program and come back here in the evenings. Maybe nothing really major at first, but if we could just give her a chance, just give it a try. . . ."

"Just what do you want me to do, John?"

"Well, I thought you might be able to check with Dr. Freund about whether he could change her medication. You know the stuff she's taking now is keeping her kind of knocked out and. . . ."

"Look, John. Carl Freund has been the consulting psychiatrist here since the word go. You come in here with a fresh master's degree and want to tell him his business. Don't you think he knows what he's doing?"

"It's not that, Mr. Fisk. Of course I think he knows what he's doing. I'm just saying that I'm seeing a subtle change in this one patient, and I think she's ready to move toward a less sheltered existence. We won't know that unless we cut down her medication. We can always change it back again if it doesn't work out. What have we got to lose?"

"I'll tell you what we've got to lose. We've got Gail Drew's fees to lose. She's a social service patient. They pay her way. But they pay her way only when she's incapacitated. If she's on her feet and out there being trained, the fees are cut to a quarter of what they are now, and we can't support her on that. And if she's out there working, her fees are cut to nothing. She can't support herself on that. Now what do you want me to do? Put this woman out there on her own in the cold? On your say-so?"

"Wait . . . wait a minute, Mr. Fisk. We can't just keep someone doped up because that's the only way we can make money off of her."

"No, now just you wait a minute. For one thing, you sound plenty noble, but I don't see you turning down your pay check on Fridays. Where do you think that money comes from?"

"I know, but. . . ."

"I didn't make this system. If you don't like the way it works, talk to the government. The thing is, I don't like seeing a patient like that lying around all day any more than you do. But believe me, we wouldn't be doing her any favor cutting off her medication, getting her out there on the streets with her hopes up, and then having her lose the support that she's got. Face it. These people are chronic. They're not going anyplace. But at least here it's clean, it's comfortable. They've got a roof over their heads and they're not piled one on top of each other in an institution like they were monkeys in a cage."

"But, Mr. Fisk, Gail Drew should have a chance."

"Have a chance for what? To starve out there on her own? Look, we need fees to run this agency. If we don't get the fees, we don't get to exist. Then what happens to Gail Drew and to the rest of those patients we've got in those beds upstairs? You think our going under is going to do them any good? Where do you think they'll go except back to State where they came from?"

1. What does this case illustrate concerning the connections between funding sources and services?
2. Is there any way out of this predicament?
3. Are there ways that differing funding patterns might be developed to make deinstitutionalization work more effectively?
4. If you were John Billings, what would you do now?
5. If you were Harmon Fisk, the director, would you be able to come up with any better answers?
6. Are there insurmountable differences between human service professionals and managers?

Case 1-2 Meeting the needs of battered women

Marcia Butler, Angela Ortiz, and Pam Collins worked together at the Department of Human Services (D.H.S.) in a fairly large city. Because they were the only women professionals in their particular branch, they tended to be the ones assigned to work with cases of battered women, and they had all dealt with a number of these situations.

Pam, the youngest and least experienced of the three professionals, often asked Marcia and Angela for advice and support when dealing with difficult problems. One such situation had just presented itself. Pam's client, a very young mother of two who had been severely beaten by her husband on many occasions, had just been referred to D.H.S. for the third time. Each time Pam worked with her, the same thing happened. Immediate, stopgap measures were taken, wounds were healed and promises made, and the young client returned to the same situation. There was no potential for change as long as this client saw herself as without resources for self-support. She could not support herself and her children economically, her self-esteem was as battered as her body, and she felt she had no future, except with her husband.

Marcia and Angela sympathized with Pam's difficulty in helping this client, but they didn't really have any answers. Each of them had seen similar situations time and again. Yet as much as they tried to help, they could see no way out, primarily because of the way services were organized.

Battered women could go to a shelter that had been organized by a nonprofit, private agency, but the shelter provided only short-term (two weeks or less) refuge for women and their children. No long-term services were offered. Women could receive vocational counseling and training through the employment service, and they could receive personal counseling through the mental health center. Either of these, however, required that the women enter into long-term programs before being able to make drastic life changes. In light of their relationships, most women did not feel safe using such programs within the context of their home situations.

Marcia, Angela, and Pam recognized the need for a more comprehensive program to deal with the needs of battered women in their locality. In order to be effective, a program would have to combine physical refuge, medical services, personal and family therapy, and vocational counseling. The purpose of such a program would not necessarily be to remove all battered women from their current homes, but to work with whole family systems and to ensure that women developed more options for their lives.

Although the general manager of the Department of Human Services recognized the need for such a program when it was presented to him, he did not see how it could fit in to the current plans and appropriations of the agency. He made it clear that he did sympathize with the aims of the program and that he would be glad to consider it further if he could see a carefully developed proposal. The proposal would need to include hard data concerning needs, as well as specific suggestions concerning program activities and funding. He would not consider reallocating funds currently being used by other programs that were already hard pressed to serve the number of clients needing assistance.

Similarly, community agencies, such as the women's shelter, shared their philosophical support for a more comprehensive program. None of the currently operating programs, however, seemed ready or able to take on the burden of providing additional services.

Marcia, Angela, and Pam began to recognize that they could not help develop this sorely needed program just by mentioning it to others. They would need to become more involved themselves. The program might be brought into being in any one of a number of ways, including creation of an alternative, community-based agency; application for a grant that might be awarded either to the Department of Human Services or to the women's shelter; or development of a coalition of existing agencies and services. The possibilities needed to be spelled out, and if Marcia, Angela, and Pam did not take the initiative on this, no one else would.

1. If you were in the situation faced by these human service professionals, would you become involved in seeking a solution? To what extent?
2. What kind of approach to solving the problem seems most promising, given the human service network that exists in the community being discussed here?
3. What steps should Marcia, Angela, and Pam take in developing, and possibly implementing, a comprehensive program?
4. What kinds of administrative functions would the three professionals need to perform in order to get the program under way?

Case 2-1 Community action and mental health

The Community Action Coalition (C.A.C.) had occupied the same storefront setting for over ten years, but the times had changed. From a small group of neighbors, shop owners, and church groups that had joined to fight successfully against the potential encroachment of a superhighway through their neighborhood, the C.A.C. had grown into a major community organization. Block clubs and community interest groups still formed the backbone of the organization, but a variety of programs, services, and agencies had spun off from the original system. The C.A.C.'s attempts to enhance the life-style of community members had resulted in the development of programs to fight against substandard housing and schools, to encourage consumer awareness, to provide recreational and training programs for youth, and to bring thriving businesses into the area.

Throughout the years, however, the C.A.C. maintained its little office in the heart of the neighborhood. And throughout the years, the same thing happened again and again. When citizens of the local community were faced with family problems, with concerns about their children, with crises in their own lives, the C.A.C. was the only place that attracted them. Although a Community Mental Health Center was based in a hospital in the immediate area, and although a branch of the Department of Social Services had been built just two blocks away, these institutions were underutilized as self-referral agencies. Going to the Community Mental Health Center meant that you were sick. Going to the C.A.C. meant simply that you were having a problem in everyday living.

The staff of the coalition's storefront office welcomed the chance to try to have some impact on their neighbors' personal lives. Sometimes troubled individuals just needed someone to listen; sometimes they needed the kind of advocacy or linkage with sources of help that the organization was best at. There were times, however, when the staff members felt inadequate to deal with the problems they were facing, times when they felt at least one professional mental health worker should be present to provide training and supervision, as well as direct therapy. The need for this kind of program became so obvious that the staff members decided that they should apply for a grant to provide seed money to get their new program started. They simply needed a way to begin to implement a more organized approach to mental health, one that would involve keeping the office open 24 hours a day, with volunteers providing help under the supervision of professional mental health personnel. The funds would provide for training, for a portion of the salaries of the trainer/supervisors, and for materials that would be needed for the immediate future. Later, they felt, the organization would be able to support the new program on its own.

They did make a good case for the need and for the concept. The foundation to which they applied for funding agreed to visit the community in order to learn more about the proposed program and about the community itself. The organization, accustomed to this kind of site visit, geared up by preparing materials, by planning a presentation, and by inviting a number of community members to present their views on the day of the visitation.

The day arrived, and the presentation began to go on as scheduled. The staff members who had written the grant proposal began to feel increasingly optimistic about their chances for funding as more and more citizens arose to express their support. Suddenly, however, a man none of them knew arose to speak.

"I've come to represent the Community Mental Health Center that serves this catchment area," he said. "As much as we have appreciated the fine organizing work of the C.A.C. over the years, we reluctantly have to tell you that the kind of service they are suggesting would be inappropriate for such a nonprofessional agency. It certainly would be a duplication of the services we are presently offering with the highest level of professional staff."

"Yes," answered the foundation representative. "We did get the letter of protest from your board of directors. It does seem as though some kind of liaison needs to take place here."

After a moment of stunned silence, pandemonium broke out in the room, as the anger of community members who disapproved of the Mental Health Center's approach rose to the surface. Amid the shouts, one thing became clear. The Community Action Coalition would not be receiving funding to meet the mental health needs of its members.

1. How could this confrontation have been avoided?
2. In what way was the C.A.C.'s planning faulty?
3. In what way was the Community Mental Health Center's planning faulty?
4. The two agencies involved in the situation seem to have differing views concerning local needs. Does this mean that their needs assessments were inaccurate, or is there some other possible explanation?
5. If you were a member of the staff of the Community Action Coalition, what steps might you take now to salvage the planning and implementation process?

Case 2-2 The model college counseling center

The counseling center of Hillsboro University had been a model of excellence in its early years. It was one of the few such centers offering long-term therapy for students who desired higher degrees of self-awareness. Only in cases of serious psychiatric crisis were students referred to outside agencies. The director of the counseling center prided himself on the fact that, with the highly qualified and credentialed staff of counselors he had hired, Hillsboro students could have all their mental health needs met within the boundaries of their peaceful, tree-lined campus.

In the last several years, however, changes had begun to take place. The number of clients presenting themselves for services at the counseling center had dropped so drastically that the center's staff—all licensed psychologists or clinical social workers—had time to spare. Waiting lists for appointments had never been long, but now the reception area was ominously quiet. This situation was surprising because any indicator that could possibly measure aspects of mental health among students showed that problems did exist. Disciplinary measures for drug or alcohol abuse had increased; the dropout rate at final exam time was as high as ever; and complaints from local police and residents showed that students were, indeed, "letting off steam" in the late hours.

In light of the situation, the university's vice-president for student affairs, Mary Belmont, initiated a series of discussions with Simon Young, the counseling center director. Vice-President Belmont's contention was that the counseling center was no longer meeting the needs of Hillsboro students.

She pointed out, "We simply don't have the kinds of students we used to. The students we have now are not here to find themselves. They're not interested in spending long hours delving into their reason for being. These young people are practical. They want help with immediate decisions, help with time management, help in developing methods for dealing with stress. They are not going to spend long periods of time in a therapist's office. Something has to change."

"But that's exactly my point," Young responded. "These students do have problems, and they're not dealing with them. They think it's not important to delve into their reasons for being, but it *is* important! They think they can solve their problems with a quick how-to session, but they can't. A good proportion of these students do need therapy—at least as many as needed it five years ago. What we have to do is get those dormitory house parents, student advisors, and professors to start referring students to the center so they can get what they need."

"We're not going to do that, Simon. We don't know what these students need unless we ask them. What I'd like to suggest is that we involve the members of your counseling staff, and then some other members of the university community, and try to implement some planning about what steps should be taken. We can't afford to be paying high salaries for clinicians to be sitting in their offices waiting for someone to remember they're there."

"Now I understand what you're really saying, Mary. It's getting near budget time again. You're not concerned about what these students need. You're concerned about the money being spent on the counseling center and you're trying to cut costs. I wouldn't mind it so much if you'd just be straight about it. Just remember this. When you hired me as counseling center director, you told me I'd have a free hand to build a quality center. You said that was what you wanted, and that's what you got. If you don't want that any more, just tell me."

"Simon, I don't want that any more."

"Then you'll have my resignation on your desk in the morning. I don't know whether the staff will join me or not."

"Simon, just wait a minute. You had some ideas about what kinds of things you wanted to accomplish with young people. You had some goals in mind, and for a long time, you met them. Now times are changing. Why is it so impossible to consider using different kinds of methods to reach students? Why not use decision-making kits that students can use on their own? Why not go into the dorms with life planning workshops? Why not train peer counselors to work with the students who live off campus?"

"Because, Mary, what you're talking about are a bunch of fads. They may save money on professional salaries, but in no way do they accomplish the same ends. These are shortcuts that don't reach the places we're trying to go. What good are they? Maybe I was hasty in talking about my resignation, but I have to tell you that I'm going to support my staff, no matter what it takes. I won't have you firing experienced therapists left and right just to bring in a bunch of kids or pieces of paper that you think can fix people up."

"I'm not suggesting that. What I am suggesting is that the plans you made when you started this counseling center were solid, and your methods worked. But you can't stay married to your methods."

"These aren't *my* methods that I just invented. These are the methods that clinicians learn as part of their professional training. They fit accepted professional standards."

"Look, Simon. I understand that. Just give me a commitment that you'll try to explore this further. We won't take any action until we've thought it through."

1. What do you consider to be the most likely outcome of the conflict between Belmont and Young?
2. What are the real issues at stake?
3. Do you see one of these two differing viewpoints as being essentially correct in terms of your own values? Would you be able to present an argument justifying the opposite viewpoint?
4. If you were to be involved in a planning process like the one suggested by the university vice-president, what steps would you follow? Who should be involved in the planning process?
5. Is there any way that earlier planning procedures might have prevented the conflict described in this case?
6. To what degree can the planning process be considered rational?

Case 3-1 The best laid plans

Katherine Wilson, the director of the Allenville Senior Center (ASC), was very much oriented toward planning. In fact, one of the first things she had done upon her appointment as director was to set a planning project in motion. A committee made up of center employees, community leaders, consumers of the agency's services, and representatives of the American Association of Retired Persons and the Grey Panthers had worked to develop a new strategic plan for the agency.

One of the first things the hardworking committee had done was to survey center members in order to assess their needs and interests. At the same time, an analysis of other human service programs in the community was also completed. A series of community meetings provided a transition from needs assessment to goal setting, and as a result of all of these procedures, a new set of agency goals had been developed.

The Allenville Senior Center's mission was to bring Allenville's older citizens into the mainstream of community life. Toward this end, the center would provide services to include:

1. A foster grandparents program, involving center members in helping care for young children in the community
2. A consultation project, through which retired center members would provide consultation to young business people
3. A placement program, assisting retired people to share part-time, paying jobs
4. An educational program, in cooperation with the local college, providing credit courses that would allow center members to work toward degrees

Many of the functions the planning committee identified could be carried out under current funding. Some, however, would work more effectively as specially funded projects. The central focus of the program was clear, and Katherine Wilson was ready to carry out her promise to the committee and to her very supportive board of directors. She would try to obtain the funding needed to carry out community-based programs. In the meantime, some of the activities could begin through allocation of part of the time of currently employed staff.

Katherine was occupied in completing a tentative budget plan based on the planned activities when she received a call from the chair of ASC's board of directors. With excitement in his voice, Jonas Pratt exclaimed that he had just been contacted by the Rodin Foundation. They were interested in funding a project to build a country retreat for senior citizens. Funding would be very generous, and they would welcome a proposal from ASC.

"Be sure to get on this right away, Katherine," Pratt bubbled. "He said he'd be interested in receiving our proposal, but you know we're not the only ones he called. The writeup had better be good. And be sure you come on strong with the needs assessment."

"But Mr. Pratt, what about the planning document we just did? That was approved by the board, and this project you're talking about doesn't sound as though it has any relationship to it. It sounds like we'd be going in the opposite direction."

"Well, I know, but this idea is so new, we just didn't think of it ourselves. The kind of funding they're talking about could keep us out of trouble for a long time."

"Mr. Pratt, it would also keep us from carrying c
involvement that we all agreed made sense. Our cente
to the woods on a retreat. They want to be involved ir
can we show a needs assessment supporting a proje
assessment we really did pointed the other way? Do y
chance at all that the Rodin Foundation might be inte
own projects?"

"Katherine, I just don't think so. They didn't sound as
for proposals. They had something darned specific in mi
in our talking about whether we want this Rodin mon
the grant. We can always decide whether we want to accept it with the strings attached
or not after we've gotten it. In the meantime, let's just put all our efforts into doing
the proposal. If we don't get the funding, no problem. If we do, then we can decide."

1. If this issue is discussed at ASC's next board meeting, what do you think will be
   the likely outcome?
2. If you were in Katherine's shoes, what steps would you take next? Would you write
   a proposal for a country retreat or try to convince the board to stay with the plan
   that had already been developed?
3. If Mr. Pratt's point of view does win out, how should Katherine deal with the
   planning committee?
4. This situation shows how easy it is to make services fit the availability of funding.
   How likely would the board be to turn down the grant from the foundation if their
   proposal were accepted?

Case 3-2 Budget cut

The Women's Agency of Schaefer City offered a full range of services to women,
including counseling, educational interventions, and career development programs.
Services were offered by a combination of professionals, paraprofessionals, and volunteers, with self-help and peer counseling important components of most programs.

The one agency program that depended solely on professional service deliverers
was the health center, located in a separate building but overseen by the same board
of directors and administration. The health center dealt with a variety of women's
health needs and offered family planning and first-trimester abortions. Although medical service was provided by physicians and nurse practitioners, all counseling was
provided by women with degrees in psychology, counseling, or social work.

For the abortion clinic, this worked very well. Each woman who came in for the
abortion procedure talked first with a counselor, who took a medical history, answered
any questions about the procedure, and explored the woman's readiness for taking
this step. The process of exploration often led women to reconsider their options;
certainly, the decision-making process was enhanced.

This program was placed in jeopardy when severe cutbacks in funding for the total agency took place. There was no consideration of eliminating the abortion clinic itself; the cutbacks, however, were to affect the counseling aspect of the program. By cutting the number of professional counselors from nine to three, enough money could be saved so that the number of women served could remain constant. The agency administrator chose to limit the intake counseling interviews to 20 minutes each. In that time, the medical information could be obtained and information about the procedure given.

The reaction to this cutback was immediate and strong. All the professionals associated with the abortion clinic recognized that the suggested change in staffing patterns would be devastating, not just for the women losing their jobs, but for the program itself.

From the patients' viewpoint, the problem involved the fact that they would be deprived of the opportunity to consider their decisions with assistance from skilled helpers. Although they would have factual information, many of them would regret their decisions, and this could have lasting effects.

The change also seemed serious in terms of the well-being of the professionals still offering services. No longer would they have the opportunity to provide empathy and help to people in crisis. Instead, they would be spending their time with person after person, giving and getting information in an assembly-line approach. They would not be able to stay with patients through the medical procedure or provide emotional support later. Instead, they would stay in their offices, maintain business as usual, and quickly burn out.

1. Given the fact that the agency had to survive with fewer resources, how could financial cutbacks have been implemented more effectively?
2. What possibilities might there be for maintaining the quality of services while cutting back on expenditures?
3. What impact might this situation have on the long-term health of the agency?

Case 4-1 The community career center

The Community Career Center (C.C.C.) had been initiated several years ago by a group of professionals who had become impatient with the impersonality and red tape that had overwhelmed their work in public agencies. All four of the center's founders had previously worked for departments of human resources or vocational rehabilitation, and their experiences had led them to think that there had to be better ways to deal with clients' career development needs.

There were a few basic concepts that had been part of the center's orientation since it had first begun operation under Department of Labor and fee-based funding. First, the founders had felt that one counselor should work with the total scope of a client's career needs, linking him or her with training programs, with educational institutions, with other needed services, and, finally, with jobs. They had also believed in using training formats to deal with the kinds of needs many clients shared. From its unassuming start, the center had provided training programs dealing with midlife career change, retirement planning, job-hunting skills, self-assessment, and a variety of other topics. These programs were offered to members of the general public, such as women reentering the job market, and to local institutions and businesses.

At first the founders of the center had provided most of the services themselves. If they felt that a particular training format had exciting possibilities or if they were invited to design something special for a local group, they would provide workshops and group sessions. In the meantime, each of the four also carried a caseload of clients to whom they were dedicated. They saw themselves as counselors, as advocates, and as placement specialists for their own clients, and the success they were having exceeded even their own idealistic expectations.

Last year the center's management had begun to get out of hand. Its size had mushroomed, and so had its funding. Local businesses had proven so supportive, especially in contracting training programs, that the initial Department of Labor contract provided only a small percentage of the agency's total funding. Each training program was self-supporting, and the number of individual clients kept growing. In order to keep pace, the center had had to hire additional staff members to provide services; so there were now a number of trainers and counselors who had not been in on the original planning. Little by little the original four center founders had become frustrated. Instead of spending all their time with clients and trainees, they were becoming involved in keeping books, in planning repetitive services, and in supervising staff members. This supervision especially bothered them. The new staff somehow didn't understand the concept of being really dedicated to their clients. These counselors did their work, but they weren't really bubbling over with creativity. They weren't seeking new challenges, coming up with new ideas, or making that extra effort that made the difference. The original founders, who did have that urge for creativity, weren't able to use it. They had become managers, and they didn't like it.

The solution they had found last year was to bring in a business manager, a recent M.B.A. who knew how to organize and control a growing firm. The center founders breathed a collective sigh of relief when management concerns were taken out of their hands. They gave their new manager a free hand and were pleased with the way he took control of the budgets and financial reports. The new organizational structure that he had created also seemed to make sense. He divided the center into departments, including the training department, where programs were designed and implemented; the marketing department, which had responsibility for selling the training programs to industrial and other organizations; the counseling department, which provided direct services to clients; the job development department, which canvased the community for placement possibilities for clients; and the business department, which took care of administrative concerns, including personnel.

This had seemed to work for a while. The newer staff, in particular, seemed pleased with the increased clarity of their job descriptions. They were no longer badgered with instructions to "be creative." They knew what their responsibilities were and could carry them out. The center founders—still the board of directors of the agency—had been pleased to have management responsibilities taken out of their hands. Now they could be creative again.

Yet that sense of renewed creativity had not taken hold. Somehow the agency's new organization didn't allow for it. Now in its fifth year of existence, the Community Career Center was in jeopardy, not because it had failed, but because it had succeeded.

Two of the four board members wanted to resign and spin off a new, smaller, more responsive agency. Monica Shannon and Paul Wilson didn't really want to make this move, but they could not see any way to carry out what they saw as their mission through an organization as unwieldy as the C.C.C. had become.

At the most volatile meeting ever held at the center, the board of directors cleared the air. Monica Shannon, one of the two original members who had decided to leave, spoke first.

"Look," she exclaimed. "Our original idea was to have an agency that would be responsive to our clients' career needs. We would stick with an individual, be an ombudsman, help meet all this one client's needs. Now we have a department for counseling and another department for finding jobs. What happened to the idea that got us started in the first place?"

"And what about the training component?" Paul Wilson chimed in. "The idea was to meet community needs by designing special sessions, not to keep repeating the same program all the time to make it easier for the marketing department. Everything we do lately is to please the marketers, to make it easier for them to sell. But what have they got to sell? We've got the tail wagging the dog."

"Now wait a minute," Mark Wells responded. "We've got a big organization here. We can't expect everything to be the same as it was. Growth and change was supposed to be one of our big aims too."

"And you were the ones who got the most excited about bringing in a manager to take the business responsibilities out of your hands," Colleen Morgan pointed out. "You can't have everything."

"I'll tell you one thing," Monica hissed. "We may be a large organization now, but we accomplished more in a day when the four of us began than that whole gang of bureaucrats we've got here now accomplishes in a month. That's what we've got here now: a bureaucracy. Why did we ever bother leaving the Department of Human Resources? We've got a duplication right here."

1. Would you describe the Community Career Center's organization as a bureaucracy? How does it compare with the structure that the agency had at first?
2. The agency grew in size over the years. To what extent does this imply a necessary change in organizational structure?
3. At this point, do you think Monica and Paul are right in wanting to leave the organization? What options do they have?
4. If you were able to create a structure for the Community Career Center right now, what would that structure be like? (Think about how you would departmentalize and what the organizational chart might look like.)

Case 4-2 The umbrella organization

The roots of the Atlantis Community Mental Health Center (CMHC) were in its inpatient, outpatient, and emergency services. Although, in keeping with the federal mandate, consultation and education services had always been included, stress had never been placed on preventive, community-based interventions until a recent major upheaval.

In response to an evaluation report showing that many groups within their highly diverse catchment area were not being reached through traditional services, the board and administrative staff of the Atlantis CMHC decided to add several new service components. The new programs were to include an outreach program for families, a drug and alcoholism program, a crisis intervention team, and several storefront outposts that would encourage service utilization by members of the minority community.

The CMHC's funding sources were uniformly in favor of this approach, but would provide funding only if a major organizational change were made. The funding sources recognized that many of the proposed services were already being offered on a smaller scale by tiny, community-based agencies scattered throughout the area. Each of these small agencies had worked independently for years, often with unknowing duplication of the services of other organizations. This new thrust of the Atlantis CMHC was recognized as a possible vehicle for a more efficient approach to human services than had been possible before. It was suggested that the human service network of Atlantis develop more effective linkages, with each agency maintaining a degree of autonomy, but with the organizations joining for the sharing of resources. The mental health center would act as the umbrella organization, offering community outreach services through existing local agencies rather than duplicating these services with the development of new programs.

Because of the obvious financial benefits to be gained through this cooperative endeavor, the mental health center and a number of community agencies made the commitment to developing a new organizational structure. A subcommittee, including a number of agency and center service deliverers, as well as funders and community members, was charged with the responsibility of drafting a suggested structure, to which the various member agencies could respond. Of course, representatives of differing organizations brought divergent viewpoints to the meeting.

Hilary Johnson, the CMHC's program officer, represented a major source of funding for the organization. Her primary concern was that services be effectively delivered in Atlantis without needless duplication of effort and without the usual endless competition among agencies for limited funds. She knew that the agencies involved all provided greatly needed services, but she knew that these services could be provided more efficiently through greater coordination. She thought it would be possible to centralize the work of these agencies in order to accomplish common goals and to divide resources equitably among programs.

Caroline Brown, Juan Casel, and Evelyn Mays were all staff members of small, community-based agencies. Each of them brought to the meeting a high degree of concern for maintaining the nature of their own agencies. They knew their agencies' strengths lay in their responsiveness to local needs and in the fact that their programs had been developed by community members. They had always resisted pressures to expand, recognizing that the smaller agency can sometimes maintain a degree of responsiveness and flexibility that a large organization cannot duplicate. They knew that fiscal realities meant they had to become part of a larger entity, but they also knew that there would be dangers involved in losing their own identities. They could not duplicate the center's lack of accessibility or they would go under.

Similarly, Nick Chan and Sally Allen, representing local citizens' groups, recognized that maintaining accessibility would be important. They knew that many of their neighbors resisted using the services of the center but felt more comfortable in their dealings with the smaller agencies in their immediate neighborhoods. They knew that the creative and open atmosphere of the small agencies needed to be maintained. Nick and Sally also knew, however, that the service consumers would be the losers if more efficient use of funds didn't begin to take place.

Nelson Richards, director of the Atlantis Community Mental Health Center, was most interested in the degree of centralization that could be accomplished. Although he would have preferred unilateral expansion of services on the part of the center, he recognized that some major benefits could be gained from using the center as an umbrella organization. He could see great possibilities for the sharing of resources. For instance, each agency could become part of the management information system so that the flow of clients from agency to agency would be enhanced. Common budgeting could mean a significant increase in the funding available for the center as a whole. Such activities as staff training, personnel, and purchasing could be centralized; so each agency would gain greatly in efficiency. Planning could be broadly based, and purchases could be made in money-saving quantities. Looking at it from a more humanistic standpoint, services to consumers would be improved, and no client would ever again be able to "fall between the cracks" because of lack of information or lack of comprehensiveness.

Melvin Hammond was also in favor of a high degree of centralization, but for a different reason. He, as a human service consultant called in by the state funding agency, knew that the best resource utilization would involve having one central agency to act as fiscal agent for funds. He recognized, however, that the direction this agency would take would depend to a great extent on the kind of organizational structure they developed. One possibility would be to departmentalize the new, enlarged organization by type of service, with all direct service deliverers in one department, all outreach specialists in another, and all community organizers in still another. A different alternative would be to divide the organization according to population served, with all drug abuse program staff working in one department, all family service professionals in another, and so on. The important aspect of the organization to Melvin Hammond was that workers should identify themselves with Atlantis rather than with their former agencies.

Each of these individuals had organizational priorities that differed. Yet the committee would need to decide on an organizational structure that would please everyone, at least to a degree, and that would work.

1. What are the major organizational issues involved here?
2. What would you see as the primary alternatives for the organizational structure? What are the potential strengths and weaknesses of each?
3. If you were asked to give input to the committee, what organizational structure would you suggest? Why?
4. What would be the implications of varying approaches to departmentalization?
5. How centralized do you think the organization should be?

Case 5-1 Director of training

When the Atlantis Community Mental Health Center became an umbrella organization, the traditional services normally offered by the center were combined, for the first time, with the more nontraditional approaches favored by the small, "grass roots" agencies in the community. ACMHC now included both "the center" and the "neighborhood outposts" that had formerly been independent agencies.

This drastic change in the organization brought with it the need for new approaches to training. Nelson Richards, director of the center, recognized this need. His response was to hire Ellis Shore, a mental health professional with experience in university teaching, to design and implement a comprehensive training program.

Richards's directive to his new training director was clear. The skills of the paraprofessionals in the outposts were to be upgraded. The center director felt that the service deliverers in the community-based agencies lacked the background and education that he would expect of professional helpers. These people were now working under the Atlantis name, and they would have to provide professional-level services. He would leave the methods up to Shore, but the mental health skills of the community agency workers would need to be enhanced.

Shore began this work with great enthusiasm. He created, almost single-handedly, a series of workshops designed to develop trainee competencies in individual, family, and group therapy. He also developed a complex schedule that would allow the workshops to be provided on-site at each of the neighborhood centers. Knowing that he could not provide all the training himself, he involved several of the mental health professionals who had been employed by the center before the creation of the umbrella organization. He asked these professionals to serve as cotrainers and made sure that he included people with varying therapeutic orientations, from psychodynamic to behavioral to existential.

He and his cotrainers agreed that the workshops he had designed would upgrade trainees' skills if they became actively involved in the process. Use of the outposts as training sites would mean that participation would be so convenient for agency workers that attendance could be purely voluntary.

With high expectations, the training director and his cotrainers began the first series of workshops. At the first workshop, 20 participants appeared. Although only 12 remained for the whole day, Shore was relatively pleased with the turnout. At the second workshop, only 10 paraprofessionals attended. The third drew only 6.

Shore, in frustration, confronted Isabel Phillips with this evidence of lack of motivation among agency workers. Phillips, who had administered one of the more successful of the city's community-based agencies and who was now coordinator of the outreach program, was in touch with the paraprofessionals in the neighborhood centers. She would know how to get these service providers more actively involved.

"Isabel, I've been given the authority to make these workshops compulsory," Shore pointed out, "but I really don't want to do that if I can avoid it. How can I light a fire under these people? You know them. Why aren't they motivated?"

"As a matter of fact, you're right," Phillips responded. "I do know these people, and what I know about them is that they're the most motivated people you're ever going to see in your life. Every one of them has put in more hours in a week than you can imagine for pay that hardly puts them over the poverty level. They do it because they believe in what they're doing and because they know how much they're needed. When you say they're not 'motivated,' I have a hard time picturing what you're talking about."

"Well, what I'm talking about is the fact that they're not showing up for these workshops that they know are encouraged by the director, that they know they have released time for, that they don't even have to step out of the doors of their agencies to get to. Now if these folks are so concerned about their work, something just doesn't fit."

"You're right, Ellis. Something doesn't fit, but the thing that doesn't fit is your training program. What makes you think they need upgrading in their therapeutic skills?"

"Isabel, are you kidding? That's what I was hired to do. When Richards gave me the job, he told me that he didn't care what methods I used, but that the skills of the paraprofessionals in the outreach programs had to be upgraded. That was the word he used: upgraded."

"Well, let me tell you something about Richards. He's completely out of touch with the community. He's always been out of touch. He doesn't know what the people need from the agencies, and he doesn't know what kind of training the workers need. They don't do therapy in those agencies. They don't have the luxury of sitting in their offices dealing with one person at a time for months on end. They're out there in the streets, getting people organized and helping them deal with real, concrete problems. In fact, has it ever occurred to you that you just might be designing all these beautiful training interventions for the wrong people? The folks in my agencies know what they're doing. It's the people in the center that need training. They don't know how to do anything but therapy, and the community isn't buying it. If you want to make a training contribution, why don't you hire yourself some paraprofessionals as cotrainers, go up to the center, and provide some on-site training on how to close the gap between the center and its so-called consumers. From what I hear, business isn't exactly booming in that big granite building uptown."

1. If you were Ellis Shore, what steps might you take to develop a more comprehensive and appropriate training program?
2. What special leadership issues might be involved in a decentralized agency such as the Atlantis CMHC?

Case 5-2 Burnout

The Valley Substance Abuse Agency provided counseling and rehabilitation services on an outpatient basis to young people and adults involved with various forms of substance abuse. Many clients referred themselves to the agency for help. Even more, however, were there because they had been sent by the court after involvement with illegal drugs. They often continued to present themselves for services because their failure to do so might result in imprisonment.

Although the agency had attracted a number of highly effective human service workers, the counselors had been complaining more and more of "burnout." Both the counseling specialists and the group work specialists tended to find themselves tiring of the sameness of their work and of their relative lack of success. Their clients were not always as motivated to receive their help as they were to give it, and they had few success stories to tell. Although the workers involved in the outreach program to schools were able to approach their work somewhat more optimistically, they also had a lack of certainty about their effectiveness and a recognition that they might continue to do the same work for many years without any concrete results.

All the agency's human service workers shared a recognition that their career development within the agency would be limited. The organization was too small to allow for a great deal of upward mobility, and the workers tended to spend virtually all their time in direct service to clients. Interactions among staff members were friendly, but not very intense.

Recently, the problem of burnout had become intensified. The turnover in staff members was so great that only one worker had been on the job for more than three years. Of the current staff, most expected to move on when they could. In the meantime, absenteeism was high, the quality of work was declining, and the pervading atmosphere of the agency showed a lack of energy and enthusiasm.

1. What factors in the agency's makeup might have contributed to the prevalence of burnout among the employees?
2. If you were in a supervisory capacity in this agency, what might you do to prevent the problem?
3. Is this kind of problem inevitable in human service agencies?

Case 6-1 The token economy

Having worked as a therapist for a number of years, Jim Forrest had developed a high level of expertise in dealing with problems related to substance abuse. His work had included jobs in several settings, including a short-term detoxification program in a hospital, a community-based methadone treatment center, and a community mental health outpatient program.

Although his work with clients had always been satisfying, two things continued to trouble him. One major issue for Jim was that his experience had convinced him that his clients' milieu was more important than any other aspect of treatment. Although one-to-one counseling could be helpful, it was always less important than the kinds of reinforcement clients got for various behaviors in their immediate social environments.

The other aspect of his work that tended to trouble him was the question of management. He had grown impatient with the pressure on him, as a professional therapist, to stick to specific time lines and methods, regardless of his clients' needs. In each agency, there had been a tendency for managers to create methods of operation based more on business principles and treatment costs than on the effects of various treatment modalities. He felt that, given the chance to do what he felt was best for his clients, he could work both effectively and efficiently.

Jim finally had the chance to try out his ideas when he was invited by a former colleague to take on a job as head of a newly funded detoxification program being set up in one wing of the local community mental health center. The program had been funded to provide short-term services, and two of the therapists from the previous, smaller program were to remain on staff. With this exception, Jim would be free to develop the program in whatever way he saw fit. There was sufficient funding to provide for the hiring of a staff of four more professional therapists and eight paraprofessionals.

Jim began interviewing potential employees, telling each of them the same thing. The program would be based on use of a token economy, meaning that clients would receive concrete and specific reinforcements for behaviors that were consistent with responsible, adult conduct. Every staff member would need to be involved in recording and reinforcing appropriate client behaviors, for only then would the clients begin to learn new ways of dealing with their environment.

Beyond this "bottom line" of commitment to the token economy as a treatment modality, professionals would be free to set their own hours and to work with clients according to their best interests. Newcomers would be more closely supervised at first. Later they, too, might have the kind of freedom already granted to the experienced professionals.

Most of the new workers started in at their tasks with a high degree of enthusiasm. It was like a dream come true, and after a few weeks Jim began to think that he was already seeing results in terms of client change. There were, however, a few problems beginning to surface.

First, Hugh Schmidt, one of the two therapists who had already been employed at the center, began to complain to anyone who would listen about the idea of the token economy. Schmidt believed that long-term therapy, insight, and intrapsychic change were the only ways to deal with substance abusers. Changes in behavior could not get at the root cause of the problem, and the token economy could change only concrete behavior, not attitudes. He continued to work with clients in the same way he always had, but the token economy was constantly being sabotaged.

Another member of the professional staff was troubled not by the token economy, but by the freedom Jim had allowed for the employees. Carol Cooke pointed out to Jim that although the staff members had been enthusiastic at first, they would not maintain a high level of commitment unless they were aware of the rules and regulations governing their own behaviors. Jim scoffed at these concerns until one Friday afternoon when he had to make a presentation at an out-of-town conference. When he realized he had forgotten something, he called the office. Not one of the professional staff members was there.

The problems Jim had begun to face were minor, but they started to make him think. Could he maintain a central focus in the program if every member of the professional staff was not necessarily committed to it? Could he trust the professional staff in the way he had always wished to be trusted? The challenges began to seem a little bit more difficult than he had really expected.

1. What do you think of Jim's approach to program administration? What are his strengths and weaknesses in dealing with his new leadership position?

2. If you were Jim, what would you do about the problem posed by Hugh Schmidt's attitude? Is it necessary for the staff to work as a closely knit team, or is there room for a great deal of variation?
3. What would you do about the problem posed by Carol Cooke? Do employees— even trained professionals—need clearer behavioral guidelines than Jim Forrest provided?
4. Do you think Jim has the potential to be more effective than the business-oriented professional managers he had experienced before?

Case 6-2 A test of supervisory skills

Sarah Stone felt a bit leery about the employee who had been assigned to work in her child abuse project. She needed workers who were highly skilled in working with families and who were able to build solid relationships with children. She knew that Bob Lawrence had a reputation for being one of those helpers with skills that could almost be described as magic. He had supposedly impressed everyone who had ever seen him work with children as one of the most effective people in the agency. Yet Sarah also knew that Bob had been close to being fired and that this transfer to her special project was seen by the agency director as Bob's last chance at "rehabilitation."

The report from Bob's last supervisor lay on Sarah's desk, and she looked it over for the third time.

"Bob Lawrence is undoubtedly skilled as a service provider. He develops instant rapport with children, and his family interventions are masterful. Yet all this work seems to be intuitive. He cannot really describe what he does, never clarifies his goals, and, in fact, interacts with other workers as little as possible. He almost never attends department meetings, although these meetings are considered crucial to our work. We also need to file treatment plans on each of the children with whom we work, and I have been unable to get Bob to make even minimal efforts to complete any paperwork at all. I do recognize that the purpose of the agency is to provide services, rather than to do paperwork, and I don't consider myself a stickler on this. Yet agency work has to be a team effort toward common goals, and Bob just has not become part of the team. When I try to work closely with him, he actually seems to resent it, preferring to carry on independently. I believe in providing very close involvement and support for my supervisees, but Bob has not accepted this. I recommend that he be transferred to another department or project. Perhaps another supervisor might be more effective than I have been."

Sarah knew that Bob's effectiveness in working with families and children would be crucial to the project. That was why she had accepted his transfer from his former placement. Yet she had doubts about her own ability to supervise him effectively. She knew that teamwork was going to be important on this project. It had been funded for the purpose of testing an innovative form of family intervention, and everyone would have to be involved in sharing ideas and in contributing data that would help in the evaluative research. She hoped she would be able to count on Bob, but she knew that her own supervisory skills would really be tested.

1. How would you feel about having someone like Bob in a program you were administering?
2. If you were Sarah, what kind of approach would you use in working with Bob?
3. What mistakes do you think Bob's former supervisor might have made in working with him?
4. What concepts concerning leadership style and motivation might prove helpful in providing effective supervision for Bob Lawrence?

Case 7-1 Evaluating the consultation and education department

At the Greenby Community Mental Health Center, the Consultation and Education Department was about to go under. Although consultation and education are required for all community mental health centers, not all centers have fully staffed and active departments. Instead, they implement consultation and education as a percentage of each professional's work. That was what Henry McDonald, the executive director, was suggesting for Greenby.

"You have to understand my position," he exclaimed to a distraught consultation and education director. "Our funding has been cut back. We're more dependent than ever on fees for service and third-party payments. Consultation and education are luxuries we really can't afford. They don't bring in the funds we need, and we've got to put our resources into programs that carry their weight."

"But you know that C and E programs are a high priority. Every center has to have one to keep up its funding," Andy Cutler replied.

"Andy, let's not play games here. You know we don't have to have a C and E department with a full-time director. We only have to provide the service. The real issue is whether your program stays in operation the way it is now, and I'm saying it can't. Now stop worrying. Your job isn't in jeopardy. You'll be able to move over to the clinical program."

"Henry, believe it or not, it's not my own job that I'm concerned about. No matter what kind of measurement you use, you have to see that the C and E department does pull its weight. We've developed liaisons with every major employer in the area; we've got preventive programs going in the schools; and our divorce and family workshops are attracting more people every time we put them on. The word is getting around in the community."

"Sure the workshops attract people—at $5 a head, why shouldn't they? The program is self-supporting, I'll grant you that, but it's not pulling in enough capital to pull its weight with the center as a whole. There's no way it can."

"But what you're not recognizing, Henry, is that this program is supporting the other programs. You've had an increase in the number of people referring themselves for alcohol and drug abuse programs. I'm telling you that that's because of the preventive programs we've been doing at the factory. You've had an increase in the self-referrals for family therapy. I think they're coming from our workshops. The programs we do help people recognize their problems, and when they recognize them, they start to come in for more help."

"That's very possible, Andy. But I've got a board of directors to deal with, and I don't know whether they're going to buy that line of reasoning. They're not professionals, you know, and they don't necessarily see those relationships that way. What they can see is the difference between what a person pays to participate in a workshop and what the same person would pay for one of the other programs. It's a good thought to say that you're feeding into the other services, but we don't really know that. We don't really know anything about the impact you're having. Give me something I can tell the board. Give me something I can tell the state. Just give me something."

1. What steps might you take if you were Andy Cutler, the consultation and education director?
2. How might a more effective evaluation program have helped the C and E program?
3. What methods might prove helpful in demonstrating the effectiveness of Andy's preventive programs?

Case 7-2 Evaluating a family intervention

The Orchard Family Service Center received many court referrals because of its reputation for dealing effectively with the families of abused or neglected children. The center's philosophy was that children should not be endangered but that families should be reunited as soon as possible, with continuing support provided by the center's family workers.

Families had always been served individually. Now Laura Brent and Audrey Rogers, two of the agency's longtime family counselors, were suggesting that they try out the idea of working with several families in a co-led group situation. They felt that one of the strengths of this approach would be that families would have additional support from one another, beyond what they could receive from professional care givers.

Ray Richards, the agency's director, could see the logic in this idea. He was concerned, though, because he felt that the agency's reputation had been built on the effectiveness of their current casework approach to working with families. He felt that it would be appropriate to try out the new approach on a trial basis, but he wasn't really sure how the trial itself could be evaluated. They couldn't very well tell a court-referred couple that they were in the control group and couldn't be served. But they had to have some kind of comparison if they were to make any kind of judgment about the effectiveness of the group approach. He asked Michelle Burke, the consultant who had helped with the agency's Title XX evaluation report, to try to develop an evaluation plan for the new service.

1. If you were Michelle Burke, what steps would you take first in assisting the Orchard Family Service Center?
2. What type of design might be helpful in evaluating the group approach to work with families?
3. On what basis would you measure the success of the family group intervention?

Case 7-3 Evaluation emergency

John Little, director of the Developmental Disabilities Training Project, called an emergency meeting of the project staff.

"You've all been working really hard on the training manual," he said. "I hate to pull this on you right now, but I've got to tell you that I just had word. The feds are sending in their evaluator. He's going to be here next week, and we've got to be ready."

Amid the groans, Jane Carlin, a staff trainer, spoke up. "What's the big problem?" she asked. "We've been providing a training session every week. We've had workshops on developmental disabilities for the teachers, for citizens; we've had the TV show; now we've got a manual for parents. It seems to me we're in great shape. So what's the problem?"

"Well, I was kind of putting this part off," John answered. "They sent along the new evaluation form so that we can complete the self-study before the evaluator gets here. That's the tough part. We're going to really have to dig to get the information ready."

"What kind of information do we need? Remember, we did that pre- and posttest with all the people at the workshops. We've got a lot of data on the learning effects from the workshop. Of course, it's not that easy to do with the TV program. . . ."

"That's the least of our problems, Jane. Remember, this is a training project. What they want is information on all participants in any training workshop. They want the ages of trainees, their sex, their employment, their income, all the demographic stuff. I just didn't think about all that because the form last year didn't ask for it. See, we're using the same kind of evaluation form as continuing ed. programs are. It doesn't make any sense, but I'll bet we can dig up that information somehow."

"Wait a minute," George Peterson called out. "I worked my tail off on that TV program, and there's no way in the world I'll ever be able to even guess who watched it. Does that mean the whole thing didn't happen? Does that mean I get a grade of zero? I flunk?"

"Now, George, you know it isn't like that. They just like to have the information so they can put it together with the data from all the other projects they funded. They've got to show results just like we do."

"That's fine to say, John, but if they're going to evaluate us on how many men, women, and children show up at our sessions, we should do the kind of stuff that can lend itself to what they're looking for. I'm feeling like my stuff just isn't going to make the grade."

"I'm starting to feel that way, too," Jane said. "What's the point of doing one thing if they're evaluating something else?"

"Wait a minute, everybody," John responded in frustration. "We're getting way off the track here. These people aren't here to tell us what we should do and what we shouldn't do. They're not going to grade us on what we did. One of the things they ask us about in an open-ended question is the content of the program, the kinds of interventions we did. There's no problem there. The problem is just in putting together the data that they want, the demographic characteristics and all that. Now I've got most of it somewhere. All I need is for somebody to volunteer to help me dig through the files and see what we can find that might relate to some of the questions they're asking. We'll be able to get the sex of participants by looking at their names on those address cards we had them fill out. The ages will be hard. That we'll have to guess at. . . ."

1. How might the agency have avoided this "emergency" situation?
2. How might the funding source have helped avoid the situation?
3. If you were John, what kinds of evaluation models would you use for this program?
4. How should the staff deal with this immediate situation?

Case 8-1 Consulting with the association for physically handicapped children

Karen Wong served as program administrator at Greenpasture, a school for physically disabled children. In this capacity, she worked closely with many of the children's families; so she was not surprised when a group of parents approached her for help.

These parents were members of the board of the Association for Physically Handicapped Children (APHC), which had served the needs of children and their parents for many years. The association had just gone through a change in structure, with the local organization becoming an independent group after years of having been an integral part of the state association. The members felt that this would be a good time to review their mission and services, and Karen Wong had been named as a possible consultant. The association asked her to consult with the board and staff concerning their respective roles and concerning the directions that APHC should take in the immediate future.

Karen agreed to act as a consultant to the association, provided that the board of directors and staff would recognize that the ultimate decisions concerning the organization were theirs. She could help them get in touch with their own priorities, but she would not give them advice concerning future directions.

With this approach understood, Karen started the consultation process by gathering data that could be used to diagnose the association's problems and to identify salient issues. She decided to interview each staff member and each board member individually because she wanted to become aware of subtle differences in perceptions and she knew that the organization was small enough to allow for this approach. When she completed this diagnostic process, she shared the results with the board and professional staff at a retreat.

The diagnostic process showed that APHC had a four-pronged purpose:

1. To advocate on behalf of handicapped children, with these efforts to include lobbying as well as interventions with schools and human service agencies
2. Community education, to inform families of handicapped children, as well as the general community, about issues relating to physical disabilities and about available services
3. Direct services to disabled children and their families, including a parents-day-off program for partial day care, as well as a diagnosis, referral, and counseling service
4. Organizing, with emphasis on empowering the families of handicapped children to assert their rights and help one another and themselves

Although the staff and board members seemed to agree on the purposes of the association, they differed strongly in terms of priorities. The board saw organizing and advocacy as the most important functions. Their primary focus was on the organization as a means for enabling families to help themselves and to have impact on public policies concerning the handicapped. In contrast, the staff had almost unanimous agreement that their most important priorities had to be on direct services and education. Although they saw empowerment as an important concept, they felt that families could advocate for themselves only if their immediate needs were taken care of first. For this reason, they put most of their efforts into providing counseling, referral, diagnostic, and day-care services, with the idea that building healthy families would mean building stronger bases for advocacy.

The board and staff members were surprised to learn that they differed so strongly in terms of priorities. They had always assumed that the focus of the association was a subject of unanimous agreement, with differences being oriented primarily toward the details of methodologies. A number of small disagreements now were understood.

Each respondent was also asked to specify what he or she saw as the primary responsibilities and duties of the board members and the human service workers on the staff. Again, some differences began to appear.

The board members tended to see themselves as people who could be most helpful to the organization by raising funds, setting policies, overseeing the staff, and providing personal support to staff and volunteers. Although staff members agreed that these functions were important, they also seemed to think that board members should be available as resource people to help initiate new programs and to perform such functions as lobbying and community organizing.

The staff members saw their own duties as involving the provision of direct services and educational programs. Although they had a number of volunteers helping perform some functions, they felt that they would be "stretched too thin" if they tried to do a great deal more than they were currently doing. They felt that one of the organization's strengths was the quality of services provided to children and families and that if these services were cut down, the organization's funding base and power would also be decreased. A related, complicating factor was that some of the staff members were actually VISTAs, funded by the federal government and not allowed to participate in lobbying efforts. None of the staff members listed organizing, advocacy, or lobbying as their own responsibilities. In fact, there seemed to be a general lack of awareness concerning specific job descriptions.

At the retreat, Karen shared all this information with the board of directors and the central professional staff. All of them appreciated their increase in awareness concerning the problems of the association, but that did not mean they knew how to solve the problems at hand. The board members appreciated knowing that the staff expected them to be more involved in association operations, but they didn't feel able to make greater contributions. Each of them had other responsibilities outside of APHC, including jobs, as well as care of their own children. Participation in the association was part-time and voluntary, and they felt they should leave staff work to the paid human service workers.

The staff members also appreciated knowing more of the expectations the board had for them. They felt, however, that they could not take on extensive political efforts without having much more help. In addition to lack of time, they also cited the fact that none of them really was trained in community organizing.

The board and staff members maintained positive views of themselves, each other, and the organization. They recognized, however, that they did have some problems in store for them. They asked Karen to give her recommendations about how they should function, using her own vast experience in the field of physical disabilities and her knowledge about children's needs.

1. If you were Karen Wong, how active would you feel you should be in providing solutions for APHC's problems?
2. What kind of approach to these problems might be taken by a consultant who tended to see the situation from a structural point of view? Are there ways that changes in organizational structure might have an effect?
3. What kind of approach might an organizational development consultation involve? Could process-oriented consultation be helpful for the association?
4. If you were faced with a consultation situation like this one, what steps would you take now?

Case 8-2 Consulting with the Peppermint County School District

The school district of Peppermint County was in its first year under a new, court-ordered desegregation plan and faced with a number of difficulties. The new plan was unpopular in the district, especially among high school students, because it required that two high schools with long-standing traditions be merged into one institution. There was fear of violent confrontations between Black and White students; on a number of occasions, students had threatened to walk out.

In the face of this possibly volatile situation, a group of school social workers, counselors, and psychologists was asked to take leave from their normal duties and act as consultants to the board. They would help develop resolutions to problems by bringing together Black and White students, parents, citizens, and school personnel. In addition, they would consult with individual schools when crisis situations were recognized.

These teams of consultants went to work, setting up numerous meetings and going in person to schools where problems threatened. One of the biggest problems they noticed, again and again, was a certain reluctance to cooperate on the part of school administrators. What tended to happen was that a school principal would ask for help when tensions threatened to explode and then back off from implementing solutions after the situation quieted down. In one instance, a team of consultants and parents had brought together junior high school students who had been involved in a rock-throwing melee. Once tempers had cooled, the Black and White students joined in an organization that would focus on joint participation of racially mixed groups of students in intramural sports and other activities. Although the organization grew on schedule, the principal of the junior high school eliminated the organization and cut down on school activities after a few weeks.

Similar situations had occurred in several schools, with administrators refusing to allow time or space for extracurricular activities and actually suspending students attempting to organize the student body into interracial councils or committees. Some school administrators were afraid to allow nonacademic activities for fear that violence might result; they wanted only to maintain quiet classrooms and to empty the hallways promptly at 3 P.M. Other administrators were really motivated by an aversion to desegregation itself; they wanted their schools to remain "quiet," but did not relish a great deal of interracial cooperation among students. Still other administrators recognized that united student bodies might tend to create problems for administrators and teachers; they knew that students who were busy fighting one another would not actively confront school disciplinary policies or advocate for student rights and privileges.

The problem of administrative lack of cooperation came to a head when a group of three consultants was asked to intervene in a situation developing at the high school. Charles Kaye, the principal of the newly unified high school, had shown himself to be one of the least cooperative of the school district's administrators. The consultants knew that, if they attempted to work at Peppermint High School, their efforts might prove to be wasted. Yet trouble was brewing; students might be hurt; and this school had a tremendous need for change.

The three consultants—all longtime employees of the school district—brought with them varying ideas concerning the approach that should be taken in this situation.

Frank Martin felt that he, as a consultant, should refuse to intervene at all unless he was assured of full cooperation from the principal and other school personnel. Frank's idea was that no consultant should ever work with an organization unless its head supports the effort. In this case, the principal had in his hands the power to nullify any movement toward solving the high school's problems. The only possible key to success of a consulting intervention would be if the principal and his faculty and staff all agreed to search together for meaningful solutions. The needed commitment to change seemed to Frank to be missing in this instance.

Ann Sewell disagreed. She felt that the issues being faced at Peppermint High School could be resolved only if the power were realigned. Her notion was that the principal should not hold so much power that he could, single-handedly, prevent the effective desegregation of Peppermint County. Ann felt that the consultants should not see the principal as their client. They had been hired by the school board to enhance the desegregation effort, and they therefore did not have the right to refuse to intervene in specific situations, especially when students might be in danger. Ann's suggested approach was to work directly with students and parents, helping forge a more united, racially mixed group that would have enough power to win much-needed changes in the school environment.

The third consultant, Ward Lee, suggested still another alternative. Their intervention, Ward thought, should focus on changing the principal's ideas. The consultants agreed that Charles Kaye, although not in favor of integration, did not really want to risk violence within his school. He was an ambitious person who did not want his reputation as an educator ruined. He wanted to get through the school year without serious difficulty. Ward thought that their most likely success would be to prove to the principal that changes in the school environment, especially the encouragement of nonacademic activities, would help maintain the peaceful climate of the school. If Charles Kaye could be convinced of this fact, he would take the initiative in making needed changes.

The three consultants knew that they could work most effectively as a team and wanted to come to some agreement on the best way to intervene at Peppermint High School.

1. How would you characterize Frank Martin's approach to change?
2. How would you characterize Ann Sewell's approach to change?
3. How would you characterize Ward Lee's approach to change?
4. What might be the results of each of the three types of intervention?
5. If you were one of these consultants, what consultation approach would you use?
6. How would you see the consultant's role in this situation?

NAME INDEX

SUBJECT INDEX